Priestley's Progress

ALSO OF INTEREST
AND FROM MCFARLAND

*Missed Signals on the Western Front:
How the Slow Adoption of Wireless Restricted
British Strategy and Operations in World War I*
by Mike Bullock and Laurence A. Lyons (2010)

Priestley's Progress

*The Life of Sir Raymond Priestley,
Antarctic Explorer, Scientist,
Soldier, Academician*

MIKE BULLOCK

McFarland & Company, Inc., Publishers
Jefferson, North Carolina

LIBRARY OF CONGRESS CATALOGUING-IN-PUBLICATION DATA

Names: Bullock, Mike, 1939–
Title: Priestley's progress : the life of Sir Raymond Priestley, Antarctic explorer, scientist, soldier, academician / Mike Bullock.
Description: Jefferson, North Carolina : McFarland & Company, Inc., Publishers, c 2017 | Includes bibliographical references and index.
Identifiers: LCCN 2017022780 | ISBN 9780786478057 (softcover : acid free paper) ∞
Subjects: LCSH: Priestley, Raymond E. (Raymond Edward), 1886–1974. | Explorers—Great Britain—Biography. | Antarctica—Discovery and exploration—History.
Classification: LCC G875.P75 B85 2017 | DDC 910.92 [B] —dc23
LC record available at https://lccn.loc.gov/2017022780

BRITISH LIBRARY CATALOGUING DATA ARE AVAILABLE

ISBN (print) 978-0-7864-7805-7
ISBN (ebook) 978-1-4766-2870-7

© 2017 Mike Bullock. All rights reserved

No part of this book may be reproduced or transmitted in any form or by any means, electronic or mechanical, including photocopying or recording, or by any information storage and retrieval system, without permission in writing from the publisher.

Front cover image of Sir Raymond Edward Priestley by Elliott & Fry (bromide print, 1949) © National Portrait Gallery, London; *background* the Terra Nova in McMurdo Sound between 1910 and 1912 (Library of Congress)

Printed in the United States of America

McFarland & Company, Inc., Publishers
  Box 611, Jefferson, North Carolina 28640
  www.mcfarlandpub.com

To my wife, Frances,
for her limitless
encouragement and support

Table of Contents

Acknowledgments ... ix
Preface ... 1
Introduction ... 3

1. The Priestley Family in Tewkesbury—Early Days ... 7
2. University College, Bristol ... 11
3. Shackleton's Nimrod Expedition ... 15
4. Between Expeditions ... 38
5. Scott's Terra Nova Expedition—The Northern Party ... 46
6. The First World War—The British Army Signal Service ... 58
7. Cambridge University—Scott Polar Research Institute ... 75
8. Vice-Chancellor—Melbourne University ... 82
9. Vice-Chancellor—Birmingham University ... 92
10. The Commission for Higher Education in the Colonies ... 115
11. Acting Director—Falkland Islands Dependencies Survey ... 123
12. West Antarctica on the RY *Britannia* ... 127
13. American Deep Freeze IV Expedition ... 145
14. President, Royal Geographical Society ... 161
15. Along the Way ... 166
16. Later Life ... 170

Appendix I. 46th (North Midland) Division During the Hundred Days   177

Appendix II. The 1907–1909 British Antarctic Expedition   180

Appendix III. The McMurdo Sound Region   181

Appendix IV. The 1910–1913 British Antarctic Expedition   183

Chapter Notes   185

Bibliography   189

Index   193

Acknowledgments

The help and advice I have received from the following has been of inestimable value during the three and a half years I have spent researching Sir Raymond Priestley's first biography, and for this I wish to express my heartfelt thanks. The list is intended to be inclusive but if there should be any omissions then I offer my profound apologies:

Michael Richardson, Special Collections Librarian, Bristol University: Dr. Suzanne Paul, Keeper of Manuscripts and University Archives, Cambridge University; Dr. John Bourne, Birmingham University; Dr. Helen Fisher, University Archivist, Birmingham University; Dame Anne Griffiths, Archivist to His Royal Highness, the Duke of Edinburgh; Dr. Meredith Hooper, author of *The Longest Winter*, an account of Scott's Northern Party; the Staff of the Foyle's Reading Room, Royal Geographical Society; Anne Howarth, who had been a pupil, teacher and acting Headmistress, respectively, at Edgbaston High School for Girls of which Priestley had been President of the School Council during his time as vice-chancellor of Birmingham University; Lucy Martin, Photo Collections Keeper and, particularly, Naomi Bonham, Archivist, the Scott Polar Research Institute, Cambridge, where a high proportion of the research was completed; Joanna Rae of the British Antarctic Survey; Ronald Ridley, author of *The Diary of a Vice-Chancellor, University of Melbourne 1935–1938*; Anthony, Alison and Alex Morbey of the Old Hall, Ely, for providing me with excellent accommodation when researching at Cambridge; Sue Edlin, Chair of the Trustees of Tewkesbury Town Museum, who shared her extensive knowledge of Priestley with me; the late David Villavoys, a local historian, for his paper on the Priestley Family in Tewkesbury; the late and legendary ice-specialist Charles Swithinbank, who I had the great good fortune to meet shortly before his death and who had known Priestley and greatly admired his work; Ellen Scrivens and John Hubert, granddaughter and grandson of Priestley, who, as well as making his diaries and papers available to me, also provided their most generous and unstinting support; Beth

Emanuel, my book secretary, for her dedicated work without which the biography would not have been possible; finally, and especially, my wife, whose previous experience as a professionally qualified librarian has been of the greatest help with the planning of my research and who, as always, has provided me with limitless support.

Preface

Sir Raymond Priestley's long and eclectic life was one of great achievement and distinction in which his unerring sense of duty, considerable physical and moral courage and personal integrity were the enduring features. Many personal tributes have been paid to him from men of equal stature but a full biography is an inexplicable omission—until the volume of research required to cover the length and breadth of his very full and unusually active life are taken into account. The primary objective of the present work, therefore, is to correct this omission.

By a happy coincidence, Sir Raymond was the inspiration for my previously co-authored book on communications during the First World War[1] based on his pioneering work as the Official Historian of the British Army Signal Service during the conflict[2]; further investigation revealed that this was but one amongst a host of equally significant and, indeed, what would later be considered as even greater achievements.

As a gallant soldier of the First World War, during which he was awarded the Military Cross, as a full participant both as an explorer and scientist during the Heroic Age of Antarctic Exploration with both Scott and Shackleton, as a leading educationalist for which he received his knighthood and with his immensely strong sense of public duty exemplified by the wide range of the other aspects of his life, it is essential that this be put on record.

In many ways, the task has been made much easier as he maintained an incredibly full and detailed—some might even judge it obsessive—diary throughout the whole of his life, in which his often strongly held views are recorded with candor but, on most occasions, distinguished by a refreshing lack of prejudice, and openness to new concepts. As a consequence, the book reflects many of the features of an autobiography endorsed by the views of many of those with whom he came into contact who, on the basis of their own high reputation, can be regarded as reliable witnesses demanding respect. It is for this reason that when, on very many occasions, quotations appear without attribution, it is because they are taken specifically from his diaries, while much of the text derives from a summation of the same source material.

As anticipated, the program of research required was very extensive and all those who have provided invaluable assistance are acknowledged, personally and with heartfelt thanks, elsewhere. Institutionally, the Town Museum in Tewkesbury, the Universities of Birmingham, Bristol, Cambridge and Melbourne, the Scott Polar Research Institute, the British Antarctic Survey, the Duke of Edinburgh's Archive at Buckingham Palace and the Royal Geographical Society are principal amongst a host of others, while members of Priestley's family have been unstinting in the help that they have provided. Equally, a wealth of literature, illustrated in the bibliography, across a wide spectrum, has augmented the research to its considerable advantage.

Finally, my previous military experience and research coupled with my own travels in Arctic and Antarctic regions have been of inestimable value in understanding the challenges of the environment in which he was so extensively involved.

Introduction

I first encountered Raymond Priestley in his role as Official Historian of the British Army Signal Service following the First World War[1]; his work was the inspiration and starting point for my recent Master of Letters thesis, followed closely thereafter by a co-authored book, on communications during this war.[2]

During the course of my research it became clearly apparent that his gallant war service—he was awarded a Military Cross—was but a short though highly significant interlude in a long life of distinguished accomplishment across an array of prestigious appointments.

This breadth of activities went some way towards explaining the almost inexplicable lack of a biography until now, though a number have taken a keen and detailed interest in his life and achievements. Not least of these has been Meredith Hooper in her excellent book, *The Longest Winter*,[3] an account of Scott's Northern Party, which drew heavily on meticulous research of Priestley's almost obsessively detailed and comprehensive diaries at the Scott Polar Research Institute. Equally enthusiastic and extremely thorough have been Sue Edlin's and David Villavoy's compilation of documents and artefacts at Tewkesbury Town Museum specifically relating to Priestley,[4] this being the town of his birth and where he spent significant periods of his life.

When consulted, along with many others including surviving members of his family, there was unequivocal agreement that a biography was long overdue.

One has only to consider, briefly, the scope of his achievements, chronologically, to reinforce the need to correct this gap in biographical historiography while recognizing that the breadth of his activities perhaps explains its omission.

Born in 1886, and having spent his early life and education in Tewkesbury, he went up to Bristol University to read geology but was persuaded to interrupt his studies to embark with Shackleton on his Nimrod Expedition

Typical pages in one of Priestley's diaries (courtesy of John Hubert, Priestley's grandson).

to the Antarctic; he followed this shortly thereafter on Scott's Terra Nova Expedition in his successful but ill-fated quest to reach the South Pole.

On his return from Antarctica he was immediately plunged into war service and spent the immediate aftermath writing both the story of the 46th (North Midlands) Division[5] and the *Official History of the Army Signal Service (France)* during the conflict.[6]

After time spent at Cambridge University completing his long interrupted studies, and early experience in academic administration, he was involved as co-founder of the Scott Polar Research Institute, now a highly regarded and respected center for all aspects of Polar scientific research, exploration and conservation.

An opportunity then arose, partly as the result of continuing geological research carried out in Australia, following on from his two Antarctic expeditions, for his appointment as vice-chancellor of Melbourne University; this was followed by a similar appointment, closer to home, at the University of Birmingham.

Following his "retirement"—a complete misnomer in his case—he was

Introduction

appointed Head of the Royal Commission in the Civil Service and immediately thereafter became Acting Director of the Falkland Islands Dependencies Survey (F.I.D.S.—later the British Antarctic Survey) in the absence of Sir Vivian Fuchs, then engaged, with Sir Edmund Hillary, in his complete crossing of Antarctica by way of the South Pole.

While still Acting Director of F.I.D.S. he accompanied His Royal Highness, the Duke of Edinburgh, on the RY *Britannia* to West Antarctica as a guide and Antarctic expert and, after only a short interval, returned again with the American Deep Freeze IV expedition.

Consequently, it was not the least surprising that he should be asked eventually to become President of the Royal Geographical Society for a two year term, an appointment he held with great distinction.

In addition, he had taken an interest in and worked with the Higher Education Board for the Colonies throughout much of his career and it was for this, specifically, that he received his knighthood.

For the whole of his life he took a great interest in his family, despite the demands of his work, and spent his later years in and around the family home near Tewkesbury, where his achievements were recognized and highly respected; nonetheless, he still made regular forays to London to help and advise on Antarctic related affairs, beyond doubt the consuming interest of his life, until his death in 1974.

Against this background, I believe it is clearly apparent why a biography of Priestley is appropriate, and should appear without further delay.

1

The Priestley Family in Tewkesbury— Early Days

There is a display in Tewkesbury Town Museum specifically related to Priestley's life[1]; it is complemented by an excellent short history of the Priestleys, compiled by a local historian,[2] providing an illustrative background to, and laying the foundations of Priestley's later achievements.

Priestley's grandfather, Joseph Priestley, was born in Brodsworth, Yorkshire, in 1829. He was a schoolmaster and came to Tewkesbury in about 1850 to teach at Tilley's School at Shuthonger. Shortly thereafter, in 1853, he became the Headmaster of Tewkesbury Grammar School.

Five years later, he resigned to set up his own Abbey House School.

He became a Trustee of the Tewkesbury Wesleyan Methodist Chapel and a Steward of the Tewkesbury Wesleyan Circuit. He died in 1876, his funeral was attended by the Mayor and Council, and the organ in the Methodist Chapel was purchased as his memorial.

Following his father's death, the eldest son, Joseph Edward Priestley, became Headmaster of the Abbey House School at the surprisingly young age of twenty-two; he had obtained a Bachelor of Arts degree at London University and had returned to Tewkesbury to teach. He continued as Head of the Abbey House School until it merged with the Grammar School, in 1899; he was then Head of the enlarged school until his retirement in 1917. He married Henrietta Rice, who he met at the Wesleyan Methodist Chapel, of which he was a Trustee, like his father; they had four sons, all of whom were educated at their father's school, and four daughters.

The eldest son, born in 1883, was Joseph Hubert Priestley, who went to University College, Bristol, and obtained a Bachelor of Science degree; later, in 1905, he became Head of the Botanical department at Bristol and eventually, in 1911, was appointed Professor of Botany at Leeds University. He served in the First World War, going to France with the British Expeditionary Force on August 9, 1914, was commissioned, and from 1915 until the Armistice was in the Intelligence Brigade of the General Staff; twice mentioned in Dispatches, he was awarded the Distinguished Service Order. Returning to Leeds after the war, he had a successful academic career and served as pro vice-chancellor. He died in 1944.

After Raymond Priestley, the second son, born in 1887, the third son was Donald Priestley, born in 1888. Very little is known of his career after education at his father's school, although he too was a strong member of Tewkesbury Methodist Church and it was there that he met his wife, Edith Broughton. She was the daughter of a prominent local citizen who was the organist at the Methodist Church, a local councilor and who acted as Mayor of Tewkesbury on no less than seven occasions. During the First World War, Donald was conscripted into the Artists Rifles while he was living in London. He was serving in the front line in 1917 as a Lance Corporal, almost certainly during the Third Battle of Ypres (Passchendaele), when he was killed in action. Although he has no known grave, his name is commemorated on the Tyne Cot memorial in Belgium, near to where he fell, as well as on the Town war memorial, the Methodist church, in Tewkesbury Abbey and on the Grammar School memorial which is now retained at the Town Hall.

The youngest son, Stanley Priestley, was born in 1889. He also served during the First World War as a subaltern in the Gloucestershire Regiment; during the Battle of the Somme in 1916 he was wounded by enemy fire while leading his men towards the German barbed wire and failed to return, presumed killed in action. His name is on the Thiepval Memorial on the Western Front in France, on the Abbey, Town and Grammar School memorials but, surprisingly, not at the Methodist church.

Raymond Edward Priestley, like his brothers, received his education at Tewkesbury Grammar School as well as becoming a member of the Methodist Church and, what he describes as, an "erratic" member of the Methodist Guild. Indeed, his pre-university world centered almost entirely around the School, the Methodist church and the cricket field, much in line with the rest of his family; this undoubtedly had a profound effect on the way in which he lived the remainder of his life.

Priestley had a fairly conventional but very happy late Victorian childhood and his recollections are full of humorous events which enlivened the otherwise fairly strict conventions of the day.[3] Inevitably, many of these involved the Church. On Sundays, he was required to attend two services and Sunday school for good measure. Sermons, in those days, would normally last for at least forty-five minutes and the only book he was allowed to read during this was the Book of Common Prayer, which included "Hymns Ancient and Modern." The "unexpected dividend from this mis-spent youth" was that he was able to put this to good use in his later experience with Scott's Northern Party in their unremitting observance of Sunday worship, despite the extreme conditions under which they lived and the precarious nature of their situation.

With lengthy sermons in mind, Priestley remembers that his father, flanked by his entire family and also boarders from his school, always maintained that he could listen better with his eyes closed and that "one day he suddenly sprang to his feet in the middle of the preacher's peroration, flung up his right hand and shouted the cricketer's appeal—How's that!—at the top of his voice" to the consternation but considerable amusement of the congregation. The same chapel is associated with memory of the Wesley appeal for funds during which a stingy pensioner, who had just pledged the sum of five shillings, immediately increased his pledge to ten shillings upon being hit on the head by a piece of plaster falling from the balcony roof; although almost certainly apocryphal, from the pulpit were heard the words, "Hit him again Lord, hit him again!" On another occasion, at a meeting of the Methodist Guild, Priestley was eating a raspberry tart "liberally endowed," in his words, with jam and cream. When his mother beckoned him to her, he placed the tart carefully onto his chair, having only taken one bite, and saw from the corner of his eye, "a formidable old lady, of whom he stood in considerable awe, clad in her best black bombazine dress, sit down four-square upon his chair." He fled the room and had to rely on eyewitnesses to record the inevitable and memorable outcome, which became part of local folklore.

Because of Priestley's father's headmastership, school and home life constantly intermingled and the playground, which comprised a hundred yards of asphalt in which a famous old mulberry tree (mentioned in early editions of *John Halifax, Gentleman*) was a natural obstacle, was the place for family games, including hockey. The walls of the school were used for ricochets, at which they became incredibly skilled, and which Priestley used to good effect when playing in similar circumstances while with the Duke of Edinburgh on the RY *Britannia* in much later life. During the summer holidays, Priestley was expected to pick the ripe fruit from the same mulberry tree, and puts down his later immunity to wasps stings to the number he received in early life. In the course of this full and happy family life, Priestley also received a very sound and broad education and taught at his father's school for a year before being readily accepted at University College, Bristol, to read geology. This set him on a path to a life of considerable, well recognized achievement and great satisfaction, through both innate ability and most fortunate and unexpected circumstances.

Joseph Edward Priestley and his four sons were passionately fond of cricket. He was secretary of Tewkesbury Cricket Club for more than thirty years and was an accomplished batsman. Moreover, there were many occasions when the Priestley family formed the backbone of the team; Stanley was regarded as a good bowler and, indeed, on one occasion took all ten wickets in one innings when playing for his school team without a run being scored against his bowling! Joseph Hubert Priestley continued his love of cricket while at Leeds University, becoming captain of the staff team, while Donald played for Gloucestershire during the 1909 and 1910 seasons. Raymond had an enduring and keen interest in cricket for the whole of his life, as will become apparent.

Of Priestley's four sisters, Joyce, Edith, Marie and Doris, very little is recorded or remembered, even by their descendants, in any detail; this is not altogether surprising given the prevailing attitude of the day, when the achievements of women, though considerable and often highly influential, were overshadowed in historical records by the often unspectacular careers of their husbands. There seems little doubt from Priestley's own records that his sisters were an important and happy element of his early life, and all eventually married and produced a total of eleven children between them.

Moreover, there was a very happy coincidence in that Edith married Sir Charles Wright, while Doris married Griffith Taylor, both of whom were included in Scott's Terra Nova Expedition, with Priestley. Indeed, Sir Charles, with Priestley, was a member of what was known as "the nursery" on the *Terra Nova*, a cabin occupied by the six youngest members of the expedition, and which also included Frank Debenham, who was later the co-founder of the Scott Polar Research Institute with Priestley. Also included was Aspley Cherry-Garrard, one of the party which made the historic journey, in the winter darkness and extremely low temperatures, to Cape Crozier to obtain the eggs of the Emperor penguin, later described in his beautifully written and epic account entitled *The Worst Journey in the World*.[4] Sir Charles, as one of only two surviving members of the expedition, wrote an appreciation of Priestley[5] and paid a glowing tribute to him at his funeral in 1974.

One great mystery remains—the spelling of the family name. In about 1908, the "a" in the name changes to "e" and both variations appear on family graves in Tewkesbury Cemetery.

2

University College, Bristol

When Priestley arrived at University College, it had not yet achieved full university status and its degrees were conferred mainly by the University of London, particularly for the sciences, and through a variety of other universities for the arts; Priestley enrolled to read Geology. His elder brother, Joseph, who had graduated as a Bachelor of Science while at Bristol, was now its Head of Botany, a coincidence that was to have an immense and lasting influence on Priestley's future life and career.

A brief history of University College reflects its altruistic inception.[1] At a meeting in 1874, the Bishop of Hereford, at that time Master of Clifton College, proposed the establishment of a college in Bristol which combined technical training with general culture to include the arts and sciences. The meeting included, amongst other distinguished contributors, the Mayor of Bristol, Dr. Jowett, Master of Balliol, Oxford, and the President of the British Association (with later significance for Priestley). The agreed objective was "to establish Bristol as a University city against the background of its cathedral status and important maritime history." In 1876, the first session of University College opened under the Presidency of Dr. Elliott, Dean of Bristol, with an affiliation to the long established and highly regarded Bristol Medical School, which was incorporated later, in 1893, with University College as its Faculty of Medicine. At this point it also had very strong ties with the Royal Society, with no less than seven of its past and present professors being Fellows.

Full university status was received eventually, with the granting of its Charter in 1909.

The University College that welcomed Priestley was, by this time, well established in its fine buildings in Tyndall's Park, still at the heart of university life in Bristol today. The College offered courses in Science, Languages, History and Literature with developing facilities for original research. Men and women were admitted separately, there were no halls of residence and degrees continued to be conferred by other establishments of full university status.

Priestley's initial registration was for Intermediate Science (Geology) leading to a B.Sc.

The regulations covering admission were demanding, as were those concerning general discipline. The Principal, who admitted students at the beginning of each academic year, required every candidate to produce a testimonial of good conduct and to sign an indemnity to obey the college rules, disorderly behavior being dealt with by him personally, which could include fines and, in some cases, expulsion. Fees were payable in advance—fourteen guineas in Priestley's case—and an attendance record was sent to the student's parent or guardian at specific intervals.

Lectures, for which strict rules of minimum attendance applied, were designed for both daytime and evening students, the latter primarily to accommodate teachers, clerks and artisans on a part-time basis although also open to those studying full-time. Professor S.H. Reynolds M.A., F.G.S., an eminent geologist, supervised Priestley's studies, covering a wide syllabus with a broad spectrum of lectures supported by specimens, photographs and lantern slides. Amongst a very full program were included subjects highly relevant to Priestley's future involvement in Antarctica: the action of ice, marine inundation, rock structures, fossils and, of particular importance in his participation on both Shackleton's and Scott's expeditions, minerals of economic value, volcanoes and volcanic rocks. In addition the geological laboratory was open daily for private work and, at weekends, field trips were available.

Scholarships covering fees relating to University College and the degree-conferring universities were also available. The College records reveal that Priestley entered for one such scholarship and had already received good marks in the additional subjects of Chemistry, Pure Mathematics, Physical Geography, History and Languages which formed part of his wider university education.[2]

The College also had a thriving Christian Union, affiliated with the Bristol College Christian Union, of which Priestley, with his strong Wesleyan background, was almost certainly a member though there is no record of this. The men's branch, which met on a regular basis, also had meetings with a similar women's organization once in each term. The Union had a keen missionary ethos emphasized by a string of lectures by existing missionaries returning from their adventures abroad. The required reading included *Studies of the Teachings of Jesus* to supplement this missionary zeal.[3]

During his second year at Bristol, it is also evident that Priestley was becoming immersed in University College life more widely. He was a member of the Social and Debating Society, Secretary of the Chemical Society and General Secretary of the Athletics Club, illustrating early characteristics, to be confirmed much more fully later, of his total commitment to any activity with which he was involved.

However, it was during his second year at University College, at which time he was living in lodgings at 72 Waverley Road in the Redland area of Bristol, that a life-changing opportunity presented itself, the result of a happy coincidence. It happened, on what transpired as a fateful morning, he was sitting in the College Library, apparently in a rather despondent frame of mind, when his brother Joseph, the aforesaid Head of Botany, was passing through and asked him, to his great surprise, if he would like to go to the Antarctic. Priestley's reply was unequivocal. "I would go anywhere to get out of this damn place." This simple agreement led directly not only to his inclusion in Shackleton's Nimrod Expedition in 1907 as its geologist but also to a lifetime of involvement in Antarctica which, in a very wide-ranging career, nevertheless remained his main focus of interest for the rest of his life.

Priestley's dissatisfaction with his life at University College was almost entirely from what he describes as being "not too hot in schools" and not due to its other more agreeable aspects. Apart from his many sporting activities, already described, he was by this time both Captain of Hockey and a member of the College's Cricket First VI, which he enjoyed to the full. However, having only "scraped matriculation in the Second Division and just passed the Intermediate," not in any way satisfying his innate sense of the need to succeed, and although, to his surprise, he had "come, strangely enough, *proxime accessi*" to an Exhibition Scholarship for which he had entered, it was clearly evident this did not fulfill his ambition. Consequently, he was entirely open to his brother's timely intervention.

A few days later he was asked to go up to London to meet Shackleton, having already discovered that he was not the first choice geologist: this had been Percy, of Bristol Museum, who had previous Antarctic experience on the Challenger Expedition but who, for whatever reason, refused the invitation. Priestley's brother had heard of this on the University College grapevine and hence his chance suggestion. As Priestley describes it, "the offer was pure chance but I was not missing any bets now."

Priestley remembered very little of the interview although he recalled that Adams, the future Second-in-Command of the expedition, was in attendance. There were only two questions from Shackleton that he could recall: the first, "Would you know gold if you saw it?"; the second, "Could he play a musical instrument?" As he records, "I made no bones about the first and could give no affirmative answer to the second." In addition, he was asked if he was fit and well, and ordered to have a medical examination from which he received a clean bill of health.

He left the interview without knowing if he had been given the job or not but even so, when back in Tewkesbury, he leaped over a tennis net in his exuberance, came down on the point of his toe and put his knee out, which was to trouble him later, and confining him to bed for the next ten days with what his doctor diagnosed as "water on the knee." Ten days later he received a letter from Shackleton demanding to know why he was not in London collecting his equipment as he had to join in the work of preparing for the expedition, in October; the "first indication that he had made the grade!"

However, he continued to harbor doubts as to why he had been chosen for the expedition as, at this stage, he lacked any real academic qualifications: this only became clear much later during an argument with Adams who told him that "he had not been taken on this show because he was a great scientist but because Shackleton did not want all hard nuts and felt that he could manage him." Priestley accepted this quite philosophically, as he did not consider himself a great scientist anyway and felt that he could also manage Shackleton; as Priestley records, "so they lived happily ever after and he even had his pay raised by £50 a year."

By this time his inclusion in the expedition had raised him to almost celebrity status in Tewkesbury and he was asked to give a lecture in its Philharmonic Hall. Although he had prepared carefully and included forty-eight not entirely relevant lantern slides, he could only spin it out for fifteen minutes. By his already high standards it was a disaster and he was devastated. Indeed, he goes so far as to record that it affected his ability to speak in public for the remainder of his career; in his view "fools rush in and his life had been shortened by a year."

Nevertheless, despite a few relatively minor setbacks, in the late autumn Priestley embarked on the *Runic*, a small and necessarily inexpensive steamer, for the journey to New Zealand with seven other members of the expedition's shore party; the *Nimrod* had left earlier, at the end of July, not only to load additional stores but also, principally, to "show the flag" in both New Zealand and Australia in the hope of raising much needed funds for the expedition. For Priestley, this was an historic moment; it marked not only the first stage of his life-long association with Antarctica, but also his involvement with a group of like-minded companions, with some of whom he would remain inextricably linked in later life; as he expressed it "Antarctic explorers gravitate towards each other like corks in water whenever they get the chance."

3

Shackleton's Nimrod Expedition

The British Antarctic Expedition of 1907–1909 was the almost inevitable result of Shackleton's earlier participation in Scott's Discovery Expedition of 1901–1903 when, with Scott and Dr. Edward Wilson, he had reached the furthest south yet recorded of around latitude 82.17 S on December 30, 1902.[1] The exact latitude, although proving a matter of later debate and, indeed, acrimony, is now recognized as being more or less correct. The expedition's failure to reach its South Polar objective had many causes, among which its lack of supplies to guarantee its safe return and, above all, the deteriorating health of the party were the most significant; Shackleton's condition was certainly of the greatest concern by far, although all were showing signs of scurvy to varying degrees. His health deteriorated still further on the return journey. Scott records in the early stages of the return from the south, "There is no doubt that Shackleton is extremely ill … I have talked to Wilson, who thinks matters are critical."[2]

The party eventually returned safely on February 3, 1903, but, as Scott describes, "as near spent as three persons can be."[3] Despite the party's failure to meet all its objectives, Scott and Wilson were able to derive some satisfaction from their achievements, not least their return from the south bearing not only the burden of their own deteriorating condition but the real anxiety for Shackleton's survival. For a man of Shackleton's disposition this was a humiliating experience, despite having shown huge fortitude in the face of extreme adversity. This was further compounded by Scott's decision to send him home, probably correctly, on the relief ship as an invalid prior to the expedition's second winter in Antarctica. Coupled with Shackleton's general feeling of being something of an outsider with his predominantly Merchant Naval background on very much a Royal Naval expedition, and despite being chosen for the Polar Party, this will have been, at one and the same time, a cause of not only great frustration but, characteristically, a spur to succeed by his own efforts at the first possible opportunity.

A brief summary of the expedition's inception and preparations are an essential prerequisite to understanding Priestley's role in its wider objectives.[4]

Shackleton believed that he could build on the achievements of the Discovery Expedition by expanding its knowledge acquired both in exploration and science. As well as defining in much greater detail the southern limits of the Great Barrier Reef, the full extent of King Edward VII Land and what lay beyond latitude 82.17 S, there was much work still to be completed in the fields of biology, meteorology, geology and magnetism. Nonetheless, Shackleton was entirely clear that one of his greatest efforts would be to attain the geographical South Pole. His declared intention was to establish his main base on King Edward VII Land and not to encroach on Scott's Discovery base in McMurdo Sound though, through force of circumstance, he too had to winter there; this remained a continuing source of controversy and, indeed, bitterness on the part of both Scott and his supporters, who felt that Shackleton's stated intentions amounted to a promise that had been broken. In their view, Scott had clear precedence in this area.

The ship that Shackleton chose eventually for the expedition was the *Nimrod*, an old sealing ship which, after considerable refitting, proved sturdy and seaworthy but was definitely small for the expedition's requirements: this was not his first choice. He would have much preferred to have purchased another sealer, the three year old Norwegian ship, *Bjorn*, but the purchase price of £11,000 was way beyond the means of an expedition for which funds were raised from private sponsors and without official backing from such institutions as, for example, the Royal Geographical Society.

The *Nimrod* cast off from East India Dock on the Thames on July 30, 1907, and after a brief stop at Greenhithe, sailed for Torquay, from where she was due to leave for New Zealand; during the voyage she was intercepted by an Admiralty tug with orders to proceed to Cowes to join the Naval Review by King Edward VII. The King and Queen were welcomed on board where Shackleton was invested with the Victorian Order and Queen Alexandra presented him with a Union Flag and the message, "May this Union Jack, which I entrust to your keeping, lead you safely to the South Pole."[5] With these good wishes, *Nimrod* set sail for the long and potentially hazardous journey to New Zealand, via the Cape of Good Hope.

Meanwhile, Priestley, having been recruited as the expedition's geologist, enthusiastically interrupting his university studies to do so, and designated a member of the Shore Party[6] (see Appendix II for details of the full staff of the expedition) joined the main group of eight expedition members on board the one class and slow emigrant ship, the *Runic* of the White Star Line, Shackleton's previous employers. To conserve expedition funds, the Party occupied one small cabin at a cost of £19 per head, something of a bonding exercise for the six weeks of the journey to New Zealand. Shackleton meanwhile took a fast ship via the Suez Canal to Australia where he recruited two further geologists; the eminent Professor T.W. Edgeworth David of the University of Sydney and, on his recommendation, Douglas Mawson of Adelaide University, though in his case as a physicist.

While both proved highly successful additions to the expedition, Shackleton's motivation was clearly aimed at gaining financial support from the Australian government towards scientific research which he, in fact, received in full measure. Undoubtedly, Priestley's status in the expedition was downgraded by these specific additions to the Shore Party, but he accepted the change with his usual good grace, recognizing his own lack of experience and, in the event, forming a working relation with David which he would never regret and from which he gained considerable future advantage.

By January 1, 1908, Priestley was on board the *Nimrod* at Lyttleton Harbor, New Zealand, awaiting the start of the expedition; it was at this point that he started his expedition diary which was to serve the primary purpose of an extended letter home to his father, though with considerable doubts that it would ever reach him. On New Year's Eve Priestley, with half-a-dozen crew members, had been invited to join the Admiral for dinner on his flagship, *Powerful*, in Lyttleton Harbor, for what he describes as "quite the nicest dinner I have ever tasted and the officers are as nice a set of men as I have ever met." On New Year's Day he accompanied MacIntosh, a member of the ship's crew, to lunch on another warship, the *Pegasus*, prior to a resounding send-off from some five thousand well-wishers and in fine weather which he describes, with feeling, "as the last fine weather until 8th June."

Prior to leaving, a chosen few were allowed to tour the *Nimrod*, among them a Lyttleton acquaintance with whom he had spent Christmas Day and who asked, undoubtedly reflecting Priestley's tender age, for his mother's address so that he could write to let her know that he was "quite well" as well as enclosing newspaper cuttings and photographs covering the *Nimrod*'s departure.

As the *Nimrod* was tugged towards the open sea, guns from the fort above the harbor were fired in salute and the ship was accompanied by a large flotilla of small yachts, fishing boats, a number of liners of the Union Line as well as four warships whose cheering crews lined the decks while their bands played "Hearts of Oak" and "Auld Lang Syne."

At this point Priestley found conditions on board ideal, with the whole ship's company living in comparative comfort and in good spirits but, as he later describes, "we were soon to experience a different turn of fortune's wheel." However, despite his diary being written mainly for his father's benefit, he had decided "to just write a plain and unvarnished account of the conditions of life on board during our first few weeks" and not to send his early editions back with their tow ship, the *Koonya*, employed to save coal which could not be stored adequately on the already overloaded *Nimrod*. Instead, he would wait until the *Nimrod* left for home, having disembarked the expedition, to avoid any speculation as to the outcome of their voyage to Antarctica. With his usual conscientious attention to detail, Priestley asked that typed copies of his diaries should be made.

On the very first day out in the open ocean, the ships encountered a very heavy swell, rolling as much as twenty-five degrees, which worsened as the voyage progressed. Most of the expedition members experienced seasickness and, for Priestley, the first five days were the worst, with the two doctors on board, Marshall and Mackay, being equally affected. During this period, the only food he was able to keep down was half-a-dozen apples and a little Bovril and on this he had to do his fair share of pumping and take six hourly meteorological readings in every twenty-four, often at night, which he describes as "no hardship" as he could never manage more than three hours consecutive sleep anyway. However, he drew considerable comfort from Wild and Joyce, two old Antarctic hands on board, who predicted that nothing they would experience in Antarctica itself would be worse than the current conditions.

Life on board was a constantly damp experience and, indeed, on one occasion Priestley was "washed out of the stern," while engaged in what he describes as "some excellent shooting practice," by the biggest wave he had ever encountered and wet through to the skin: no sooner had he changed into dry clothes when the whole unpleasant experience was repeated immediately and on numerous occasions thereafter, with the result that he was wet through and through, "both in and out of bed."

He lived in what were described as the "Scientists Quarters" in which he contends he would not have kept ten dogs, let alone fifteen of the Shore Party. He quite evidently felt this very strongly as, in his view, "it can be compared to no place on earth and is more like Hell than anything I have ever managed," with no opening portholes, no ventilations, every blanket wet with salt water, unbearably smelly and with the door shut on most occasions because of the weather. The only place for the occupants' personal baggage was on the floor which was subject to constant flooding and their luggage ruined in consequence. However, with typical foresight, Priestley had obtained a deed box in Lyttleton which protected photographs, letters, notebooks and diaries.

Fortunately, he had little time to dwell on the miserable living conditions as he was involved in a constant round of duties, mainly with his co-geologists, David and Mawson. These involved a constant chain of hourly readings of the barometer and the dry and wet bulb and maximum and minimum thermometers, as well as recording seawater temperatures, weather conditions and wind direction more often than not in disagreeable and, at night, dangerous circumstances. At the same time the barometer was going down and a gale predicted from the south-west, a bad omen for the ship's progress south.

The ponies on board were a cause of great and continuing concern for other members of the Shore Party; they required day and night attention, and those providing it receive praise from Priestley for looking after "those poor brutes who are having a much worse time, despite great efforts by the horse guards." At this point Priestley has evident concern for the ponies' survival and, indeed, expresses the view that the expedition's chance of reaching the Pole would die with them. Anxiety for the dogs was of almost equal concern although, through the tireless efforts of Joyce and Marston, their conditions had been improved by a "snug shelter" forward of the bridge. Above all, the entire ships company "was praying for conditions to improve from bearable to comfortable."

Now that Priestley was feeling the effects of sea-sickness less acutely, and despite the rough seas persisting, his diaries begin to show some references to and interest in the food on board. He accords high praise to William Roberts, the cook, who worked in the most difficult conditions in the galley, in which Priestley records "he could not even have made a cup of cocoa." At lunch and dinner, a good stew was served, with the addition of soup at dinner and "duff" for pudding at both meals. At breakfast he most enjoyed the hard-boiled eggs with bread and marmalade and porridge. However, it was not always possible to make bread in the rough conditions, and it was replaced by ships biscuits which were hard and "require much mastication." In addition, tinned meat was replacing fresh meat, which would not be available again until seals and penguins could be captured. All Priestley's meals were taken in a very crowded wardroom where twenty-one members of the Shore Party used a space designed for no more than eight!

He describes life on board as harmonious and "nobody would wish to be anywhere else except nearer the Pole." None of the party had "turned a hair physically," and morale was high and clearly evident in their regular musical evenings ("Chantys"). Priestley had also come to appreciate the value of swearing, a constant feature of the sailors' vocabulary, which appeared to help them overcome the often extreme conditions in which they worked though he is at pains to point out "that he does not intend to swear himself and still finds it repugnant." On a personal level, after a week at sea Priestley is keenly aware of his disreputable and unwashed appearance and having grown a thick black beard takes the view that "if put in the dock, any jury in England would give me ten years without enquiring what I was accused of."

At this point, Priestley had sustained a knee injury, although the circumstances in which it occurred are unclear; this may well have prompted his decision not to send his diaries home as he felt they would worry his mother. It is also evident that he was suffering the pangs of homesickness and missing the dances in Tewkesbury. However after almost two weeks at sea the party experienced its first dry day, which followed an "horrendous gale"; blankets and bedding were placed on deck to dry, the scientists' quarters were cleaned and disinfected and a party atmosphere prevailed. Shackleton went so far as to "splice the mainbrace," handed out cigars and cigarettes and organized a musical evening, with some "very original individual performances." It was also at this moment that Shackleton confirmed that Professor David would remain with the expedition for its whole time. Priestley records, again with good grace, even if he lost some prestige he took the view that it would be "vastly more valuable for geology and that he was sufficient of a scientist to be glad."

Around mid–January, Priestley reports perfect weather and his first sighting of icebergs; they were tabular, crevassed and about one hundred fifty feet out of the water, indicating their ice barrier origin. This was the appropriate time for their tow ship, the *Koonya*, to return to New Zealand. Priestley therefore took the opportunity to send letters home that would have King Edward VII stamps and postmarks for the first time, noting, in typical Priestley style, that they will be valuable and recording the name of intended recipients in case they did not arrive. Their dispatch was to be entrusted to Kinsey, Baines and Co. Shipping Agents in Lytlleton. He goes further in recording "may the curse of the whole Expedition rest on anyone who intercepts the letters for the sake of the stamps!"

The captain of the *Koonya* was also given an autographed copy of the menu of a farewell dinner given in his honor in the Wardroom, at which a very good whisky was served; this was hearsay so far as Priestley was concerned, in view of his unique teetotaler status on the expedition. Furthermore, he will almost certainly not have been aware that this was the special MacKinlay's Rare Old Highland Malt Whisky that had been liberally supplied to the expedition, although only moderate quantities were consumed, and a case was unearthed at the Nimrod Hut a hundred years later in perfect condition and, no doubt, improved with age.[7] At the same dinner, Priestley was very amused by Dr. Mackay's recitation of *David and Goliath* as told "by a worthy Scotch bailee at a Sunday School prize distribution."

As the *Nimrod* progressed further into the ice regions, at around latitude sixty-three and a half degrees, the decent weather continued with good sunsets and sunrises and bird life in profusion. The first pack ice was sighted, though being detached from the main pack the ship was able to maneuver through without much difficulty. As a novice to the Polar Regions, Priestley was fascinated by his first sighting of killer whales and seals of many varieties, including Leopard, Ross, Crabeater and Weddell. The bird life was equally prolific, predominantly Antarctic and snowy petrels, but also including Antarctic terns and sooty albatross.

The ship was now heading for Balloon Bight, some seventy miles from King Edward VII Land, which Priestley considered bad news for the geologists as rock specimens would have to be transported a similar distance back to the ship. At the same time, an unpleasant southerly gale was blowing up in the Ross Sea, unheralded by a corresponding fall in the barometer, which could be unreliable in such conditions in southern latitudes; the sea and air temperatures were almost the same at around twenty-eight degrees Fahrenheit respectively.

Priestley experienced his first taste of real seamanship, including its traditional language, at this stage having been prevented from being of much use in earlier adverse conditions due to sea-sickness. All hands were called to "bout" ship, "wearing" her, that is bringing her round into the wind, and then "tacking" into the wind. Priestley records that "the exercise was of great benefit to his digestion which had suffered through lack of it, so far."

As January drew to a close, and "in the land of the midnight sun," the ship approached the expected location of Balloon Bight. However, there was considerable confusion as to its location by comparison with its position detailed in Scott's *Journals of the Discovery Expedition*.[8] Eventually Shackleton, in agreement with Captain England, was forced to the conclusion that Balloon Bight had been destroyed and floated out to sea. Consequently, it looked certain that a landing could not be made on King Edward VII Land and, while the ship could work west along the Barrier to try and locate another suitable landing site; in its absence recourse to Scott's Discovery base in McMurdo Sound would be the only viable alternative. Finally, at seventy-eight degrees, forty-one minutes south, the farthest south that any ship had yet reached, the fateful decision to retreat and head for McMurdo was taken, at which point, one of the greatest and most bitter controversies of the Heroic Age of Antarctic Exploration had its inception.

For Priestley and his fellow geologists, this was a decision that could be taken with a clear conscience and much to their advantage, as McMurdo would provide a much better location for geological exploration. Indeed, anticipating the landing, the geologists were already developing plans to spend two to three weeks exploring the Ferrier Glacier, which should yield some interesting fossils and enable them to explore its dry valley, which had been described as "beautifully glaciated" by the Discovery Expedition.

In the event, while a landing was made in the vicinity of the Discovery Hut, the sea-ice prevented this being close enough to haul one hundred fifty tons of supplies across the intervening distance; in fact, Joyce, Wild and Adams had made an exploratory journey to the Discovery Hut, which they had found in a wonderful state of preservation, but it had taken them fourteen hours to make the return journey even with a sail hoisted on their sledge to take advantage of the following wind.

However, Priestley who reports "feeling at the top of his form both physically and mentally" and in company with Professor David and Mawson, had not wasted his time. As well as trying out skis "quite successfully" for the first time, the three geologists had their initial excursion on the ice with a trip to Tent Island, and their first real sighting of Mount Erebus about nine miles distance (to have greater significance for Priestley in his subsequent ascent of the mountain). During this short trip, it is clearly evident that theirs was anything but a starvation diet; their lunch, for example, comprised a tongue, sardines, bread, butter, biscuits and a knuckle of ham, together with two bottles of cocoa and three lemons, given to Priestley in Sydney! Nonetheless, the walking was some of the hardest that Priestley had ever done and he returned back on board after eighteen grueling miles with what Shackleton described as "a good sledging appetite."

The expedition eventually moved the relatively short distance to Cape Royds (see map, Appendix III) as the chosen site for the expedition's hut and base. After a false start when a southeast wind thwarted their initial landing, in Priestley's words, "Man proposes but God disposes," the party commenced landing stores including the motorcar, the ponies and dogs and the parts for the hut. In geological terms, the site was composed of "basalt with feldspar crystals and, strewn about, erratics of granite, in addition to gneiss and aplitic rocks." At the end of the first week in February, the work of the expedition was about to begin in earnest.

During the remaining days of February, Priestley, together with all members of both the Shore Party and the Ship's Company, was fully employed in setting up the expedition base. Initially, he was involved in sledging fodder for the ponies and cork for the expedition hut while Dunlop, the engineer, sunk holes in the lava and cemented in foundation poles; meanwhile, he continued to sleep on the ship which was eventually brought nearer inshore and a block and tackle set up at the top of the hill approaching the hut site, which could pull up six sledges at a time using steam and the ship's winch. Unfortunately, this operation had to be interrupted quite frequently due to a temporary break-up of the ice.

Nonetheless, by about February 7, the hut was more or less complete and, with a good quantity of stores landed, it was decided that the Shore Party could remain even if the ship had to move out from time to time. Unfortunately, Priestley twisted his knee quite badly again on February 9 which kept him on board ship until he could finally land, with his personal luggage, on February 21. This continuous movement of the ice because of the southeast wind was causing England, the ship's captain, considerable concern; he was keen to leave for New Zealand as soon as possible. However, with only eleven and a half tons of coal landed, this would allow for only one stove for heating to be kept alight throughout the winter and, even then, unless situated in close proximity to it, the temperature would be below freezing elsewhere in the hut.

For the moment, however, Priestley was enjoying the "picknicky" existence with "plenty of stores, a good chef and some physical work." There were still no facilities to wash but "the dirt peels off" and "getting up in the cold was unpleasant but he felt fine after a good breakfast." From mid–February onwards, the Hut was almost complete. The walls were decorated with autographs and photographs of the King and Queen. They had a functioning clock, a self-registering thermometer and a Robinson's of Tewkesbury calendar, which he provided, given to him by his Uncle Sam. He had also taken the opportunity to walk along the valley, with Macintosh, to where the ponies were tethered and where slightly brackish water was collected from a small lake, for drinking purposes. At the same time, he collected and labelled several geological specimens which he stored in special collapsible cardboard boxes which he had bought from the aforementioned Robinson's. He also noted an interesting phenomenon. Spray from a storm "dashed right over the cliffs for hundreds of yards and caked all the rocks and stores nearby with ice as much as twelve to eighteen inches thick."

Finally, on February 22, the *Nimrod* left for the winter; for Priestley this was where his specific scientific role in the expedition really began. Nonetheless, during the first day of the Shore Party's now complete isolation, he was involved in the more prosaic duties of helping Shackleton to clean the hut and moving iced-up stores. Of crucial importance, the *Nimrod* had been able to leave a total of fifteen and a half tons of coal for the winter; sufficient, but only just, for the party's requirements until its return. A good omen for the party's winter comfort was some very good cakes that Roberts had made using a cake tin improvised from Coleman's flour boxes.

The final days of February were spent in settling into the hut and its environment. Priestley "earned his keep" in a round of duties but was prevented from joining the remainder of the expedition in preparation for a penguin foray because of continuing problems with his twisted knee. The interior of the hut was divided into nine cubicles, with improvised divisions, though only two, for the darkroom and Shackleton, had been properly "walled off"; the consequent reduction in space in the middle of the hut made it much warmer which was a most welcome improvement. Apart from areas left for the chef and stores, the cubicles measured approximately six foot six inches square, each allocated to two of the Shore Party. Priestley was to "dig" with Murray, the biologist and he expected that "we are likely to get on first rate."

He also took the opportunity to organize his personal gear which, with his customary attention to detail, had been meticulously prepared for the expedition. His books and photographs had traveled safely as had his geological hammer and ice-axe, in his view "the most useful tools in the Expedition." His chemical apparatus, including an agate pestle and mortar, a platinum crucible and some foil and wire, were all in perfect condition despite their packing cases getting wet during the *Nimrod's* voyage.

Some of the cubicles were already exhibiting the characteristics of their occupants. Dr. Marshall had stained the "walls" of his cubicle, shared with Adams, with permanganate of potash, which gave it an excellent walnut color. Joyce and Wild, however, illustrated their natural practicality by providing their cubicle with extensive shelving. Meanwhile, Marston and Day decorated their walls with Antarctic sketches and "it looked very nice." Murray and Priestley contented themselves with "arranging their stuff on the floor until Murray could be released from his duties, as carpenter, on the roof of the hut."

Overall, the hut was proving "luxurious" with meals now taken at a proper table and chairs and with wash basins and baths on stands, one for each cubicle. Priestley was also amused "to hear the talk and snoring that goes on in the night and, even more, by the recriminations in the morning." Priestley was more acutely aware of this as he volunteered to act as the almost permanent night watchman; this arrangement suited him very well as he could work much better in the relative quiet which prevailed; his strong work ethic was already very well established even at his comparatively young age. However, interruptions to his watch, when they occurred, came mainly from either the dogs or the ponies. The former were habitual fighters while the latter would often gnaw through their traces and go on the rampage, often eating the compressed fodder stored outside the hut.

Importantly, geological work could now begin in earnest as February gave way to March. A short walk along the coast from their winter quarters to a small bay provided very good results. Erratics, many of great size, littered the mainly moraine-like material. Olivine basalt containing very fine porphyries crystals was also discovered, by Murray. Equally productive was Backdoor Bay, another short walk from the hut, and an adjacent lake carpeted with reddish brown algae on the bottom with air bubbles which appeared to have frozen as they streamed to the surface. Nearby was a gravel terrace with erratics of an unidentified darkish green close-grained rock. Priestley had already labelled forty different specimens while David was reserving some of the most interesting for sectioning during the long winter night.

At this stage, Shackleton proposed that the specimens be given to the principal universities of Europe and the Colonies. While both David and Priestley fully approved the plan, they realized that it would involve an exhausting collecting program which would, however, be more than offset by its value to scientific research.

Priestley records, to his great satisfaction, that the first Sunday in March was the first "to be kept up properly." On all previous Sundays, since their landing, the weather had been fine and had to be utilized for essential work. Now that the Party was much better established, Shackleton took the opportunity to read an abridged version of the morning service and, apart from essential routine, the day was kept free. It was also something of "a red letter day" as the Party was issued, "liberally," with its woolen winter clothing. Priestley received "six pairs of mittens and gloves, six pairs of stockings, three pairs of bed-socks, a pyjama suit of jaegar wool, three singlets and three pants, three woollen outer-shirts, two woollen caps and a scarf; in addition, a pair of warm house-boots and a pair of Russian felt boots."

The first sign of a later cause for great concern and anxiety was the unexplained death of one of the ponies; it was thought that it was poisoned by eating wood shavings and refuse within its reach. However a hut for the ponies was completed shortly thereafter which added to both their comfort and safety. Nonetheless, Priestley records in his diary that the walls were constructed mainly of fodder bales, which appears somewhat incongruous!

Preparations were now in full swing for an ascent of Mount Erebus, an active volcano of around thirteen thousand feet in height, making it of great scientific interest, and within easy reach of winter quarters. David, Mawson and Mackay were chosen as the assault party, with Adams, Marshall and Brocklehurst in support. Priestley felt certain that, as the remaining geologist, he would have been chosen as a member of the assault team and greatly regretted that his troublesome knee prevented him from taking part.

On March 5 the Erebus Party set off with sledges carrying up to five hundred pounds and Shackleton, Joyce, Wild, Day, Murray and Armitage, with Priestley, went with them to help over the initial stages of difficult ground; by the following day the sledging parties could be seen clearly making good progress at around five thousand feet and hopes were high that they would achieve the summit.

Meanwhile, the news was not so encouraging with regard to the ponies. "Sandy" was ailing, and despite being dosed with the unlikely combination of syrup, brandy and beer, hopes for his survival were slim; indeed, he died on the following day. An autopsy illustrated that he had swallowed as much as fourteen pounds of volcanic dust, indicating that the ponies had been picketed in an area where this was all too readily available for their consumption. Any problem with the ponies was of the greatest concern as their continuing good health was considered essential to the expedition's success in reaching the Pole.

Priestley drew much greater encouragement, however, from the progress of the Erebus Party, spotted by Armitage, using his telescope, on March 7 and indicating that the support party had decided to go for the summit as well. Consequently, Priestley was not surprised when, only four days later on March 11, both parties returned, having reached the summit, with the exception of Brocklehurst, who had been "pretty well knocked up." Geologically, the ascent had also been a success. David had found the old crater covered with millions of feldspar crystals, some of which he had secured, and the fumaroles had built up "chimney like structures with cowls of ice" owing to the unique climatic conditions.

Elation quickly turned to dismay again, however, when another of the ponies, "Billy," was showing symptoms similar to those from which "Sandy" had died; it seemed almost inevitable and, indeed, proved to be the case that he too would not survive. Priestley expresses the view, strongly, that in these circumstances the chances of reaching the Pole will be "chimerical."

For the remainder of the month of March and throughout April, life continued with the same now well established routine of activities, enlivened by some notable variations. Around the middle of March, Murray called him at 3:50 a.m. to view the sky on the western horizon, which showed an amazingly full spectrum of colors, arranged in the shape of a bow, which affected him profoundly. He also continued to be greatly troubled by the deteriorating state of the ponies, with others having to be shot. On one occasion, when it took two revolver bullets to dispatch a pony, he reports that "I don't think I have appreciated any half-hour in my life less than that which I spent watching a dying horse knowing all the time that he was sure to go and there was nothing I could do for him." Towards the end of March, this was also a most productive period, geologically, mainly on the lower slopes of Mount Erebus, especially at around the one thousand foot level; elsewhere, the position of some granite erratics "proved to be the best method of establishing the former extent of the Great Ice Sheet." In addition, he was impressed by the movement of pieces of "screw-ice" sliding over each other "accompanied by one of the weirdest noises I have ever heard though at times they remind me of certain concerts I have heard!"

With the help of other members of the party, including Shackleton, who, as a matter of leadership policy, involved himself in all aspects of the expedition, good progress was made in digging trenches which, at progressively increasing depths, produced some interesting results. Priestley reports, for example, on one occasion "that the bottom of the trench consisted of a layer of evil smelling ooze several inches thick resting on ordinary volcanic gravel and that there was no need for examination to prove that hydrogen-sulphide was a considerable factor pointing to organic material in a decaying state, later revealing vegetable material." He also helped David to photograph ice flowers which resembled stalkless white chrysanthemums, two to three inches across, with perfectly formed petals.

During the same period, life in and around the hut was both varied and lively, if not always in the best of circumstances. Brocklehurst's condition had deteriorated to the extent that Marshall had to amputate one of his toes to "quite a gallery of onlookers." This gave way to even greater concern when post-operative suppuration suggested that further amputations might be necessary. On the brighter side, Priestley very much enjoyed the gramophone after dinner and records that "while it is going I close my eyes and can easily fancy myself in the Pit at the Bristol Theatre listening to the orchestra playing the overture to the *Mikado*." Moreover, he was delighted that, even at temperatures well below freezing, he was able to work outside without mittens and without sustaining any frostbite, "indicating good circulation." Work was also progressing well with the collection and packing of geological specimens, with ten boxes filled at this stage.

The duties which formed an essential feature of life in the hut, and especially that of mess-man, by his own assessment found Priestley wanting. He records, with some feeling, that on one occasion when stoning raisins "it is a moot point I think whether there are more stones on the surrounding country or me when I have finished while I fancy that there have been stones in everything ever since from the soup to the sweet!" However, a highlight was the celebration of Wild's birthday on April 18 when a liberal allowance of luxuries was produced, including birthday cake, Christmas pudding, crystallized fruits, turtle soup, grouse, champagne and whisky. Priestley suggests that "the hardships of the Antarctic were therefore excellently represented at the table!"

Finally, as April drew to a close, the days were beginning to shorten, with the first earth shadows appearing and a gradual decrease in the light anticipated over the next two months, heralding the onset of winter.

May opened with a blizzard of great force, confining the party to the hut for three days; though not of such intensity, the poor weather continued until the middle of the month, when much calmer and clearer conditions prevailed, enabling Priestley the luxury of walks after supper, evidently to his considerable satisfaction as illustrated by his diary. "If one goes to the highest point on the promontory the Peninsular stands out beneath like a map and Mounts Erebus and Bird are both clear. The moon and its reflection on the water both being of a golden colour whilst, last but not least, round the Northern horizon there is a fairly well defined spectrum caused by the rays of the sun; then the scene will take some beating in any land."

Furthermore, at this point Priestley is of the opinion that the increasing hours of darkness were having no detrimental effect on the party and, personally, he felt on top form, to the extent that he broke his teetotal commitment by taking a glass of champagne to celebrate David's birthday. In addition, by the month's end, the party experienced some of the best aurora displays to date, which Wild and Joyce judged as far superior to any witnessed on the Discovery Expedition.

Although, by the beginning of June, the darkness prevented geological work, Priestley was very fully employed with the routine of winter survival and "time passes very agreeably." The party's doctor also took this opportunity to weigh and measure its members; Priestley's weight illustrated some deliberate loss, by "taking less dinner to avoid indigestion and he was now in decent condition." Less agreeable was his involvement in killing and cutting up seals on what he describes as "Bloody Sunday" on June 14, in which every part of the seal was utilized in some way. The highlight of the month was Midwinter's Day, which was celebrated in great style on June 23. There was an exchange of cards, presents and a larger and more varied meal than usual accompanied by a liberal flow of alcohol, as if it were Christmas, roommates Wild and Joyce being singled out as the most enthusiastic participants.

In mid-July, Priestley's morale continued at a high level; as he expresses it, "I have never experienced the joy of merely being alive as much before as I have done tonight." However, while the majority of the party continued to cope well with the winter darkness, a few incidents illustrated that some were experiencing difficulties. Brocklehurst fell out with Wild and left the hut for about an hour, causing considerable anxiety, but returned in a better frame of mind later. This was followed, in early August, "by the first really disagreeable fracas of the Expedition between Mackay and Roberts over a minor incident which might have escalated into physical confrontation had Mawson not intervened."

By the beginning of August, with the advent of the return of some daylight, sledging preparations were in full swing with Joyce busy creating harnesses and other equipment on a foot-treadle sewing machine, while Day had parts for the motorcar "all over the place." It was also at this time that Priestley records his great satisfaction at having "two faithful companions" among the dogs to look after, "Cissie and Boy," the latter thought to be a bitch despite her name and resulting in some ribaldry by his companions due to his insistence in retaining this nomenclature. However, he was later vindicated when it was discovered that "Boy" was, in fact, a male! Meanwhile, Shackleton confirmed that Priestley might retain "Cissie" as his own at the conclusion of the expedition, which he subsequently did, and at this point had already "been at pains to teach her the folly of her ways and the wisdom of mine." This was also the moment when Shackleton advised him that he would lead the geological effort in the Western Mountains in September, as David, Mawson and Mackay would be heading north to locate the South Magnetic Pole, a decision much welcomed by Priestley.

During the month, the pace of preparations gained momentum, with Priestley actively involved in dismantling the dog kennels and building a garage for the motorcar, on which great hopes still relied, with a party of no less than seven expedition members required to push the car uphill to its new home. In addition, by the end of August, geological specimens of considerable interest had been collected which, on examination by David and Priestley, illustrated "trachyte, *in situ*, occurring as a flow beneath basalt, confirming the volcanic nature of the area fairly conclusively."

September and October proved to be equally busy months with Priestley very actively involved in laying depots for both the Southern Party's attempt on the Geographic Pole and the Northern Party's journey to the Magnetic Pole. Over the same period, his duties in looking after the ponies and dogs proved very demanding and, while he carried these out with his usual conscientiousness, it is evident from his diary that this was at the expense of his official role as a geologist, which he was beginning to resent.

Fortunately his resentment, most unusual in itself, was short-lived as November started with "a great day scientifically" at Pram Point and also marked the beginning of the sledging season routine. Consequently, on November 3 he left for seven or eight days in support of the Southern Party then, as he describes it, "Ho back for Cape Royds." The first day out was over twelve fairly arduous miles of rotten surface with the ponies sinking up to eighteen inches into the snow which was "telling horribly on them and they were done up though he was feeling fit and well." However, conditions improved somewhat immediately thereafter, until they reached a crevassed area which called for considerable care, especially with the ponies. On November 7, "he said goodbye" to the Southern Party and his Party returned to the hut as quickly as possible, including a forced march of no less than thirty miles. On returning to the hut, they arrived just in time to join the members of the expedition still in residence in "broaching a keg of beer" in honor of the King's birthday and while the teetotaler Priestley suffered no ill effects, many showed a little extra "pig-eyedness" the following morning. For the next few days, Priestley continued with local trips mainly of a geological nature interspersed with the usual and more prosaic tasks of harvesting seals and penguins for their larder; this included the eggs of the latter, which were much enjoyed and very nourishing.

However, on November 23, Priestley with Joyce, Murray, Marston and Marshall started up Erebus with a view to adding to the scientific work completed during the first Party's successful summit attempt. In the event, in taking only one small tent to accommodate five people, this came uncomfortably close to a total disaster in which Priestley was the most acutely involved and during which he was to exhibit his developing powers of endurance, both physically and mentally, to the full.

After valuable help from Armitage and the dogs in the early stages of their journey, the party set up camp at around fifteen hundred feet, unfortunately alongside a nunatak, which diverted any wind directly at their tent. Although by the afternoon a strong south-east breeze was picking up, Priestley reports the party as "doing well and very cheerful" and, in view of the anticipated cramped conditions in the tent, he volunteered to sleep outside. Drifting snow began almost immediately after Priestley had turned in. He took the precaution of covering his Burberry trousers and jackets, left outside his sleeping bag, with rocks and drew some comfort from the fact that Joyce was aware of his precise location. As the drift worsened, his position became increasingly untenable and he advised Joyce that he was moving to the top of a hill nearby where he could find better shelter and where he could be found next morning.

Thereafter, conditions deteriorated rapidly and he was constantly covered with drifting snow "sweeping in a continual cloud over his head." He decided, in these circumstances, that the tent party would have great difficulty in finding him in the morning. Consequently, after dressing fully with the greatest of difficulty and discomfort, he made his way back to the sledge where he, once again, got into his sleeping bag wrapped around by the cloth which usually housed the tent. In this position he remained for the next seventy-two hours in constantly drifting conditions, being gradually blown downhill by the wind towards the glacier and in constant danger of being carried right over the hundred foot drop into Horseshoe Bay.

On three occasions, members of the tent party were able to pass him some biscuits, raw pemmican and "some Rowntrees chocolates from his rucksack" but lack of water provided him with real difficulties, particularly as he had taken only half a cup of tea before his ordeal started, not being thirsty at that time. Almost incredibly, this resulted in his going without water apart from "such névé as he could prise up with the point of a safety pin" for no less than eighty hours; moreover, this prevented him from eating even all of the small amount of food that he received. On one occasion, from faint memory, during the third day of his lonely sojourn, Joyce reached him briefly with the far from comforting news that his Party were themselves in some difficulty with the tent torn and in constant threat of being blown away by the increasing wind. Joyce completed his successful though frostbitten return to the tent only by receiving shouted advice from his companions; any further attempt to reach Priestley was out of the question.

Finally, towards the end of the third day, with a slight lessening in the wind and drift, he was able to contemplate a return to his comrades though he had the greatest difficult in getting out of his frozen sleeping bag and was eventually dragged "half in, half out," by Marston, back to the tent. Priestley found that "five men in a three-man tent was fearful" and he had great difficulty in sitting down. He was also suffering from some frostbite to his hands and feet but his circulation soon recovered. Furthermore, although he swallowed some tea with great enthusiasm, he was sick almost immediately, through a combination of weakness and paraffin in the tea, which had affected the whole of the tent party.

Priestley (right) with Murray at Green Lake, Cape Royds, during the British Antarctic Expedition 1907–09 (The Scott Polar Research Institute Picture Library).

Sleeping between Murray and Marshall he survived the next few hours in acute discomfort and eventually the party were able to get under way with the wind in their favor, having christened their erstwhile and miserable location "Misery Nunatek"; indeed, Priestley was "as glad to leave a place as any soul can be." The journey back to the hut was made more difficult by their enfeebled condition, especially Priestley who was feeling the effects of his ordeal severely. However, to their great relief, they finally reached the hut on November 28, having had to dump the sledge to be collected later. Undoubtedly, this short but acutely dangerous period was a character-building experience for the even greater and extended challenge of his role in the survival of Scott's Northern Party.

The final day of November was spent recuperating, "feeding up," and preparing for the long-awaited Western Party's scientific exploration on the Ferrar Glacier. This would complete the expedition's overall objectives, although the success or failure of Shackleton's Southern Party and David's quest for the Magnetic Pole were entirely a matter of speculation at this stage. The plan thereafter was to return to Butter Point by January 7, 1909, to meet David, Mawson and Mackay, when the parties would split again, with Priestley, Mawson and Brocklehurst working in Dry Valley while David, Armitage and Mackay would return to the hut at Cape Royds.

Consequently, the Western Party started for Butter Point on December 1 to lay depots with six hundred pounds of supplies, and by the 5th reached their first objective. The difficult sledging conditions over poor snow and in mainly bright and warm sunshine had made Armitage snow-blind, which Priestley treated with cocaine and zinc sulfate. He describes their journey as "slow and monotonous and our sledging habiliments, when the sun is out, border much more on the punitive," although one great improvement had been the addition of Bovril to their pemmican!

On reaching Butter Point they found not only an established depot of four hundred fifty pounds of supplies but, more significantly, a letter in a milk tin from David, Mawson and Mackay. This illustrated that the Party did not now expect to return to Butter Point until around January 15 but, meanwhile, requested that such diverse items as "baccy and a muffler, photographic plates and cooking oil" be depoted to await their return. David's letter expressed the view that Priestley would find Dry Valley interesting geologically and "wished him the best of luck ... and thank you for all your kindnesses."

At this stage of the journey, Priestley concentrated some of his scientific efforts on meteorology and was fascinated by the different cloud formations, which included cirrostratus, cirrocumulus and cirrus, all of which were much affected by the air current with Erebus constantly coming in and out of the clouds. Nonetheless, geology remained his principal preoccupation; when camped at the foot of the Ferrar Glacier, he noted "a good deal of water inundation and transportation along the sea cliffs whilst the dust of the moraine was quite remarkable with a surface of bare ice and patchy snowdrifts."

With the depot laid, the Party returned to the hut at Cape Royds by December 8, finding "everybody fit and well"; supplies for three men for five weeks, and the laying of depots, had to be arranged in preparation for the next journey which, as Priestley's diary illustrates, comprised very heavy loads; they included fifty tins of pemmican, thirty-two pounds of sugar, twenty-four tins of matches, sixty-three pounds of biscuits, five pounds of tea, seven tins of cooking oil, twelve pounds of oatmeal, salt, fourteen pounds of Bovril, two tins of pepper, eleven pounds of chocolate, eighteen pounds of milk and eight pounds of cocoa, in addition to any personal preferences.

Their journey back to Butter Point that they attained again on December 4, had been relatively straightforward over fairly good surfaces. Hereafter their progress should be very fruitful, particularly in geological terms, so far as the ever fully committed Priestley was concerned. Having fulfilled David's party's itemized requests, the group left Butter Point on December 15 and over the ensuing few days, as they approached Descent Pass and Cathedral Rocks, Priestley was "enthralled by ice formations, ice cascades and glaciers in profusion."

For the remainder of December, approaching Christmas Day, Priestley was in his true element, collecting geological specimens and mapping glacial features, with particular reference to the rapid thawing of the ice which was taking place as he worked, supported by detailed sketches and diagrams of the rock formations. His research revealed that the previous records available were untrustworthy in many respects.

By Christmas Day, the party was established on a good camping site in a sheltered position, and it was declared a rest day. Their dinner menu included a plum pudding and a toast to the donor who had given this to Wild when in New Zealand, although its unaccustomed richness lead to some of the party having vivid dreams which were recounted, with gusto, on the Boxing Day. Priestley also records his appreciation of Darwin's *Voyage of the Beadle*, which he read for half an hour each evening.

The first day of the New Year of 1909 found the party within sight of Butter Point again, where they would continue with their scientific work while waiting for David's Northern Party to return. However, when they had not returned by January 6, with all really useful work completed, Priestley's party left Butter Point temporarily, leaving their camp fully provisioned, but returned on January 8 to find still no sign of David's party.

Consequently, after waiting anxiously until January 12 and with still no sign of David, Priestley's party decided to take a week's provisions to work in Dry Valley where some very useful geology was completed. This included "large patches of gravel mixed with boulders of every description and size, with a chaos of sedimentary, volcanic, plutonic and metamorphic rocks." It was here, while taking a stroll after dinner with Armitage, that Priestley revealed some details of his future hopes and plans. This included, crucially, his willingness to remain in Antarctica for a further year in the event of the non-arrival of the Southern or Northern Parties before the date that the *Nimrod* could leave safely for New Zealand. At the same time, Armitage promised to visit his home in Tewkesbury to "give some account of me and to exercise any commissions I might have him do." His philosophical outlook for one so young and his decision to volunteer for another winter in Antarctica is reflected perhaps in the quotation, noted in his diary at this same period, from the small compilation of his favorite poet, Stevenson, which he had with him, specifically his *Requiem*.

> Under the dark and starry sky,
> Dig the grave and let me lie.
> Glad did I live and gladly die,
> And I laid me down with a will.
>
> This be the verse you grave for me:
> "Here he lies where he longs to be;
> Home is the sailor, home from the sea,
> And the Hunter, home from the Hill."

At this point Priestley makes constant reference to feeling hungry despite eating his "full whack" and felt that this was because he was still growing—a reasonable assumption in view of his age. He also had another opportunity to volunteer for a second winter when he learned that, in the event of the Southern Party not returning, Murray had instructions to ask Mawson "to stay down" with two volunteers. Also he felt that he had withstood his first winter well, with no further trouble with his knee, no frostbite or snow-blindness and without requiring any medication, even for his anticipated indigestion.

Alternatively, if all went well with both the Southern and Northern Parties, and the expedition was able to return home intact, he hoped to be associated with David, as a salaried assistant, in the publication of the results of the expedition; failing this he was perfectly happy to return home with his private geological collection, to spend a year or two at University College while waiting for a further chance to enhance his practical experience. In the event, much of this ambitious plan was brought to fruition.

By January 20, Priestley was bemoaning his fate at having to sit around waiting for the Northern Party, but life changed dramatically on the 22nd; the floe on which he, Armitage and Brocklehurst were camped broke off from the glacial moraine and went out to sea. He describes while completing his diary "more from habit than anything else" that the Party were as near death as they could be with only fifteen days provisions and oil, on half rations, and one chance in a thousand of being picked up by the *Nimrod*."

Miraculously, the party was back on land at Butter Point by January 23 but only after "twenty-four hours that felt like a fortnight," and after an experience that even Priestley had difficulty in describing with his usual objective clarity. While on the detached floe, the Party investigated every means of salvation, all of which proved impossible until, with the turning of the tide, they drifted back towards Butter Point, their only realistic escape route from their perilous predicament. This had been pressed home particularly as killer whales were common in this area and, with their usual line of attack being breaking up the floes on which their prey could be found, would no doubt have viewed Priestley and his companions as a welcome change to their diet.

In the event, the floe eventually returned to its original location adjacent to, but not hard up against, Butter Point. It was only after a flurry of activity, born of desperation, that the party was able to bridge the gap with their sledge and scramble onto land with most of their supplies intact. Priestley describes this very near-death experience, "may I never have such an experience again, I shall dream of Killer whales for weeks!" Undoubtedly, this event, over which he had no control and in which good fortune was the deciding factor, could easily have ended, most abruptly, Priestley's distinguished life at a very early stage.

The very next day, adding to their great sense of relief, the *Nimrod* was sighted and the party was taken on board to return to Cape Royds. By January 28, Priestley had all his private collection of specimens on board ship and, meanwhile, had absorbed most of his mail and the newspapers from England. He was dismayed that "the English newspapers seem to be full of lies about the relations between Shackleton and England on the voyage down" and was of the authoritative opinion that many "were by a lot of fools who seem to be making themselves conspicuous on subjects of which they know nothing and only know what is wrong." He felt that it was entirely erroneous that Shackleton should have been condemned in his absence while shouldering the heat and burden of leading the expedition, in which he had never hesitated to bear his full part. While it is historical fact that Shackleton and England disagreed, mainly on account of the latter's perceived timidity, it is generally recognized that Shackleton was vindicated by the outcome of his decisions and, in Priestley's view, "England has acted like a rotter in not denying these reports at once." With his mail he found no such dissatisfaction and had received letters from everyone he expected to write. His was particularly grateful to Joyce, who had returned home with the *Nimrod*, and whose series of letters "read more like a novel." To these, his father filled in the gaps with local news from Tewkesbury, including that of his beloved cricket.

It was also becoming clear, from both the newspapers and his letters, that Shackleton's decision to set up his expedition base at Cape Royds, *force majeure*, which Scott regarded fundamentally as his preserve, was being given considerable publicity, universally to Shackleton's detriment. Priestley was clearly upset both in relation to the truth of the accusations and their effect on Shackleton. His views, which he expresses without reserve, are worthy of consideration because of their historical significance when made by one of whom the test of time has proved to be a most reliable witness. He contends that "he is one of the most sensitive men I have seen and will feel them awfully. I think we will all stand by him however for he played the game by us and has taken his share of hard work and done a good deal personally to help with the scientific work."

In a much lighter vein, and in typically Priestley style, on hearing of his brother Bert's engagement he felt that he would make a very good uncle and "had been patronising some penguins in a very avuncular manner."

The first ten days of February were spent somewhat in limbo as the return of the bay ice had forced the *Nimrod* to put out to sea temporarily but it enabled the ever conscientious Priestley to catalogue and pack his geological specimens, preparatory to loading and return to New Zealand. However, his future was still uncertain as neither the Northern or Southern Parties had returned until, to the intense relief of all the members of the expedition then resident at Cape Royds, David and his companions arrived back safely having reached the South Magnetic Pole "in spite of all difficulties."

Over the next few days, it was Mawson who had recovered sufficiently to give an account of their trip. They had covered almost one thousand three hundred miles, man-hauling sledges and without a support party, a record that Priestley felt worth having for the expedition in itself. Furthermore, he goes on to add that "they must have been nearly on their beam ends at times and had gone for days living on only a few biscuits and the animals of the country." To add to this good news, the *Nimrod* returned to Cape Royds towards the end of February landing the Southern Party's Support Party and by March 1 the Southern Party itself had returned.

The expedition was now fully reunited, and although Shackleton and his companions had not reached the Pole, they had come within less than one hundred miles of attaining it at eighty-three degrees thirty minutes south, or thereabouts; indeed they might have reached the Pole had Shackleton not judged the risk of some or all of them not surviving as too great, even though they were so tantalizingly close. They had endured extreme hardship in their climb up onto the central plateau, reaching an altitude of eleven thousand, five hundred feet, in constant danger from hidden crevasses, on short rations from dwindling supplies and with Marshall suffering from acute dysentery.

By March 3, the entire complement of the expedition was on board *Nimrod* which set out on its journey home. Both the expedition and Priestley had attained much and gained greatly from the experience. The expedition, as a whole, had made the first ascent of Mount Erebus, the South Magnetic Pole had been attained, the Southern Party had almost reached the Pole and in doing so establishing a feasible route for future attempts, while Priestley's party had carried out a detailed survey of the mountains west of McMurdo Sound. Furthermore, as a result of the expeditions' combined activities,

3. Shackleton's Nimrod Expedition

extremely valuable work had been completed in the fields of geology, biology, magnetism, meteorology and physics.

For Priestley, while the expedition must be considered as a "baptism of fire," he had proved, beyond doubt, his ability to endure great hardship and danger during two life threatening experiences, and to become a valued and highly regarded member of the expedition team by his contribution towards not only the advancement of scientific knowledge but also by his commitment to and involvement in all aspects of expedition life. Above all, it established Antarctica as the central interest of, and quite possibly the catalyst for, his later long and distinguished life.

4

Between Expeditions

By mid-March 1909, the *Nimrod* with Priestley on board arrived back in New Zealand to universal acclaim and overwhelming hospitality; on this occasion Shackleton's success was not overshadowed by the threat of war which "stole the limelight" from the launch of his second Antarctic venture.[1]

The ship had paused, briefly, at Stewart Island on the return journey to prevent the evening papers in New Zealand "scooping the news that later gripped the world." Here, Priestley "tasted the joys of more temperate climes when the expedition members were decanted onto a sandy beach" where he fished for blue cod, bathed and lazed about in the sunshine of a perfect day. As he describe it, the expedition members, lulled by this unusual pleasure, were "fed on by insects feeding on carcasses that had been free of bites for a whole year" with a most uncomfortable and painful aftermath. At their first of many official banquets later in Christchurch, those attending could easily recognize the expedition members; "they were never still." Priestley and his fellow sufferers were "covered with tiny suppurating pimples which made them writhe and shrug unceasingly as they scratched and swore!" As a result, while the food was very acceptable, the numerous and lengthy speeches were purgatory.

Because Professor David wisely missed the first banquet, Shackleton unexpectedly passed Priestley a note telling him that he would be required to reply to one of the many toasts on behalf of the scientists; together with strict instructions to touch on the importance to the world of Antarctic meteorology, geology, magnetism, oceanography and botany, with a few words on the significance of Mount Erebus, "but on no account for more than five minutes." Priestley records, with his customary self-deprecation, that he has no recollection whatsoever of what he said but "that he filled the assignment very ill."

Nonetheless, the banquet reminded him of a last and celebratory dinner before the expedition left Antarctica. It appears that Frank Wild had disgraced

4. Between Expeditions

himself by "doing himself too well." In the middle of Shackleton's speech, he had risen unsteadily to his feet and leaning heavily on Priestley's shoulder had shouted "bugger Scott." A dumbfounded Priestley had been commanded in a sibilant whisper by his neighbor, Joyce, to "drag him down and muzzle him you bloody fool"; he did and was thanked by Wild the next morning. Wild was, of course, very partisan in the controversy which marred the Scott-Shackleton relationship and Priestley's view, at this early stage, of what was later to become a major and divisive issue in early South Polar exploration, is particularly pertinent and influential, as he served with both protagonists.

Priestley felt that the entire affair was "quite unjustified" and based on false premises. On the one hand, he took the view that Shackleton believed, quite wrongly, that Scott attributed his own comparative failure in 1902 to Shackleton's illness while, on the other hand, Scott never forgave Shackleton for making his Headquarters on Ross Island, his previous base, though Shackleton did everything possible to settle elsewhere. While Priestley puts it in an uncomplicated and straightforward way, the issue grew to huge proportions with the passing years and caused great divisions with the protagonists' supporters becoming either "Scott or Shackleton men."

As this was to become an issue of such extensive dispute and historical debate, it is worth digressing to record Priestley's considered view as it evolved.

He and Day were the only two to serve with both Scott and Shackleton "under the footing of Officers." Both agreed that "while by all ordinary moral standards, Scott was the better man, Shackleton was the more inspiring leader." This was Priestley's considered and settled view, though he qualifies it by stating that he did not know Scott at the height of his powers and thinks that he may have been a different man on the Discovery Expedition when he was younger and "more buoyant."

Nonetheless he does not believe that even Shackleton could have left the written record that Scott did, in the face of his inevitable death; in his view, clearly a man who was very different when faced with disaster and death compared with his tendency to worry over trifles in circumstances where things were actually going well. By way of illustration, Priestley recalls a lecture given at Cambridge when he got into quite serious trouble during some fairly mild criticism of Scott to a generation of students to whom "he was a hero without blemish and without par."

Returning to 1909, the *Nimrod* steamed into Lyttleton Harbour with more than 30,000 people on the foreshore and wharves to greet the expedition members. This followed a very brief stop at Akaroa where Priestley had been able to send a cable to his father who would be, in his view, "already making a nuisance of himself to his fellow citizens proclaiming the safety and vicarious fame of his son!" Amongst the Lyttleton crowd was a burly woman who, holding a baby a few months old at arm's length, shouted "I've called him

Shackleton Nimrod Jones!" While this must be regarded as the ultimate compliment, Priestley felt it was at the expense of the child who in later life would, almost inevitably, be known as "Shacks."

Priestley stayed in New Zealand for only a few days before embarking on the *Paperoa*, as a first-class passenger, bound for England via Cape Horn, Montevideo, and Rio de Janeiro in company with Wild, Joyce, Day and Marston, his "comrades in arms." He felt on the crest of a wave as a "not unimportant member" of what he certainly considered was the most successful South Polar expedition thus far. In his view, it had made the greatest leap forward towards attaining either Pole, coming to within ninety-seven geographical miles of its goal, had crossed the longest valley glacier yet known, had climbed to over ten thousand feet attaining the summit of Mount Erebus and had reached and located the South Magnetic Pole. For him it had certainly not been without life threatening moments, principally when adrift on the ice floe at the mercy of killer whales, in addition to seventy-two hours without shelter and exposed to a blizzard with virtually no food and water, on the slopes of Erebus; overall he felt "he had measured up," undoubtedly a modest understatement.

However, in his unequivocal view, he benefited most from the opportunity to work with Professor David who he considered was a "master of his science" and, undoubtedly, had a marked effect on the young Priestley's developing character and future life.

To Priestley and his companions, life aboard the *Paperoa* was a complete joy. The pleasures of civilization had not yet palled and to him "a beef-steak was a feast." The nine-thousand ton vessel was in stark contrast to the two-hundred twenty-ton *Nimrod*. Indeed he records that, when disembarking from the thirteen-thousand ton *Runic* at the commencement of the expedition and boarding *Nimrod*, he had "mentally checked his stride lest he should step across into the sea beyond!"

Life on board was not without incident, one of which was to have a fundamental and lasting effect; amongst the second class passengers was a young lady who was later to become his wife. They did not meet for some time as Edwardian mothers were very wary of explorers. Furthermore, he had asked other girls to dance but had been rebuffed. Consequently, when Joyce told him that he had found a "peach" for him, he was "so fed up to the teeth" he turned the opportunity aside and did not meet his future fiancée for another week.

Priestley enjoyed the entire journey home including all their ports of call, especially Rio de Janeiro, but recalls few specific incidents; however, he mentions one of considerable future scientific interest. It appears that Joyce had taken more than a fancy to a young woman on board and, to impress her, had presented her with one of the more attractive rock specimens from the expedition's collection. Priestley immediately recognized this as a piece of limestone breccia covered with intriguing marks similar to Egyptian hieroglyphics. He quickly substituted it for a piece of white granite with small red garnets splashed though it and advised Joyce "to tell her it comes from further South!" As a sequel, he retained the retrieved stone until it could be analyzed at Sydney University, almost a year later; when sectioned it was found to be full of archaeocyaths, a common ancestor of sponges and corals and the only recognizable fossil from the entire expedition. Later an important memoir was written about it and Priestley records that "perhaps it is just and right that a small surviving fragment is now on the seal ring worn by his youngest sister who married the author of the memoir." This was, of course, Griffith Taylor who had served as chief geologist on the Terra Nova Expedition, and who was later to become something of a geographical legend.

On arriving back in London, this proved to be a testing time for Priestley and all the returning members of the *Nimrod* party. Shackleton's fame was at its peak, sustained by a commanding personality and enhanced still further by his friendship with Edward VII. While his comrades shared in the reflected glory of his achievements this came at the price, to Priestley at least, of a demanding and seemingly never ending social round.

In reflective mood, Priestley dwells more generally on the pressures of post-expedition life, which for some resulted in mental problems and, in some cases, even suicide. As one of the most notorious example he specifically cites Johansen, who shot himself in Christiana after the Amundsen South Pole triumph, from which he had been specifically and, some hold the view, vengefully excluded after serious and irreconcilable disagreement for which both parties were, in part, to blame. At the same time, he takes the opportunity to record his strongly held and often later repeated view of Amundsen's success as "the greatest geographical impertinence ever committed" after what he considered as his duplicity in raising money to fund his drift across the Arctic Ocean when his well-concealed intention was always to go south. Overall he felt that "the plunge from austerity into untrammelled luxury and fame" created real and, sometimes, insuperable problems of readjustment.

While spending the ensuing four months in London, Priestley shared a single room in Blackfriars Road with Wild, Joyce and Day, sharing two beds between them! During the day there was little work to occupy them, which was particularly difficult for someone of Priestley's energetic temperament. However, the boredom was occasionally relieved by the opportunity to sign deluxe copies of Shackleton's recent book of the expedition, *The Heart of Antarctica*,[2] at Heinemann's, where they were liberally supplied with whisky and cigars, although both were of no comfort whatsoever to Priestley, a non-smoking teetotaler.

By contrast, every evening they dressed for dinner and entered into an entirely different world; as Priestley records, "they were lions of the London

Season." As an example, he recollects an occasion when Shackleton marshalled a party of twelve to attend a dinner at the Park Lane home of Eckstein, of De Beers diamond mining company fame, where they were among thirty guests. On each place setting was placed a model of the *Nimrod* made in the unusual medium of white heather, at a cost which Priestley felt "would have kept them in clover for a week." This was escalated still further by the entertainment provided, by amongst others, Clara Butt, a noted diva of the day, at a total cost of some two thousand pounds, a huge sum in today's values; as Priestley notes, "what they would have given for their individual share of the cost, in cash."

Fortunately, a safety valve for the demands of the London Season was provided for both Priestley and his companions, apart from Marston, with occasional retreats to his parent's home in Tewkesbury for rest and recuperation; Shackleton was a not infrequent addition to their number. Although both of Priestley's parents were good Methodists, they were incredibly tolerant of his sailor friends and had cause to be so during their often quite extended stays, which were never without incident. On one such occasion, they were entertained to a cider party by the Mayor when Wild, misguidedly considering this a teetotaler drink, had to be helped home by Priestley, "while his blue eyes shone like stars." At another event, a Celebration Ball given in their honor by the Mayor, they sung sailor songs on the steps of the Town Hall late into the night; the chemist living opposite later wrote to the Mayor in protest at his interrupted sleep but received short shrift because the Mayor, his wife, their daughters and other members of the town elite "had helped to swell the chorus."

There was also the attraction of two dances each week, held in the Art Room of his father's school, to which all the local young people flocked and learned new idioms and songs which, as Priestley describes, were "decorous versions of sea songs that would, in their normal dress have turned the parson purple and the ladies pale!" While at home, Priestley had the opportunity to play cricket, on an occasional basis, for Tewkesbury "A" team and, despite lack of practice, still achieved some useful innings. In addition, both he and his companions bathed in the Severn, at Sandy Point, and boated on the Avon while, during one notable and "never to be forgotten" week-end, there were no less than seven Antarctic explorers living at his parents' home, as well as Shackleton and his wife in attendance for Sunday afternoon tea; all provided autographs for a constant stream of small boys.

The short interludes at home were a great antidote to his rather unnatural London life and among other things, as he puts it, "saddled him" with two Antarctic brothers-in-law. Overall, he felt that it had been a beneficial experience for the people of Tewkesbury who he felt were notably more tolerant thereafter with a greater "joie-de-vivre and breadth of view."

4. Between Expeditions 43

However, in October 1909 everything changed, very much to his satisfaction and good fortune, as Priestley headed for pastures new at the behest of Professor David, who had asked if he could be released to work in Sydney on the expedition's geological findings; an opportunity which Priestley was never to regret and, in the event, led to extensive future involvement in the Antarctic and, indeed, a much fuller life.

Priestley's recollections of his voyage to Australia on the *Marmora* via the Suez Canal are fairly sketchy but included a stopover in Colombo where he was briefly reunited with Dr. Eric Marshall, a member of the *Nimrod* party, who was on his way to New Guinea as part of another expedition. It was also in Colombo that he records the strange combination and hazy reflections of seeing a conjuror with a basket of snakes and hearing of Shackleton's knighthood, to which he responded with a cable of congratulations and best wishes.

On arrival in Sydney, Priestley entered into a new and fascinating life and was employed as a research student working, ostensibly, for a B.A. (Research) degree. In reality, he spent his entire time working with David, examining sheaves of notes and tons of rocks, in microscopic detail, in the early stages of a very significant book, which became the standard work, and was not finally published until 1914, with parts delayed still further until after the First World War.[3] He lived at 28 Rose Street, Sydney, with David at times in residence as well. Together they worked, often far into the night, with "a coterie" of specialists to help them. Among these was Frank Debenham, who later, with Priestley, went south on the Terra Nova Expedition. He would become his colleague at Cambridge for many years and was instrumental in founding the Scott Polar Research Institute, in which Priestley played a very significant part (of which more in a later chapter) before becoming its first director.

Priestley, who throughout his diaries records the highest admiration for David, details a number of tales of his mentor during this period. On one occasion, at a lecture given by David in Sydney Town Hall, with no less than six thousand people in attendance, singing what Priestley records somewhat cryptically as, "*The Ballad of the Professor's Return.*" Apparently David's wife arrived late, was at first refused entry but later let in with the philosophical words, "pass in woman, pass in—you're the seventh Mrs. David I've let through this afternoon!"

It was also David's practice to arrange picnics for *Nimrod* sailors while awaiting their return to Britain. In the intervening period, they were voracious hunters for souvenirs from the ship, which could even include the rigging itself, for pecuniary gain. After one such excursion, on the train journey back from the Blue Mountains, one of the sailors, Bill Nodder, in Priestley's words, "taking full advantage of Providence's well known care of the drunk," climbed out of his compartment and along the foot-rail, to join David and his wife to thank them for the seventy pounds, in one week, that he and his mates had made selling Kiarma basalt—from David's collection—to souvenir hunters.

"Life was not all work in the halcyon days of 1910," as Priestley describes it. He spent time under canvas with geological students from Sydney University and made many new friends "tramping the countryside and singing songs around the camp fire." In addition, a camp with more serious intent introduced him to Australian wildlife and at the end of its week's duration he was "nearly hopping himself as he routed out kangaroos, wallabies, and grasshoppers on all sides." Another excursion, with David, on a geological trip to the wilder areas of New South Wales illustrated the Professor's great popularity as they were greeted at every household with bottles of wine; they eventually returned to Sydney "much the worse for wear!"

The best trip of all however, the "king-pin" as he puts it, was to both New South Wales and South Queensland in an effort to raise funds for the publication of Shackleton's book on the expedition, which included a hectic lecture tour and some unforgettable experiences. On one occasion, an old Scots goldminer wanted to take Priestley into partnership as he had a "lucky face." On another, at Mount Morgan, Priestley's party had the manager's house to themselves but, in return, were expected to give champagne lunches to his staff, which led to subsequent enquiries about the cost of running the mine. And finally, at a weekend at Government House, he remembers tales by the Governor "of the subjugation of Papuan natives by the power of the human eye!"

Having raised several hundred pounds, the party returned to Sydney well satisfied with their efforts until they received the distressing news that Armitage, their expedition colleague, had committed suicide on his return from Sydney to Melbourne. After dressing in his evening suit and wearing all his medals, he "blew his brains out" in his room at his club. Priestley felt that, given the opportunity of seeing him beforehand, there was a good chance that this might have been prevented.

Overall, this had been a very fulfilling year for Priestley even though he had still not completed his first degree. In fact it took him fifteen years to complete it, which must be something of a record for someone who later became vice-chancellor of two universities!

However, in December 1910, a fateful telegram arrived from Scott asking if David, and crucially Shackleton, could release him to go south again on the Terra Nova Expedition. Shackleton's reply was characteristically generous and helpful—"Certainly" while David's kindness included gifts of both gear and books. Within a week, he was aboard the *Moeraki* bound for Christchurch followed by a week collecting gear together for what he describes as Scott's "somewhat neglected" Eastern (later Northern) Party to which he had been assigned. His somewhat partisan approach to his task earned him an admonishment from Scott but praise and gratitude from Victor Campbell, the Eastern Party's designated leader.

Thereafter he embarked on "a second chapter of adventure, twice as long, twice as exciting and twice as profitable as before." However, sea-sickness remained his "chief foe" and he records that "I think the only brave thing I ever did was to embark for the second time for the Antarctic well aware of what I had to go through before I set foot on shore"; a comment he would have every reason to revise in the light of his subsequent experience.

5

Scott's Terra Nova Expedition— The Northern Party

As outlined, immediately following his return from the Nimrod Expedition, Priestley accompanied Professor David to Sidney University, where he occupied the chair of geology, to work on the rocks they had collected.

Their joint monograph to be published later, in 1914, as one of the scientific reports of the Shackleton Expedition, was the first attempt to draw the main lines of the structural geology of South Victoria Land.[1]

However, Priestley had scarcely settled down to this task as part of his B.A. research thesis when, by pure chance, another opportunity for Antarctic exploration presented itself. Working with Priestley was Allan Thomson, a Rhodes Scholar from New Zealand, who had been chosen by Scott to be part of his Terra Nova Expedition, which was due to sail from New Zealand in late 1910.

At the very last moment, Thomson unfortunately contracted tuberculosis and Scott immediately asked David to release Priestley to replace him. David agreed without hesitation, but felt it necessary to consult Shackleton in view of Priestley's commitment to work on his last expedition's results. Shackleton's wired reply (previously mentioned), although very brief, was characteristically generous and helpful, but the longer term implications for Priestley were immense and ones that he treasured for the remainder of his life.[2]

For most of the journey from Littleton, New Zealand, to Antarctica, Priestley was virtually paralyzed with sea-sickness until, on January 26, 1911, Scott's party landed at Cape Evans in McMurdo Sound, named after Commander Evans—Scott's previous second-in-command—as the site for its winter quarters preparatory to its activities in the following spring; this followed two unsuccessful attempts, due to unremitting sea ice, to reach both Cape Crozier and Cape Evans (the site of Shackleton's last base) which had been chosen originally as better suited and more convenient.

After helping to establish the main party, it was from Cape Evans that six of Scott's expedition, designated the Eastern Party and of which Priestley was one, set sail eastwards on the *Terra Nova* along the Ross Ice Shelf to King Edward VII Land with the intention of exploration in this area; the ship's company also included members of the Far Western Party who were separately assigned to a different location. At this stage the Eastern Party was blissfully unaware that, for a prolonged period, they would be forced to live together in circumstances of unimaginable intimacy and privation which would test to the utmost both their physical and mental capabilities.

In the light of subsequent events, the Party could not have been better chosen to meet the challenges that they faced, and comprised[3]: Lieutenant Victor L. Arbuthnot Campbell RN, leader, aged thirty-five, known as "the wicked mate"; Dr. George Murray Levick, surgeon, RN, aged thirty-three, known as "the Old Sport" or "Tofferino"; Raymond E. Priestley, geologist, aged twenty-four (his lack of a nickname appears to have no special significance); George Percy Abbott, Petty Officer, RN, aged thirty, known as "Tiny"; Frank V. Browning, Petty Officer, RN, aged twenty-eight, known as "Rings"; Harry Dickason, Able Seaman, RN, aged twenty-five, known as "Dick." It is relevant that Scott's expeditions were subject to naval traditions and discipline and, against this background, the first three men above were classed as "officers" while the remaining three were regarded as "men." Priestley, although technically falling into the first category as the only non-naval man and without rank, was in a unique position that he used to great effect to resolve difficulties to the mutual benefit of the party as it faced its period of severest strain.

Their initial plans, however, were completely thwarted. Firstly, the *Terra Nova* was forced to turn back by thick pack ice. Secondly, while sailing along the massive barrier rounding the eastern cape of the Bay of Whales, the ship's company to its complete amazement encountered another ship. This was in fact the *Fram*, the ship of the renowned polar explorer Roald Amundsen, who had abandoned an expedition to the North Pole to come south for an attempt on the South Pole, which he was, of course, eventually successful in reaching ahead of Scott. Although he had given very belated notice to Scott by wire of his revised intentions, the generally held contemporary view was that Scott had clear precedence and Priestley felt this very strongly; indeed, he goes so far as to view it, as previously described, as "the greatest geographical impertinence ever committed," leaving no doubt as to his feelings.

The ship's company spent a day visiting the other expedition's members, who were equally surprised to encounter another ship in such remote waters, on board the Norwegian vessel. Their exchanges were friendly and left Priestley with the impression that they were "men of distinctive personality, hard and evidently inured to hardship, good goers and pleasant and good humored—

all qualities to make them dangerous rivals." He goes further in his opinion that "our Southern Party will go far before they permit themselves to be beaten by anyone and although both parties are likely to reach the Pole next year, God only knows who will get there first"—prescient indeed! What was absolutely clear was that a race for the Pole was now on and those aboard the *Terra Nova* saw it as an imperative to retrace the four hundred miles to Cape Evans to acquaint Scott with the situation with the utmost speed, being unaware that he had already received this disquieting news.

This was duly accomplished before the Eastern Party set out once again to find a secure home for the coming winter, preparatory to their intended work program during the following spring and summer, on this occasion setting their sights further north. The scope of the Party's areas of investigation were severely limited; the *Terra Nova* had only very limited coal supplies available over and above those required for the return journey to New Zealand. Indeed, if a suitable location for what had now become the Northern Party could not be found quickly, then it would have to return to New Zealand with its mission completely unfulfilled.

In very heavy seas and gale conditions, the ship reached a point some ninety-six miles from Cape Adare where the Party eventually found its winter quarters. At first sight it was far from an ideal location, as there were limited sledging opportunities in all directions. Nonetheless, it was the best on offer given the limited scope for maneuver. Moreover, when the first landings were made, it was clear that it had many redeeming features, with its proximity to the Admiralty Range of mountains and an abundance of wildlife. Priestley felt that "our luck had turned at last."

The first priority was to established its winter hut, the constructing of which revealed their glaring lack of experience, but this was accomplished eventually and, in fact, in Priestley's words, "withstood some of the fiercest blows that it had ever been my lot to experience." During the year that followed, the party lived in relative comfort and accomplished a great deal in geography, meteorology and geology before the *Terra Nova* returned to take them back to join the main party at Cape Evans after first dropping them off for a few weeks' exploration some two hundred miles down the coast. This is the moment when the truly amazing survival story of the Northern Party begins, which was to take its place amongst and justify comparison with the epic experiences, in different circumstances, of Scott, Shackleton, Mawson and Amundsen.

The party was dropped off on January 8, 1912, at Evans Cove, subject to an arrangement that the *Terra Nova* would call for them as soon after February 18 as possible. Consequently, stores sufficient only for a six-week sledging journey were taken ashore, plus an emergency food store of two weeks' pemmican, fifty-six pounds of sugar, twenty-four pounds of cocoa and five

5. Scott's Terra Nova Expedition

The Northern Party at the Cape Adare Hut during the 1910–13 British Antarctic Expedition. Priestley is seated on the left, beside Victor Campbell and Murray Levick. Behind them, left to right, are George Abbott, Harry Dickason, and Frank Browning (The Scott Polar Research Institute Picture Library).

forty-two pound tins of biscuits, together with—crucially fortunate as it transpired—a few spare clothes, reindeer skins, several cases of Oxo bouillon and a small amount of other assorted gear. This was regarded as entirely sufficient, as any difficulty in collecting the party on or around the arranged date seemed entirely remote.

From February 18 onwards, the date when the *Terra Nova* was due to return, a severe gale blew constantly for several days keeping the sea free of ice, adding to their growing puzzlement that the ship had not appeared. In fact, and unknown to the waiting party, the ship's arrival was thwarted by sea ice some twenty-seven miles offshore and, although three attempts were made before the approach of winter, these were unsuccessful and the *Terra Nova* was forced to return to New Zealand. The party's demeanor turned from mere concern to very considerable anxiety as, in their minds, they searched for catastrophic causes for the ship's absence. These included the possibility that the ship had foundered or, even, the loss of the Southern Party in its bid for the Pole.

Faced with the alarming prospect that they might have to endure an Antarctic winter, totally unprepared and in an extremely hostile environment, the party nevertheless sought to rationalize the situation and kept their hopes alive with other explanations for the ship's late return, bad weather or the late return of the Southern Party prevalent amongst the many possibilities. Meanwhile, the gale conditions continued unabated and their sledging rations were coming to an end, before they had to fall back on their slim reserve of supplies.

By February 23 the party's hopes of the ship's return had all but faded, and Lieutenant Campbell took the crucial decision of asking Priestley to take complete charge of rations, given the now almost inevitable circumstance that they would have to winter at Cape Adare. It was a decision that Campbell was never to regret, and one that almost certainly ensured the survival of the Northern Party.[4]

Priestley's immediate response was to prepare for the worst and, in improved weather conditions, immediately set out to look for seals which would be the mainstay of their survival strategy; fortunately a crabeater seal was quickly discovered and butchered, the first of many to be added to their winter larder. With his duty clear before him, Priestley found his designated task "much more of a blessing than a curse" as it gave him something to think about constantly and prevented him from dwelling on the precariousness of the party's situation. Furthermore, he drew great comfort from having five resolute companions who had spent the previous winter together successfully and harmoniously, albeit in conditions that would be considered safe and luxurious by comparison with their current predicament.

Now that the date by which any chance of the ship's arrival had passed, Priestley, with Campbell, set about preparations for a full winter with two critical priorities: the collection of food and the provision of winter quarters. The tents used for the last seven weeks of summer sledging were fast being destroyed by incessant gales and alternative shelter had to be found for, at least, the ensuing winter months. A snowdrift had been identified on the island on which they were marooned—later named Inexpressible Island, reflecting their subsequent experiences—in which it would be possible to dig a snow cave of sufficient size to accommodate the whole Party, though in very cramped conditions. In this they were extremely, indeed critically, fortunate, as the island, being geologically composed of granite and gneiss, was almost devoid of snow other than the one isolated drift available for their selected home.

The work of digging out the cave was arduous, in bitterly cold conditions and very high winds that continued more or less unabated for the next seven months. The first of March was a typical day. Starting early, the Party captured two seals and eighteen penguins which they killed, cleaned and stored,

5. Scott's Terra Nova Expedition

although it was clearly evident that securing sufficient meat for the winter would be a constant priority. They worked in gale force winds, in inappropriate and badly torn summer clothing, weak from inadequate rations, and sustained numerous frostbites.

At this point Priestley had to consider the overall provision of rations to cover not only the forthcoming winter but also to take account of the fact that they would not, in all probability, be picked up by the *Terra Nova* in the spring and would therefore have to sledge the two hundred miles to the expedition's main base at Cape Evans in October, a daunting seven months ahead. Consequently, their rations were reduced immediately to accommodate the anticipated timetable. This made the task of digging out the cave even harder and hunger was a constant companion, despite fairly generous quantities of seal and penguin meat, the forthcoming scarcity of which was not fully anticipated at this time. However, their lack of carbohydrates resulting from a severe restriction in the biscuit ration at least helped them to overcome their initial distaste for blubber.

The snow cave was completed finally in early March, measuring twelve feet by nine feet and five feet high, an incredibly small and cramped space for a party of six but viewed by Priestley, both at the time and in retrospect, as a home and refuge of warmth and comfort by comparison with their former existence. The three officers, including Priestley, set up their quarters in one half of the cave while the three other ranks occupied the remaining space available. Life immediately assumed an agreeable and harmonious atmosphere, with much friendly banter, as the Party enjoyed their seal hoosh (basically a stew containing meat and ground down biscuit with a variety of random ingredients available) and cocoa, followed by the singing of their favorite songs in the flickering light of their blubber lamps until the cold drove them to their sleeping bags; the cave, of course, had to be maintained at a temperature below freezing to prevent it melting, with catastrophic consequences.

At an early stage in the cave's occupation, Campbell made a decision which would perhaps seem strange to anyone not involved in their precarious situation but which, in fact, contributed greatly to the good relations and spirit of understanding which held for the whole of their incarceration. Drawing a line with his boot down the center of the cave and pointing to the side occupied by the other ranks, he said "that becomes the mess deck" and pointing to the area housing the officers, "and this becomes the quarter deck"; after indicating that both decks, for the sake of good order, would be inspected weekly but, meanwhile, indicating that conversations within either deck would be deemed to have not been heard by the other. In Priestley's words, "from that day forward each of us knew exactly where we stood and this contributed enormously to our tranquility."

With the entire winter ahead, the imperative was to secure sufficient seal meat to allow for at least half-rations. Priestley calculated that a minimum of fifteen would be required and with only half a dozen captured so far, this was, in truth, a life and death issue which could not be easily overcome in the constantly prevailing fierce winds. Even shorter rations were the inevitable outcome, although their small stock of Adélie penguins occasionally enhanced their morning hoosh.

Apart from the party's reduced biscuit ration, they had a few other ingredients in their diet, the scarcity of which made them symbols of real luxury. Half of the stock of biscuits, sugar, chocolate and cocoa were set aside for the sledging journey to Cape Evans at the end of winter, leaving only a meager allowance in the meantime. However, Priestley still found it possible to serve out twelve lumps of sugar to each man every Sunday, one and one-half ounces of chocolate every Saturday and every alternate Wednesday, and two small tins of cocoa for the group each month. This left a small margin for the celebration of special events. Abbot's birthday on March 10 was such an occasion, when an extra biscuit ration was allowed, and Priestley considered these "a godsend during the next seven months and more than once they brightened our spirits when the outlook was bleak."

By April 1, the party was well established in a more or less waterproof home and living in relative comfort, although their interior equipment was at an early stage of development; this was particularly true of their cooking stove, which was central to their requirements. Overall, the party's prospect of getting through the winter alive now looked more hopeful, although it was highly dependent on them obtaining sufficient seal and penguin meat to augment their otherwise meager supplies. Priestley, with great foresight and wisdom, continued to mark special days with an increase and variation to their diet. He kept the last day of each month as what he describes as "a fete" and served out twenty-five muscatel raisins to each man. He regarded these as "the cleanest tasting food we have had so far and none of us will ever enjoy the taste of raisins so much as we did then." Despite, and in Priestley's view because of their short rations, the party's health remained fair, although the forced use of seawater instead of salt and a diet of only slightly boiled meat did cause some initial problems. However, the majority of the party overcame these quite quickly, except for Browning, for whom it remained a continuing problem with later repercussions.

In the early days of the party's isolation, they undoubtedly suffered from mild symptoms of depression and, as Priestley makes clear, it was providential that they were not aware of the tragic death of their five close friends and colleagues on the Ross Ice Shelf following their successful attainment of the Geographical South Pole, although beaten into second place by Roald Amundsen and his Norwegian Party. A further indication of their heightened mental state was the incidence of very vivid dreams as time progressed, to the extent that Priestley felt "that there was a complete distinction between their waking and dreaming hours." At first, their dreams centered round the two issues of food and relief from their current predicament but soon dreams of food predominated; Priestley describes this graphically. It seems that every night one or more of the Party's dreams included the vision of a sumptuous banquet which was whisked away on the point of eating, or of a shop where everything they wished to eat was available, but the shop was closed for business. The exception to this general rule was that their doctor, Levick, invariably was able to enjoy the fruits of his food dream before waking, giving him, quite understandably though illogically, an unfair advantage in the eyes of his colleagues; nonetheless, they still listened with relish to his description of the meal!

As winter approached, the wind continued to blow at sixty miles an hour or more and, with only thin and worn summer clothing, members of the party only ventured outside for essential purposes and had little opportunity for pure exercise. However the search for seals, the daily collection of food from the ice foot where it was stored, improvements to the shaft into their cave and the collection of seaweed for the insulation of their home were all essential tasks that had to be carried out, come what may. Consequently, their evenings were, by far, the most enjoyable part of their days; after the evening meal Priestley reports that "they would enjoy themselves in singing and reading aloud from the Bible, David Copperfield and the few other books they had brought along with them."

The greatest cause for concern at this time was that the continuing high winds kept the seals away so that their food intake, on a reduced meat ration, was barely sufficient for them to carry out their essential tasks. Nevertheless, when the sun finally set for the last time on April 27, Priestley calculated that they had sufficient food available at the reduced level to keep them going until its return in August, although with the frequent occurrence of frostbite in current circumstances, it seemed unlikely that the party would be in good enough condition to sledge back to base on the sun's immediate return but would have to wait for comparatively better conditions of both wind and temperature.

Before the sunlight finally disappeared, the party experienced a strange phenomenon; Priestley reports that they spotted what appeared to be four figures about half-a-mile away "in extended order as if they were a sledging party and our imaginations supplied the sledge." Thoughts of a relief party sprung instantly to mind although, on reflection, their direction of travel made this difficult to explain. The reality, when the light improved, was four Emperor penguins "advancing in their usual stately fashion." Despite their disappointment, the blow was softened by the addition of more than one hundred pounds of meat to their winter larder, as the birds were caught and killed with all speed.

The task of cooking meat so easily secured was in sharp contrast to the difficulties of preparation for cooking after it had frozen; the space available was incredibly restricted within the cave and the floor coverings became indescribably filthy from the thawed chippings of frozen meat. Much of this had to be picked up and used in the hoosh; often even the gnawing pains of hunger made this impossible to eat and Priestley describes his own feelings of revulsion at their personal and living conditions.

Due to the extreme winter conditions, members of the Party only ventured outside when absolutely essential and because the cave was very cold, despite the heat from the blubber stove, spent the vast majority of the time in their sleeping bags, with meals taken *in situ* and served by the cook for the day. While the days were spent in either day-dreaming or sleeping, the evenings were a time for more general conversation and Priestley continued to be amazed that six normally extremely active men could " settle down to an inert and vegetating existence without fret or protest." Indeed, the Party exhibited good humor and even temper throughout and, in Priestley's view, demonstrated that the luxuries of civilization only fulfil the wants they create. This did not for one moment infer that the party would wish to endure an experience which, if repeated, they would almost certainly either not survive or during which go mad but they were undoubtedly able to find solace in the simplest of pleasures.

In arriving at this accommodation with their situation, there is no doubt that the small luxuries which Priestley was able to manage and produce, such as chocolate and sugar at appropriate and often critical moments, made a huge contribution to the overall morale of the party and marked out his appointment in charge of rations as a great success. There were other variations to their diet which also contributed to their general acceptance and satisfaction with their situation. An Oxo hoosh every Wednesday for breakfast was looked forward to with keen anticipation, as were the seal liver, heart and kidneys used to flavor the Sunday meals. Furthermore, with the exception of Browning, who never satisfactorily adapted to the use of seawater in the hoosh, the Party kept remarkably fit. Priestley had no doubt that the frugality of their diet, paradoxically, contributed towards their survival, where with so little exercise and in such foul conditions, a more meat intensive diet would not have done the same.

As the winter progressed and the difficulties of their living conditions, by improvisation and ingenuity, were gradually overcome their enduring optimism that they would survive had taken permanent hold and the arrival of Midwinter's Day was looked forward to as a moment for great celebration; in Priestley's assessment "Petronius never had so much pleasure from a

Roman Feast." The hoosh was flavored with the carefully saved livers and hearts of Adélie penguins, their only bottle of wine—Wincanis!—was drunk from horn mugs impregnated with blubber but was ambrosia to men deprived of any form of alcohol for many months, and each man had four biscuits, four sticks of chocolate, twenty raisins, fourteen lumps of sugar and a full ration of cocoa. The smokers (Priestley being the only nonsmoker) each had a cigar and a sixth of a plug of tobacco. Priestley records a long and cheerful evening with the most rewarding thought that, from now on, the sun would come a little nearer each day until, on August 10, it would show above the horizon.

By this time, all members of the party experienced aches and pains, mainly as the result of their confined circumstances but also attributable to the imbalance in their diet; Priestley mentions particularly what they referred to as "igloo back," an "infernal crick" from never being able to stand upright in the five foot high cave. However, from late July onwards as the light began to reappear, their spirits rose with it. It was also becoming clear, if not certain, that they would have sufficient supplies of meat to survive as a number of Weddell seals had appeared that could be expected to come up onto the ice foot where they could be caught fairly easily.

The time had arrived for their preparation for the long trek across the ice and snow back to the expedition's main base at Cape Evans; in Priestley's words "between us and salvation"—a heartfelt description. The immediate priority was to improve their fitness after their long, extremely cramped and, indeed, squalid confinement. This was achieved by doing Swedish calisthenics, as best they could in the cave, when the necessity became clearly evident; at first, one set of exercises alone left them entirely exhausted. Fortunately, the party benefited crucially from the inclusion of both a naval surgeon from the physical training department and also a gymnastic instructor.

At first, the party made good progress with the exception of Browning; although remaining in good spirits, his physical condition was far from satisfactory. Priestley attributes this partly to the enteric fever which he contracted during the South African Boer War and which had permanently weakened his constitution, but even more so because he had never adjusted to the limitations of their diet and had, in fact, been ill throughout the whole of the winter. This had been a matter of growing concern to both Campbell and Levick, especially in regard to their forthcoming arduous journey to safety.

Then, in September, all of the party with the exception of Campbell developed ptomaine poisoning as a direct result of what Priestley describes as the "abominable" composition of their hoosh—spoiled meat, rope fragments, seaweed, penguin feathers, and sometimes even beach pebbles! Nonetheless, their hunger drove them to accept the tainted food until they discovered, fortuitously, a small pool of blood and meat scraps in the corner of a bent tin which had harbored the bacteria. Nonetheless, the diarrhea this caused was severe and everyone suffered from acute thirst as the result of dehydration.

Finally however, on September 30, they had recovered sufficiently to leave the cave and start on their march to safety. Dressed in the new clothes which they had reserved for the journey, this was their first change for seven months and a great comfort and relief to them all. Although spring sledging was not usually anticipated with any degree of pleasure because of the inevitably very low temperatures and consequent incidence of frostbite, on this occasion there was great relief amongst the whole party that they were finally moving away from the cave. They were also now able to allow themselves a full ration of pemmican, which had been reserved for the march and although initially this was more than sufficient, the effects of the cold conditions and the extremely hard work of sledging soon made them crave for even more than the full ration. Indeed, Priestley records that he would have sacrificed almost any delicacy for its same weight in pemmican.

In the initial stages of the march, the party found great difficulty in making headway in the incessant gale conditions and after sledging around one hundred miles they were in a debilitated condition, with their survival in serious doubt. However, by the greatest of good fortune, at Cape Roberts they stumbled across a cairn with flags flying, containing not only much needed stores of food, including many luxury items, but also a matchbox containing up-to-date news. This, to their intense relief, informed them that the *Terra Nova* had been prevented from picking them up as it had been blown away by intensely strong offshore winds and not because it had met with an accident, thus removing one of their greatest fears. Consequently on that day, October 29, the party enjoyed a veritable celebration feast and, on the following morning, suffered very sore mouths; this was partly due to eating large quantities of biscuits in addition to three days of sledging rations, a whole week's ration of butter, raisins and lard together with a tot of medicinal brandy, but probably much more because they were already suffering from fairly advanced scurvy, evidenced by sores, blood blisters and chipped palates in their mouths.

The note that they had discovered left the party in no doubt that they had been given up for dead, months ago, by the rest of the expedition and, almost certainly, the depot discovered at Cape Roberts saved Browning's life as the change in diet had an immediate effect on his general health and well-being.

Finally they arrived at Cape Evans and the expedition members in residence were astonished and overjoyed to see them, as they had given up all hope of seeing them alive. It was also then that they received the news that

Scott's party had not returned from their southern journey the previous winter. During the their recuperation, and with considerable difficulty, they managed to avoid overeating but instead had many small meals augmented by numerous snacks, often in bed. Their physical condition on arrival told its own story. They were completely free of fat reserves and their skin incredibly wrinkled, but this quickly changed. In Priestley's case, after weighing one hundred forty pounds on arrival, this increased to one hundred seventy-three pounds over the course of six days. But their overall condition confirmed that their scurvy was fairly advanced, as they were all suffering from edema, which is a marked symptom of the disease.

The group searching for the Polar Party had been unexpectedly successful in finding the bodies of Scott, Wilson and Bowers in their tent one hundred sixty miles from the hut at Cape Evans; included in the search party was Charles Wright, Priestley's friend and, later, brother-in-law. The search party had found the now historic records of the Southern Party's last days and had buried their bodies beneath a snow cairn before reading the burial service over their comrades.

Priestley's summing up of the Northern Party's experience is characteristically understated but leaves no doubt that, while none of its members would have any wish to repeat the experience, it had been in so many ways life-changing; his own words cannot be improved upon to describe why. "The very discomforts and privations I endured with stalwart companions have only served to convert otherwise commonplace comforts into exquisite pleasures and privations have been glossed over and pleasures enhanced by a very perfect comradeship. The Northern Party was regarded by their other companions as thick as thieves and well we might be, for if ever men knew each other inside and out, it was the six of us who dwelt together for seven months in a hole in the snow."

As a footnote it is interesting to record that during a later radio interview about his exploits in Antarctica, Priestley described his experiences with the Northern Party[5] as "a pretty stiff time" reflecting not only the "stiff upper lip" understatement of his day but also, and very much more so, the inherent and growing toughness, courage and self-confidence of the man who had played a central role in the survival of his comrades.

6

The First World War— The British Army Signal Service

The pattern of Priestley's military career was determined in October 1913[1]; encouraged by his Antarctic colleague on Scott's last expedition, Charles Wright, (later knighted and to become his brother-in-law), he joined the Wireless Section of the Signal Company of the Cambridge University Officers' Training Corps. Wright had been a graduate student in the Cavendish Laboratory; now they both arrived at Cambridge together, Priestley to Christchurch and Wright to Caius where they collaborated on the Glaciology Memoir of the Nimrod Expedition. This became the standard work on the subject and later formed part of the Ice Manuals at the Scott Polar Research Institute.[2]

His first Commanding Officer was Colonel F.J.M. "Chubby" Stratton who, coincidentally, later occupied the rooms in Caius where Priestley and Wright had prepared their Glaciology Memoir, while his Lance Corporal was Henry Thirkill, later a most distinguished Master of Clare with a finely tuned understanding of undergraduate life. Indeed, Priestley records a later occasion when with his wife he attended a dinner party given by Thirkill which was severely disturbed by what he describes as the noise of a "near riot" from undergraduates practicing rugby football in the rooms above. With apologies to Priestley's wife, Thirkill summoned the College Porter and asked to him to convey the message "that if they wished to call upon him, would they please come through the door!"

Priestley's short period with the Wireless Section was not without incident. He spent his Field Days, with what he describes with some authority as the later Official Historian of the British Army Signal Service,[3] as "positively the first army portable wireless telegraphy set."

It was a very early crystal set with "cat's whiskers" and worked by an alternator fixed to the frame of a strong and heavy push-bike, the whole very much in the experimental stage. During their summer camp, this was either pedaled furiously around the Hampshire countryside, or in a stationary position, while an enthusiastic operator tried, almost always without success, to make contact with Headquarters. Later, the set met its end from a direct hit while being used in the trenches by a Dismounted Cavalry Division in the spring of 1915, over which Priestley and his comrades would certainly have "wept no tears."

There were also lighter moments to Priestley's pre-war interlude. He and a brother-in-law who lived in the New Forest played "military tennis" in army shirts and braces, to the word of command; a most difficult exercise but much to the entertainment of the assembled family. Priestley's passion for cricket also found an outlet in the Cambridge O.T.C. The unit beat a strong Ringwood team when he renewed his acquaintance with Kenneth Caldwell; he was the local parson whose father had been a competitive rival Headmaster of Barbourne College, Worcester, when his team played against Tewkesbury Grammar School during his father's Headmastership. He also scored his first century, covering himself with what he contends was "strictly temporary glory" against a Bournemouth military side.

Then came the outbreak of war. Almost all that was left of the Cambridge University O.T.C., after the initial rush to enlist, went into training in Pembroke College under Captain Carter, an officer from Repton School O.T.C. Almost immediately Priestley gained a temporary promotion when the Regimental Sergeant-Major of the Engineer Company to which Signals were attached, fainted at a T.A.B. inoculation parade. Priestley, as the most mature-looking and prospective Lance Corporal in sight, marched the parade home and he records, "the acting rank stuck for months."

Priestley was undertaking entirely infantry training at this time which coincided with the arrival of the Sixth Division for final divisional training before joining the British Expeditionary Force in France. On one field day, Priestley's unit was marched off to the Gog Magog Hills to take up a line just below the crest which the Sixth Division was to assault. The O.T.C. uniform was field-grey and as the regulars swept forward with bayonets fixed—"a magnificent sight"—someone, in serious error, gave the order for the O.T.C. to counter-charge. When the O.T.C. appeared cheering and waving their unloaded rifles, after a slight wavering by their opponents a private was heard to cry out, "My God! Here are the bloody Germans." Priestley was preparing to do what he records as "the first four minute mile" when officers from the Sixth Division dashed across the front line knocking up the bayonets.

The O.T.C.'s field-grey uniform figured in another incident recalled by Priestley. Frank Potts, a "rather rotund gentle" zoologist and Fellow of Trinity Hall, had finally obtained his commission after many weeks of struggle with, what were to him, the meaningless and banal mysteries of the Army Drill Manual. The day he joined his battalion coincided with a General Inspection and Potts was posted, a lonely figure in field-grey, in the rear rank. When the inspecting Brigadier arrived, he exclaimed, "Good God, Colonel, what have you got there? A German prisoner?" "No, Sir," replied the Colonel, "a professor from Cambridge," in a tone that implied something a good deal worse.

Finally, in September 1914, Priestley was offered simultaneously a Captaincy in the South Wales Borderers and a Second Lieutenancy in the London Wireless Section T.F. The Adjutant had endorsed his application form in red ink, "Wireless Expert," which, at this time as a practicing geologist, he certainly was not; in the event, he was given no choice and had to accept the Wireless posting. This proved highly fortuitous as, within a month, twenty of the thirty officers in the battalion of the South Wales Borderers to which he would have been posted were either dead or wounded and Priestley felt that his chances of survival would not have been great. With only a passing knowledge of physics, Priestley found this a difficult assignment, particularly as he no longer had Charles Wright as his mentor; Charles was by this time a leading light in the Scottish Wireless Section and, with Henry Thirkill, was being introduced to horse-riding. It came as no surprise to Priestley that, after one halt, Thirkill managed to get himself hoisted back on to his horse by a passing farmer, but back to front!

Priestley was dispatched to join the Londoners in Bury St. Edmunds, when an incident with a horse figured almost immediately. Like Priestley, his immediate superior Henry Chittick, another Second Lieutenant, was not very much at home on a horse, but nonetheless had to parade mounted for a General Inspection which followed shortly after Priestley's arrival. When Chittick gave the words of command, "Present Arms," the consequent slaps on the rifle butts behind him proved too much for his charger which bolted for its stable, dislodging him in the process. As Priestley records, with strong feelings, "what we all went through, including horses, for King and Country in those stirring days!"

Thereafter, the Wireless Section moved from Bury St. Edmunds to Bewdley in Worcestershire, much nearer to Priestley's family home in Tewkesbury. This proved something of a crossroads in Priestley's life. Firstly, Henry Chittick embarked with the majority of the Wireless Section for Gallipoli, leaving a very disgruntled Priestley with half-a-dozen drivers and a dozen horses to look after and very little else to retain his interest and attention. Secondly and as a consequence, in his words, "I took a week's leave and got married almost out of spite."

In late July of the previous year, anticipating the approach of war, he had traveled down to Ringwood to persuade the brother-in-law of his fiancée, Phyllis Boyd, to cable her in Austria, where she was a governess to an Austrian count's family, to come home at once. In fact, she was not free to return until December 1914, by which time she was fully apprised of Priestley's desire for an early wedding, and this eventually took place in Ringwood, in April 1915, during his week's leave. Priestley was married in uniform and took with him a brother officer's sword, which he borrowed for the occasion. Under the impression that tradition dictated that the wedding cake should be cut using the sword, in doing so he left a large brown Vaseline stain which ruined a significant proportion of it. Nonetheless, in spite of Priestley's typically light-hearted references, this was, in fact, the beginning of a very happy marriage which went on to produce two daughters.

Another turning point in Priestley's army career followed, almost immediately, when it was decided to brigade all the Territorial wireless sections in one unit as a wireless training center at Worcester. The Commanding Officer was Major Handley of the Southern Army Troops Wireless Telegraphy Section and he chose as his Adjutant a very personable and well respected officer, Captain Rathbone of the Northern Section.

Fortunately, but only so far as Priestley was concerned, Rathbone went absent without leave for a weekend on the Wireless Section motorbike, had a head-on collision and broke his arm. As a result, he was stripped of his post and, although Priestley was only a junior Second Lieutenant, his Antarctic Medal again marked him out for promotion and he was appointed to the fill the Adjutant's vacancy. The Worcester Section grew rapidly and with it Priestley's promotion, first to full Lieutenant and then to Captain shortly thereafter. Over the course of the following two years, this loose conglomeration of wagon and pack wireless sections grew into a training center which, before it left Worcester in 1917, numbered some two thousand men, two hundred officers and two hundred horses and included a Riding School, a Signal School, a Motor Cycle Section and an Interception Station.

Priestley's tenure of office during 1915 and 1916 were both strenuous and eventful. The Section adapted an old corn store in St. Martin's Gate, Worcester, as its Headquarters with stables, at a weekly rental of ten shillings The Section also enlisted a number of staff from both the King's School and the Royal Grammar School in Worcester, including Spencer Humby, later a distinguished senior science master at Winchester but, meanwhile, a first-class wireless instructor, as Priestley had anticipated of a good physicist. Priestley, in his role as Adjutant, scoured the local countryside for both stations and billets for various sections and established Signals units with the Royal Worcestershire Regiment at their depots at both Norton and Great Malvern; in fact, during the harsh winter of 1916, it was a common occurrence for six-ton lorries, with wireless stations on board, to slide backwards on the icy slopes of the Malvern Hills.

Colonel (previously Major) Handley, the Section's Commanding Officer, had a well-deserved reputation as a reckless driver and Priestley records that "he was responsible for the only time I ever heard a General shriek"; it happened when the Inspector General, Royal Engineers, with Handley at the wheel of an Armstrong-Siddeley car, was being driven to inspect the Malvern Depot. The Colonel was doing thirty miles an hour between high hedges on the wrong side of a country road when, on a sharp bend, their vehicle met a three-ton lorry doing thirty miles an hour but, by the greatest of good fortune, also on the wrong side of the road. While Priestley had become inured to Handley's driving, the Inspector General had not, and rose in his seat and shrieked at the top of his voice!

There was yet another such occasion when visiting, with Priestley, a brother Colonel at his country house which had been requisitioned as a Company Headquarters. On leaving, Handley stepped on the accelerator instead of the brake and completely demolished one of the Colonel's gateposts in front of his eyes. Indeed, Priestley records that "I had more hairbreadth escapes in those two years in that Armstong-Siddeley than I ever had in the Antarctic where my first motoring experiences took place" (on the Nimrod Expedition with Shackleton).

Colonel Handley figures again for less salubrious reasons. He was, apparently, a director of a small family firm selling electrical accessories and his keen business drive sometimes caused him to be, in Priestley's words "carried very near the wind"; for example, if a new ammeter was required, it would often be bought from his family business at a price very near to the maximum that the Army would sanction but, on his express instructions, without the name Handley appearing on the invoice.

Priestley's recollections of 1915 and 1916 at Worcester are many and varied. During this period, he lived in lodgings at Commandery House in the center of Worcester where he had "Woodbine Willie" as a near neighbor in St. Martin's Gate, on his rare leaves from the Western Front. Paradoxically, cricket continued to demand his attention as in the course of his duties he assumed responsibility for Worcester County Cricket Ground and where, occasionally, he played himself. On one such occasion he scored a "delirious" century against Norton Barracks Headquarters Staff, finishing his innings with five fours from successive balls from an aged and plump RSM, much to the glee of the assembled soldiery, only to be bowled by the last ball which bounced no less than three times on its way to the crease!

During 1916 as the section increased in number, its quiet and efficient Territorial Sergeant Major Shepard was outranked by the arrival of Regimental Sergeant Major Newland, "a mountain of a man" who had returned from the Western Front. Though he wore a wound stripe, it was rumored that this was not sustained in the course of his duties but "through the collapse of a cellar lid late in the evening!" These suspicions were later confirmed beyond much doubt when, at a Bank Holiday Fete on the Worcester County Cricket Ground, Priestley was asked to sanction the use of the Section van to transport the RSM back to barracks, as he had played host all day "not wisely but well." Nonetheless, Priestley considered him a truly authentic RSM who, while he terrified the rank and file, had theirs' and the Section's best interests at heart.

The RSM was also very much involved with Priestley in his role as Adjutant. On one such occasion the RSM brought a sapper, by the name of Taylor, up on orders before Priestley for a minor offense; Taylor refused to say anything in his defense and so received seven days confined to barracks. It later transpired that he was not the correct Taylor and was well aware of that fact, but was too much in awe of the RSM to say so and preferred to let matters take their course.

On another occasion, the RSM met his match when he and Priestley were in the Adjutant's office dealing with a sapper who had been absent without leave. Suddenly there was a great commotion in the outer office when a very small woman forced her way through "the serried ranks" of clerks and N.C.O.s, slapped the RSM hard on the cheek and left with, what transpired, was her husband, never to be seen again. In fact, Priestley records that crime was not common in the Wireless Training Section though it was not entirely free from it. On one occasion, for example, a subaltern facing a charge of passing "dud" checks was successfully defended by a brother officer who was a solicitor. Unfortunately, his defense involved importing a witness from Scottish Command for which the defendant paid with another bad check and for which, this time, he paid the penalty.

The Wireless Section grew rapidly and on occasions needed to parade up to a thousand men, for which a new and beautifully asphalted parade ground had been built; "there were some queer soldiers among them." In one instance, a draft of thirteen sergeants, on parade in resplendent new uniforms, caused a near riot amongst the assembled troops. When given the command to dismiss, the new squad of sergeants failed to move off as they did not know how to "form fours"; they were, in fact, specialists destined for a new intelligence station in Egypt, and owed their rank to their scarcity value as intellectuals.

This was not an unusual situation and the Wireless Training Centre (W.T.C. as it had now become), was called upon to send drafts to all theaters of the war with inevitable and unusual consequences. For instance, a squad of Glasgow telephonists, who had never been outside the United Kingdom, were sent to East Africa to establish a wireless station at Tsavo, famed for its inclusion in the book *The Man-eaters of Tsavo*, in which a pride of lions decimated a gang of navvies.[4] Some of the Glaswegians had read the book and when, after dark, lions were heard roaring, decided urgent action was required. The squad had seven days' emergency rations of "bully beef," in seven-pound meat tins, which they proceeded to open and place in a circle around their camp fire in the hope that the lions might prefer the bully beef to them! No lions, in fact, came near the camp but, in the African heat, the meat went bad and the squad had to survive on army "hard tack" biscuits alone, for the next seven days.

Only once in Priestley's tenure did the W.T.C. receive a complaint about one of its drafts. This was when a new draft was sent to France after only six weeks intensive training, was immediately put into quarantine for measles and then overlooked for two months, by the end of which its members had forgotten almost everything they had been taught. In addition, the W.T.C. had an excellent series of Inspection Reports in which Priestley's Polar Medal, yet again, often played a key role. He was placed in a prominent position near the front of the parade and, although all inspecting generals felt that they ought to recognize all medals, Priestley's, being Naval, usually called for an explanation. When provided, the remainder of the parade was usually spent in discussion between the colonel and the general about Shackleton and Scott, with little attention given to the inspection of the parade.

By now, Priestley had completed almost two years' service and was pleased with the fruits of his labor. The W.T.C. was the only source available to the Army of trained personnel. There was a constant amount of hard work requiring a good deal of dedication to his duties. For example, he records that, on arriving back from leave at Kidderminster at one o'clock in the morning, he then walked through twelve inches of snow to Worcester to take the six o'clock parade. He also devoted his first long leave to join the W.T.C. Riding School to set a good example, in the course of which he was thrown by his horse and quite badly concussed. With his customary humor, he acknowledges that the blow to his head provided a "logical answer for some of the things I did and said in later months" to those who observed the accident!

He also made many friends throughout all ranks during these two years and the only grouse appeared to be about his insistence on well-trimmed hair. Indeed, one sapper was heard to say out of the corner of his mouth; "'e's only jealous mate, look at 'is own 'ead," a remark he felt it diplomatic not to hear.

In early 1917, one of his main preoccupations was the continuing progress of the Young Officers School which he had established. Though it was increasing in strength, its youthful participants required careful watching, especially in their attraction towards female company. This was given particular emphasis on a day when Priestley was walking down Worcester High Street with the colonel, who was complaining volubly about this specific issue. Suddenly he spotted a young officer approaching with a glamorous young female on his arm—in fact, a lieutenant who would go on to become a Group Captain. "There's that young devil again" stormed the colonel and, a moment later as the couple drew near, "My God! It's my daughter."

By this time, Priestley was becoming rather frustrated and considered that he had earned a change of duties, particularly as both his younger brothers had been killed in France. Moreover, although he made a number of applications to be sent overseas, the colonel always turned them down on the fairly justifiable grounds that his local knowledge was invaluable. However, the W.T.C. was now due to join the main Signal Service Training Centre (S.S.T.C.) at Fenny Stanton in Bedfordshire, where Priestley was quick to point out he would have no local knowledge. Still his request was refused, but by going over the colonel's head to General Boys, Commandant of the S.S.T.C., it was finally agreed that, subject to further general signals training, he would be posted overseas in his existing rank of captain, which duly took place.

He left an unusual but poignant legacy at Fenny Stanton. His father had been looking after a dog for Priestley named "Glennie Nos" (Long Nose) who had been the leader of one of Scott's Antarctic dog-teams. When his father retired, Glennie Nos had to be returned to Priestley's care. In effect, it joined the army, had its own sergeant, one Sergeant Butcher, to look after it and apparently enjoyed army life. However, in the spring of 1918, dogs were considered a nuisance and an Army Order decreed their destruction. To avoid this, Glennie Nos was trained to hide behind a pigwash barrel outside the Sergeants Mess whenever a member of the military police or anyone who was a stranger approached. In due course, this ruse became common knowledge to all but those bent on his destruction, including visiting generals and staff officers who liked to test it out and, in the process, helped to contribute to good reports by minimizing their attention to detail elsewhere. Once again, Priestley felt that his Antarctic experience had made a valuable contribution. In January 1918, Priestley left Fenny Stanton for Haynes Park to complete his full Signals training before being posted to France.

However, before passing on to this entirely new and, undoubtedly, life-changing experience, it is important to reflect on his military career so far, most particularly the importance of his contribution towards wireless training throughout the army. By 1918, the British High Command had been forced to overcome its previous antipathy towards and suspicion of wireless communication. Furthermore the replacement of spark by continuous wave sets had made wireless a much more viable means of communication; continuous wave sets were lighter, less visible to the enemy, had a greater range, were less subject to interference, and easier and less demanding on personnel to operate. Above all, they were not subject to the limitations imposed by cable communication lines.[5]

This would be a crucial factor in the much more mobile warfare which characterized the war in 1918, exponentially as it progressed towards its conclusion. Wireless had been championed mainly by the Royal Flying Corps, enthusiasts recruited from Marconi, and those within the British Army Signal

Service committed to its development and training in the face of at best, indifference and more often prejudice at High Command level. Even so, it was much more the exigencies of the situation rather than enthusiasm for wireless which demanded its more extensive use. In the *Official History of the Signal Service*, which he wrote in 1921 shortly following the end of the war, Priestley emphasizes this point to a degree. However, it was only later when, understandably with the passage of time and less proximity to the conflict, a more objective analysis revealed the extent to which a much earlier and entirely possible development of wireless would have had a profound effect on both the strategic and operational conduct of the war, to its considerable advantage.[6]

Priestley had occupied a central role in wireless training in the army from the very beginning of the war and as it progressed, the numbers in training had increased dramatically in line with the general increase in the size of the army as a whole. From here forward he would be involved, first hand, in the critical phase leading up to the Hundred Days[7] and the eventual breaking of the Hindenburg Line in which all aspects of signal communications, but predominately wireless, played a crucial role.

On Priestley's arrival at Haynes Park, his first encounter was with an immaculately dressed adjutant, "Sticky" Glew, and seated at a far less impressive desk, the colonel, his new Commanding Officer, in the "quieter" uniform of the Rifle Brigade, neither of whom seemed pleased to see him. However, once again Priestley contends that his Antarctic Medal came to his rescue to the extent that he was invited to join the colonel for dinner that evening, which went well.

Apparently, Glew was something of a legend, which certainly owed much to his rise through the ranks and he epitomized and reminded Priestley of a well-known army story which summed this up precisely, along the following line: A ranker Royal Engineer's Captain was exercising his company at a time when the army was very conscious of observation from the air. An inspection was due and the company commander had his men drawn up to the rear of a really impressive line of trenches they had excavated but, unfortunately, the displaced turf had been turned the wrong way up, and the resulting brown scar across the country would be visible by any scouting aircraft for miles around. "Good God, man," said the inspecting general, "you've got all those sods turned the wrong way round." Without a moment's hesitation the company commander drew himself up and shouted "Company, About Turn." Priestley felt that "this was Sticky to the life, he would never have thought twice about it."

At Raynes Park, Priestley immediately renewed his never altogether comfortable relationship with horses. At his first "stables," at which the major in charge of the Riding School was not present, Priestley asked a passing sergeant where he might find him. The sergeant indicated that he was in hospital with a broken leg and it was, in fact, the horse that Priestley was grooming that had kicked him. Priestley records with some feeling that never had a horse been so carefully groomed from the midriff backwards than during the four weeks it took him to complete his second Army Riding School. Within four months, Priestley had qualified as a fully-fledged Signal Officer, including proficiency in Cable, Airline and, of course, Wireless Telegraphy. Thereafter, he entered a new and dramatically different phase of his war service with his immediate embarkation for the Western Front in May 1918 to join the 46th (North Midlands) Division which had seen brave and tenacious service in France since February 1915; a short summary of this period provides an essential background to Priestley's service.[8]

The 46th was one of the pre-war Territorial Divisions and in peacetime was known as the North Midlands Division, comprised of men from the counties of Derby, Nottingham, Lincoln, Leicester and Stafford, commanded at the outbreak of war by Major-General the Hon. E.J. Montagu-Stuart-Wortley, C.B., C.M.G., M.V.O., D.S.O. At the commencement of hostilities the division was mobilized with its headquarters first at Derby and afterwards at Luton and Bishop Stortford. After only seven months training in England, it embarked for France in February 1915, with the distinction of being the first Territorial Division to be committed for action on the Western Front.

After only two weeks, the division was placed in reserve for the Battle of Neuve-Chapelle, although not used, but received its baptism of fire at Ploegsteert and thereafter occupied the British front line at both Kemmel and Neuve-Église before it moved to the Ypres salient in Belgium; it remained there for four months with time spent in front of the infamous enemy stronghold known as Hill 60. It was while in this area that the division was subjected to the first of the enemy's "Flammenwerfer" (flamethrower) attacks, resulting in the temporary recoil of the division's left flank, which was retrieved only by stubborn and heroic resistance by its 139th Brigade.

The division's next move was to the Bethune area where, on October 13, 1915, it relieved the Guards Division and made its first attack of the war on enemy fortifications known as "The Quarries" and "Fosse 8," sustaining extremely high casualty levels and reducing its total strength by almost half. Later in 1915, in December, the division was selected for service in Egypt, and while two brigades eventually arrived there, the order was countermanded; the two brigades were recalled, and the entire division reassembled in Northern France in February 1916, taking over the lines in front of Vimy Ridge, at that time held by the enemy, from French troops.

On July 1, 1916, the division took part in the opening phase of the Battle of the Somme, on the most westerly portion of the enemy's front line at Gommecourt; their attack was anticipated and rebuffed with, once again, very high casualty levels. As a result, the division was forced to regroup and was not involved in any significant action until March 13, 1917, when it was called upon to attack a strongly defended wired area known as Rettemoy Graben which, after an initial heavy bombardment, was assaulted by the 5th North and 5th South Staffordshire regiments with Bucquoy as their objective. Unfortunately, and not unusually, the bombardment had only partially cut the wire, the enemy put up a stubborn rearguard action and the two battalions suffered heavy casualties in the course of this unsuccessful attack.

Later in March 1917, the division relieved the 24th Division at Lens and remained there for the following four months, where it was involved in the continuing war of attrition in some very hard fighting. By July 1, 1917, the line had advanced by an average of two thousand yards, and captured of the tactically important Hill 65.

Over the next fourteen months, the division was involved in trench warfare in the Cambrai-Lens sector of the Western Front and assisted the Canadian Corps, with Divisional Artillery, in its successful capture of the strategically important Hill 70. The division completed this long spell of trench warfare in the Givenchy area where "raiding" was the order of the day spurred on by the division's new commanding officer, Major-General W. Thwaites C.B., a keen disciplinarian and respected leader who encouraged the offensive spirit in his men. This undoubtedly improved the divisional morale, led to some successful local actions with the capture of numerous enemy prisoners and helped to expunge the memory of some difficult reverses that the division had endured,

Priestley in uniform as a major while serving with the 46th (North Midland) Division during the final Hundred Days of the First World War (The Scott Polar Research Institute Picture Library).

albeit in circumstances of often heroic resistance. Consequently, by the time that Priestley joined the division, preparatory to its crucial and successful involvement in the final "Hundred Days" offensive and the breaking of the Hindenburg Line, it was, as Priestley describes, "as hard as nails and fit for anything"; from his point of view, a good and auspicious time to join the division under its new commanding officer, General G.F. Boyd.

When Priestley arrived at Le Havre he made what he describes as "a good start" when his brother, who was an Intelligence Officer, met him and "introduced him to some good cider." Nonetheless, he was not entirely happy when his seniority placed him in charge of the draft, of which he was one, as Officer I/C Train on its way to Abbeville but which, with the help of a competent group of N.C.O.s, was concluded successfully. For a few days he was Acting Chief Wireless Instructor of the B.E.F. at Abbeville, as the present incumbent, Rupert Stanley, who had been with him at Worcester, had taken the opportunity to arrange "Paris Leave." However, almost immediately he found that, due to past connections, local influence was being used on his behalf to his considerable satisfaction. Colonel Stratton, his commanding officer while at Cambridge, was staff officer to the Chief Signal Officer, 2nd Army, and had asked for Priestley, initially as a supernumerary. He was first attached to the 6th Division and then the 1st Division, spending the following two months in the Ypres sector learning firsthand the extreme and often insurmountable difficulties of laying signals cable. It was one of the most enduring and intractable problems for the Signal Service throughout the whole of the war and especially in Flanders, where the water table was very near to the surface. Indeed, to withstand the impact of a direct hit by a 5.9 inch shell, cable needed to be buried at a depth of at least six feet, which was entirely impossible in this sector. Serious and ongoing problems of maintaining communications which was not solved satisfactorily until the advent of more readily available, effective and acceptable wireless sets.[9]

During this period, Priestley was called upon to supervise parties of disgruntled infantry who thought, "poor devils," that they had been taken out of the line to rest. Instead they found themselves employed in laying cable overnight, in the muddiest and most miserable of conditions while, at the same time, coming under heavy and indiscriminate enemy artillery fire. With his blue and white Royal Engineers' (R.E.s) Signals armband, Priestley became well known very quickly but not always in ways that he would have wished, but nonetheless understood. On one occasion he overheard an infantryman remark, with considerable depth of feeling, "If I were digging graves for bloody R.E.s, mate, I'd be 'appy." A similar incident, reported to him by a subaltern of the Sherwood Foresters, echoed this prevailing sentiment. As the subaltern passed down the line in torrential rain and under heavy enemy fire, a Sherwood Forester expressed his feelings to his companion thus: "Bill, in six days God made the Earth. The seventh day he made the Notts' and Derbys' to dig the whole bloody lot up again." Then he spat on his hands and got on with the job, which Priestley regarded as "the P.B.I. (Poor Bloody Infantry) at its best."[10]

The two months undertaking these duties were full of incident for Priestley. On one occasion he was returning to his billet when a 5.9 inch shell came down practically between his legs, knocked him over on impact and covered him with mud but didn't go off; immediately after, he recollects hearing similar shells falling "whilst sitting anxiously in the officers' latrine!" On another occasion, a Douglas motorcycle fell to pieces under him on a hard paved road; at that point he swore to limit himself to "push-bikes" in the future—which he did for the rest of his life, including never driving a car. Priestley's role with a battalion of the division's Portuguese allies, who he was supervising in digging signals cable trenches, provide a final insight into his experiences during this period. Apparently, although the Portuguese infantrymen "worked like hell, they immediately went to ground when a shell came within a hundred yards of them" while their officers "never stirred all night from a shell hole where they sat playing cards." In general, while Priestley regarded their infantrymen as good workers, he considered their officers as ill-trained and irresponsible. Nonetheless despite this he perfectly understood, for the sake of good order, the need for a Battalion Order to the effect that, "In future the troops of Britain's closest ally will be known as our noble allies the Portuguese and not those bloody Portuguese."

In August 1918, Priestley was transferred to his first permanent job since arriving on the Western Front, as Second-in-Command of 46th Divisional Signal Company, Fourth Army. At this time, the division was in very active preparation for an attack on the Hindenburg Line, which initially involved a crossing of the St. Quentin Canal in the face of heavy enemy resistance, and was scheduled for September 29, 1918, as the opening phase of the Battle of Bellenglise. (Appendix I provides a brief outline of the main phases of the 46th Division's involvement in the breaking of the Hindenburg Line and thereafter, until the Armistice on November 11, 1918.) In his new role, by this stage of the war, Priestley had at his disposal the full and wide range of signals communications including, critically, the latest and most effective continuous wavelength wireless sets as well as the well-tried Carrier Pigeon Service; in fact, the use of pigeons predated the current conflict and had been used in the war almost from its inception.

By this time some ninety thousand personnel had been trained as pigeon handlers and the service had grown exponentially since its first real involvement in action, at the Battle of Loos in early 1915. At that time, the Director of Army Signals had gone to the Army pigeon loft in order to be present when the first message was received. Although the battle opened at dawn, the first message did not arrive until dusk. When the message was delivered to the Director of Army Signals, Priestley records that when opened, it read tersely, though with a complete absence of military significance, "I've carried this blinking bird far enough. Signed Pte J. Smith."

On his appointment to 46th Division Signal Company, Priestley considered it his good fortune to be placed in charge of forward signals, the role usually reserved for his commanding officer but who, in this instance, had been in France since 1915 and chose to exercise command from rear signals Headquarters. As part of his duties, almost inevitably horses figured yet again as the "Horse Lines" became part of his responsibilities. They were an area beloved and readily understood by inspecting generals and consequently received more than their fair share of attention. With the preparations for the forthcoming battle in full swing, Priestley had no men who could be spared to keep the horses in inspection trim but, fortunately, he had a good and experienced team of N.C.O.s that contrived to overcome these difficulties.

On another occasion, in late October, while on horseback in the Cambrai area, Priestley encountered a general and his attendant staff approaching. Preparing to salute and with his eyes firmly fixed on the general's party he, although not his horse, was unaware of a concealed dug-out in his path; the horse stopped short and Priestley was thrown over his head to the barely suppressed amusement of the staff officers. However, Priestley recounts that the general himself stopped immediately, smiled and congratulated him on having performed the ultimate duty of a mounted officer in such circumstances—"not to let go of the reins."

Though Priestley's anecdotal accounts for this period reflect his ability to find some humor, even if ironic, in the worst of situations, this was in the face of the harsher realities of the Battle of Bellenglise, in which his division was now fighting with great fortitude and distinction against determined enemy resistance established in defensive positions which, until now, had been considered as virtually impregnable. The enemy was concealed in deep and well protected dug-outs which withstood a seventy-two hour barrage from the divisional support of no less than twelve brigades of field artillery, with minimal casualties although, crucially, its supply lines were severely disrupted.

The responsibility for communications support for the twelve Brigades of attached Artillery rested with the Divisional Signals Company, adding greatly to the pressures placed on its already stretched resources, with which Priestley was very actively involved. Each Brigade Headquarters had to be interconnected and also provided with links to the attacking infantry. The result was huge pressure on the cable and airline sections as, paradoxically, although sufficient continuous-wave wireless sets were probably available at this late stage of the war, they were not matched by enough trained personnel to operate them, despite the best efforts of Priestley and others before his posting to the Western Front.

Worse was to come. A cavalry brigade arrived in the divisional area to await the expected breakthrough although, it has to be acknowledged, cavalry had been held in reserve for this very purpose since the commencement of the war and yet had never been deployed successfully, as indeed they were not on this occasion. Nonetheless they made their presence felt. Their horses had to be picketed and one cavalry unit cut and used two hundred yards of the signals cable to make a picket line, on the night of September 28, 1918, at a critical period when communications were of vital importance, preceding the opening of the Battle of Bellenglise on September 29, 1918. Coincidently, the commanding officer of the offending unit was the well-connected Major Nigel Haig; as a result, Priestley records, the division's subsequent complaint "did not make much impact at General Headquarters" (and Field Marshall Haig).

While for those with a specific interest, Appendix I provides an outline of the 46th Division's performance from the opening of the Battle of Bellenglise through until the Armistice, the forcing of the German's last prepared line of defense, the Beaurevoir-Fonsomme line during the Battle of Ramicourt was the division's last involvement in trench warfare and had particular significance for Priestley. Once again, the cable sections under his command had to interlink nine Field Artillery Brigades, three Infantry Brigades and Divisional Headquarters, the task being completed successfully only minutes before Zero Hour and, by contrast with the Battle of Bellenglise, communications worked perfectly from this point onwards for the remainder of the attack. Priestley's contribution to this strenuous, often dangerous but very successful operation was recognized by the immediate award of a Military Cross.

The citation for Priestley's award appeared in the London Gazette dated October 4, 1919, as follows[11]:

> Lt. (T./Capt.) Raymond Edward Priestley, 46th (N. Mid.) Div.Coy., R.E.,T.F.
>
> Near Bellenglise on 2, 3 and October 4, 1918, he was in charge of the executive handling of the signals communications and was mainly instrumental in keeping touch with the units during the attack on Ramicourt and Montbrehain. His efficiency and enthusiasm were, most marked. He showed utter disregard of danger during his duty on the lines over the whole of the shelled area.

But, as Priestley records, the success was not achieved without some subterfuge. The Battle of Bellenglise, and more especially the demands of the Cavalry Brigades, had exhausted the division's cable supplies. Priestley was "at his wit's end" when he was advised that Corps Headquarters had just moved leaving behind its whole communication system intact. Priestley immediately mobilized three six-horse wagons and his signalers removed no less than sixty-eight miles of twisted cable just in time to complete the network. At this point, Priestley records that as his cable wagons rumbled over the horizon he held a Corps Signals subaltern in conversation as to the extraordinary mischance—the disappearance of his complete cable network overnight. It was a "steal but not a conscienceless one." His excuse appears to be that Corps Headquarters was nearer to Army supplies and consequently could replenish stores more easily, there was still a good airline system in operation and, in any event, Corps Headquarters moved less frequently than that of Division. There seems no doubt that good communications will have been fundamental to success in the battle and made a major contribution towards reducing casualties.

As a footnote to his award of a Military Cross, Priestley notes that quite ludicrous mistakes were sometimes made. In one instance Corps requested two lists: one for officers who refused to be inoculated; another for recommendations for the immediate award of a Military Cross. Each list contained twelve names, there was a mix-up at Corps Headquarters, and the twelve officers who had refused inoculation gained the award.

The Battle of Andigny, the third and last action of the division during the Hundred Days, brought its contribution to a close; it had been one of almost unparalleled success during the whole of the war on the Western Front. The division, with a fighting strength of only eight thousand men, had captured six thousand men, sixty guns and spearheaded the critical breakthrough of the Hindenburg Line. Throughout the entire war, however, the severity of the fighting in which the division was involved between February 1915 and the Armistice on November 11, 1918, tells its own story: 1502 officers and 28,067 other ranks were killed, wounded or reported missing.

It was at this point that the Divisional Commanding Officer, General Boyd, decided that the Divisional History of its service during the Hundred Days must be written without delay and advertised in General Orders for an author. An officer on the general's staff—"until then a friend of Priestley's"— told him that there was an officer in the Signals Company who had written a book on Antarctic exploration. Priestley was summoned and asked to do the job but declined on the basis that he wished to return to Cambridge to resume his studies. The general asked him not to decide immediately but have dinner with him in the mess[12] that evening—"a Royal Command" no less. At dinner and after four glasses of port, in his words, "he would have written anything." He was immediately relieved of all regimental duties and in the surrounding devastated area wrote *Breaking the Hindenburg Line* and, as a direct result, was asked to follow this by writing the *Official History of the Signal Service* during the war.

A final spell as Deputy Director Signals, First Army, in Valenciennes, followed by a few months at Imperial Defense Headquarters in London brought his military career to a close, and ushered in his return to Cambridge.

7

Cambridge University— Scott Polar Research Institute

Although Priestley returned to Cambridge briefly in 1913 following his return from the Terra Nova Expedition and matriculated as a pensioner in Christchurch College for a course of research study, the First World War intervened, and he did not return to resume the work on the scientific results of Shackleton's Nimrod Expedition, which he had interrupted to join Scott, until 1919. Consequently, at this point, he had still not completed a first degree and his return to Cambridge had been further delayed in writing the *Official History of the Army Signal Service* following the end of the war.

Consequently, it was not until late 1920 that his thesis under the general title of *Antarctic Glaciology*[1] was approved, earning him a B.A. and recognized as a very valuable and scholarly work. It was based on the scientific investigations of Shackleton's Nimrod Expedition, written in conjunction with his fellow and highly regarded geologist, Professor Edgeworth David, covering the glaciology and tectonic geology of South Victoria Land, with short notes on paleontology by Griffith Taylor, another expedition member. Subsequently, he completed sections of the British (Terra Nova) Antarctic Expedition 1910–1913, written jointly with Charles (later Sir Charles) Wright, also a fellow expedition member, published in 1922 entitled *Glaciology*[2] and thereafter considered a classic of early glaciological literature. At the same time he studied agriculture, for which he was awarded a diploma in 1922 before becoming a fellow of Clare College in 1923. It was also during his early years at Cambridge that discussions took place, in which he was very actively involved, that led eventually to the establishment of the Scott Polar Research Institute (SPRI) This is dealt with separately in view of its profound importance in polar exploration and research, in which SPRI has developed exponentially and today is one of the leading research establishments in its field.

From that moment, in 1924, Priestley embarked on what would be a continuous career in academic administration, culminating in his eventual appointment as vice-chancellor of the University of Birmingham. In his first post at Cambridge, as Assistant Registrary, he was immediately faced with a wide variety of demanding duties that would test his inexperience to the full. These included, among an extensive range; the supervision of the list of candidates for all examinations including the application of fees, the management of the examinations themselves and, thereafter, Matriculations and Congregations; acting as deputy to the Registrary whenever required and at short notice; being available at the Registrary daily during terms and especially on the days of Congregation, Matriculation, General Admissions, and meetings of the Senate. In addition, he was expected to be present in Cambridge for significant periods during the Easter and Long Vacations. His success in this post led subsequently to his appointment in 1927 as First Assistant Registrary and Secretary to the General Board and then, in 1934 for one year only, as Secretary General to the Faculties. His recognized success in these posts, in which student welfare was always his first priority and continued to be throughout his career, resulted in his appointment as the first vice-chancellor of the University of Melbourne, in 1935.

We must now turn our attention to a vitally important part of Priestley's legacy, both to Cambridge and the future of scientific exploration and research in the Polar Regions, in the establishment of the Scott Polar Research Institute (SPRI). Although Frank Debenham, its first director and previously a colleague on the Terra Nova Expedition as a geologist in its Far Western Party, receives much of the credit for the establishment of SPRI, there is no doubt that Priestley was very much involved from its inception through to the project's realization. This in no respect devalues Debenham's role, which was crucial. He continued his work in the field and spent a major part of his professional life at SPRI, whereas Priestley left Cambridge to complete a varied career covering a wide spectrum of activities.

Indeed, in an article written by Debenham for SPRI's twenty-fifth anniversary, this is made abundantly clear,[3] as it is in Peter Speak's more recent biography of Debenham.[4] While admitting that it is rarely possible to state precisely when a new concept arises, he is in no doubt that the first seeds of the idea were sown in November 1912, when Debenham and Priestley were on Mount Erebus in Antarctica, making a geological survey designed to complement a similar exercise carried out by Professor David, Douglas (later Sir Douglas) Mawson (later the leader of an Australian Expedition) and Priestley when on Shackleton's Nimrod Expedition. A discussion ensued about how their findings could be compared with those of previous studies and a subsequent debate about the need for a central depositary for all field records, as well as other related matters, such as improvements in sledging gear and camping equipment, for example. It is also clear from written evidence, discovered later by Debenham, that Shackleton had similar though embryonic thoughts, probably as the result of over-wintering discussions that were very much the result of enforced inactivity and, more often than not, proved to be no more than pipe dreams.

With the intervention of the First World War, the idea of some type of Polar Institute to centralize scientific information was swept aside, along with many others, due to the extreme exigencies of the situation but, fortunately, resurfaced when both Debenham and Priestley returned to Cambridge in 1919. Their first step was the preparation of a paper outlining their ideas which was sent, in the first instance, to Sir Arthur Shipley, Master of Christ's College who they considered a kindred spirit, and consequently receptive to their ideas. The immediate response was all, and indeed more, than they could have hoped for; Sir Arthur immediately forwarded the correspondence to Sir William Soulsby, Honorary Secretary of the Scott Memorial Mansion House Fund who, in turn, passed it on as "an interesting statement" to the Trustees of the Polar Research Branch of the Fund. The result was that £10,000 was set aside for a Polar Research Fund from the incredibly generous and immediate response to the Lord Mayor of London's appeal of behalf of the Scott Memorial Mansion House Fund. This had been set up following the "Message to the Public" from Scott on behalf of the dependents of himself and the four men who died with him on the return from the Pole, raising a magnificent overall total of £76,000.

In making the grant for a Polar Research Fund, the Trustees envisaged "that the funds would be devoted to an endowment in aid of future polar research, the income to be applied either annually for the encouragement of such work as may arise or allowed to accumulate until such an occasion presents itself."[5] Some time previously, Debenham and Priestley had taken the precaution of consulting Lady Scott and also fellow members of the expedition, who had approved their plan, and in order to maintain its momentum they prepared an article outlining their ideas in much greater detail, forwarded to the Trustees on January 29, 1920. In this, both Priestley and Debenham, as petitioners, though not anticipating such a generous sum, were at pains to make clear that their original expectation was that the grant would be available for capital expenditure as well as running costs.

Thereafter on May 5, 1920, Debenham was summoned to a meeting at the Mansion House with the Lord Mayor in the chair, at which the renowned explorer Sir Francis Younghusband was also present, at which he was faced with some very searching but nonetheless sympathetic questions. The hugely important and, indeed, historic sequel was a letter from the Trustees dated May 6, 1920, to the vice-chancellor of Cambridge University stating that "the Trustees were prepared to grant £6,000 towards the provision of a suitable Wing or Annex forming part of a larger building devoted to Geography that was also a separate beneficiary from Scott Memorial Mansion House Fund."[6]

Consideration of the proposals were delayed by the "Long Vacation" but, finally, on November 20, 1920, its council made the following recommendations: that a Polar Research Institute be established at Cambridge in association with the School of Geography; that temporary accommodation be provided in the Sedgwick Museum and that, in the meantime, funds be allowed to accumulate. The recommendations were approved by Grace on November 26, 1920, and the Scott Polar Research Institute was launched. So far so good, but with money agreed for the building only and not for maintenance, there were many problems still to be overcome, in which the ensuing five years were critical. However, through the continuing goodwill of the university and many donations from friends and well-wishers, the trustees felt able to make an official announcement of the new venture in the *University Reporter* simultaneous with the presentation of a paper by Debenham, with Priestley in attendance, entitled "The Future of Polar Exploration" covering the aims and the layout of the new Institute, to the Royal Geographical Society, on December 20, 1920, and published in its *Journal* in March of the following year.[7]

The fledgling Institute was helped enormously by the important and strong support of Shackleton, who promised to give such records and equipment that were available from his own expeditions and, thereafter, began to take shape and to amass an impressive collection, amongst which contributions from former members of Scott's expedition were, not unnaturally, at the forefront. Nonetheless, Debenham records that "even so, the most prominent exhibit for some time was a large blue and white advertisement of a polar bear swimming after a seal in a rough sea. The colouring and action of the picture were excellent, but I was always rather ashamed of it in our collection since polar bears can never catch a seal in the open sea and do not attempt to do so!"[8]

During the early days of SPRI's existence, its reputation tended to be somewhat ahead of what it could realistically provide to meet the many demands immediately made upon it. Nevertheless, from the very beginning, it had the support of a large number of men with extensive polar experience who could be consulted and were rarely at a loss to provide answers; in essence, SPRI became a clearing house for information on a wide variety of technical and other issues. In addition, SPRI's founders were keen that the Institute should cover all polar activity and not be confined to mainly Antarctic matters on which its establishment was based, there having been only very limited recent British activity in the Arctic. This problem was quickly overcome by a surge of British interest in Arctic regions during the 1920s, especially those led by George (later Sir George) Binney of Oxford University and J.M. Wordie of Cambridge University. During the course of these expeditions a large number of well qualified young men were "infected by the polar bug"[9] and went on to continue the work with huge enthusiasm and greatly increased momentum.

The early days of the Institute, which relied heavily on a group of very willing volunteers, were usually referred to as its "attic period"[10] because included in its premises was a large attic holding a wide variety of related books and equipment that became something of a magnet for those with a shared interest leading, frequently, to debates about polar travel, equipment, and its historical background, with related exhibitions and even occasional parties.

However, the prospects for a new Geography building, despite early enthusiasm by the Trustees of the Scott Memorial Mansion House Fund, had begun to fade, in which case the future of SPRI was also in jeopardy as this was scheduled to become its permanent home. The inadequacies of the temporary facilities in the Sedgwick Museum were already becoming apparent. The major stumbling block was the understandable reluctance of the Trustees to release building funds before those for its future maintenance were provided for. In an attempt to overcome this difficulty, Debenham, with Priestley's support, approached the Trustees of the Research Fund, that part of the Memorial Fund under which SPRI benefited specifically, in a letter to its Honorary Secretary, Sir William Soulsby, dated February 10, 1925, proposing that from the £6,000 already promised to the university, a quarter of this should be used as a capital fund for maintenance. Moreover, Debenham and Priestley, because of the excellent relationship that had been maintained with the Trustees, felt able to express the hope that all the funds promised to SPRI could soon be released.

After a good deal of diplomatic maneuvering, but accompanied by much goodwill on all sides, the vice-chancellor of the University of Cambridge received a letter indicating that the full allocation of funds could be released and his reply on May 9, 1925, marks a truly historic moment in SPRI's history; "the University of Cambridge gratefully accepts the generous offer of the Trustees of the Scott Memorial Fund to present the University with a sum of money for the erection, endowment and maintenance of a Captain Scott Polar Research Institute."[11] For Debenham and Priestley, what had been little other than a dream on the slopes of Erebus had become a reality. For this reason, Debenham records, "Priestley and I spent the evening more in reminiscence than planning."[12]

The actual planning, inevitably, took some time and it was not until January 27, 1926, that the first meeting of the Management Committee was convened; its membership had been carefully and, in the light of its future success, wisely chosen. Professor Seward, as the Committee's first Chairman was an inspired choice, having regard to his keen interest in polar exploration, his recent journey to Greenland and his influence as vice-chancellor of the

University; his success in this office can be measured by his re-appointment as Chairman, on an annual basis, for the following ten years until he left the university. The Royal Geographical Society nominated Dr. H.R. Hill to be its representative, the remaining members being Priestley, Debenham and, in addition, J.M. Wordie, later to be acclaimed for his prominence in Arctic exploration.

The Management Committee immediately laid out the aims of the Institute which were published in the Royal Geographical Society's *Journal* in its July 1926 edition. Preceding this, an opening ceremony took place on May 22, 1926, in the form of an exhibition of what had been collected by the fledgling Institute in the previous five years before its official inauguration. At the dinner that followed, no less than sixty-five attended including nine men from Scott's and five from Shackleton's expeditions. Notable amongst the attendees were Lady Scott and also Sir T.W. Edgeworth David, a member of the Party that first reached the South Magnetic Pole and the doyen of South Polar exploration; as Debenham records, "David's reply to the toast to 'The Guests' was the most memorable both for its dramatic quality and for the personality of the speaker, who might well be called the Nansen of the Southern Hemisphere, so varied were his interests, so skilled his science and so kindly his outlook on the world"[13]—certainly sentiments that Priestley would have echoed and amplified as a result of the close working relationship and enduring friendship he had developed with David in Antarctica.

While initially the Management Committee was able to approve significant grants to those working up the results of recent expeditions, entirely in line with its avowed objectives, this generosity had to be tempered following the Institute's move of premises from the Sedgwick Museum to those in Lensfield Road, recently purchased by the university, in which SPRI established its headquarters. In general terms, the move was of great advantage to the Institute's work but carried the additional burden of increased overhead expenditure which, although shared with the School of Architecture until 1929 when it moved elsewhere, nevertheless constrained it financially.

Unfortunately, this coincided with a period of ill health for Debenham but, fortuitously, a chemistry mistress from the local County School and a volunteer at SPRI, Miss W.M. Drake, stepped into the breach and as well as cataloguing all its equipment, maps and books, also acted as hostess during both term time and in the school holidays; fundamentally, she was instrumental in creating a continually welcoming atmosphere and, even though not theoretically qualified, nevertheless quickly became proficient in directing technical questions to their most appropriate source. It was only during her final year at SPRI, in 1930, that the Committee was able to formally appoint and pay her in the post of Assistant Director; furthermore, to her immense credit, she left behind what Debenham describes as "Hints to Future Assistants,"[14]

7. Cambridge University

which was to prove of immense value to those who followed, as well as bringing out the first number of the *Polar Record* which was published in January 1931 and continued as the record of all major Polar events in subsequent years.

Finally, in 1934, after seven years in its temporary building, the SPRI was able to move to its new and custom-built premises, which it occupies to this day and where its history of outstanding success as a center of excellence for polar exploration and scientific achievement is both acknowledged and well documented. For the purpose of this biography, there is no doubt that Priestley played a major, if not sufficiently acknowledged, role in SPRI's inception and development up to the stage where it could be confidently left to others to continue the good work thus begun, while he departed for a significant new challenge as the first vice-chancellor of Melbourne University.

8

Vice-Chancellor—Melbourne University

Priestley was recruited to be the first salaried vice-chancellor of the University of Melbourne against the background of his proven experience and success in academic administration at the University of Cambridge; as previously described, he had held various posts at Cambridge, culminating in his role as Secretary-General of the Faculties, acting as secretary to the Board responsible for all matters relating to both teaching and research, equipping him admirably for this newly created role.

The University of Melbourne, founded in 1853, was by the 1930s in need of considerable reform to bring it into line, and indeed reputation, with its international counterparts. The instigation of its reforms are accredited, mainly, to Professors of Law and Commerce, respectively Kenneth Bailey and Douglas Copland, whose principle recommendation was the appointment of a full-time salaried vice-chancellor requiring an amendment to the University Act of 1928, which was successfully guided through the Victorian Legislative Assembly by the then Attorney General (later Prime Minister) R.G. Menzies, culminating in a new Universities Act in 1933.[1]

The Act made the newly appointed vice-chancellor effectively the University's Chief Executive Officer with overall responsibility for its educational and administrative affairs including discipline and any neglect of duty, misconduct or inefficiency; this being, undoubtedly, the greatest shake-up of administrative affairs in the university's history, it was perhaps not surprising that those who had become accustomed to exercising power and control resented the changes and sought to avoid or, even, ignore their implications at every opportunity.[2] It was into this emotionally charged environment that Priestley arrived, in company with his wife, Phyllis, and his elder daughter, Jocelyn, on Sunday, February 17, on board the *Nestor*, after a five-week sea voyage, preparatory to taking up his official duties on Monday, February 18, 1935, aged forty-eight.[3]

While at sea, he had prepared himself with his customary thoroughness that involved an extensive reading list, including a wide variety of subjects covering Australian history and its constitution, its economy, the inception of the University of Melbourne and its professoriate, together with the more recent minutes of its Council and Finance Committee, in addition to visiting the universities of both Fremantle and Adelaide at scheduled stops during the voyage to Melbourne.

On Sunday, February 17, his last day at sea, Priestley admits his usual apprehension at taking on a new challenge, particularly one of this magnitude, likening it to the time spent before going out to bat in an important cricket match but feeling, nevertheless, that its absence "might imply a change of outlook and character that would not necessarily be for the good though he could do without the nervousness."

From the outset, Priestley set himself a schedule that would have defeated a less driven individual, involving a six-day week at the university, often augmented by additional work on Sundays, in addition to the busy and vital social round which was an absolutely essential aspect of establishing his new role in the wider community; all this, as well as working at home in thorough preparation for a multiplicity of meetings, speeches and presentations, which formed part of the vice-chancellor's unremitting duties. However, his overriding guideline for his first year was, predominately, to look and listen.

He also established specific targets from the very beginning of his tenure with the clear objective of achieving these within a realistic timescale, set at around five years; with equal clarity, he anticipated that if he failed to make very significant progress towards these goals within this period, then this would almost certainly precipitate his departure.

First, and of primary importance, was the establishment of a strong Students' Union. Indeed, he was appalled by his first impression of both the student accommodation and the students' view of the university as merely a means to an end in achieving a satisfactory degree and little else; the much wider benefits of a university education, derived from the constant student interaction that a robust Students' Union would provide, had, hitherto, been entirely neglected. In Priestley's view, a spirit of social cohesion was as essential to the value that students gained from their time at the university as the quality of the lectures they attended. Second was the need to provide a new chemistry building, in order to meet the university's aspirations to be a leader in the field. Priestley viewed this as not merely a physical requirement but, much more, as a cooperative interaction between staff, students and the wider community including, crucially, both the media and the government; in this, he was heavily influenced by his recent and successful experience at Cambridge.

Staff matters also demanded his immediate attention, with competitive salaries, which had suffered severe cuts during the 1931 recession, as an essential prerequisite to attracting the best academicians; in addition, opportunities for individual research, which until now had been allowed only parsimoniously, had to be made much more freely available and recognized as a critical measure of the university's success.

As part of his overall objective of developing the university into a much more united and coherent establishment, Priestley felt strongly that the vice-chancellor should live on campus. He also believed that his residence should be designed to allow students easy and welcoming access to their vice-chancellor. In addition he believed, of equal importance, in creating strong links between the students and the university, was the creation of an Appointments Board to assist students in finding suitable postgraduate employment that fully recognized their potential. This was particularly the case in the area of public services where Australian universities as a whole were very poorly represented, Priestley felt, much to their detriment.

To accompany these developments, Priestley was determined to improve relationships with members of parliament, which currently ranged from, at best, apathetic to often highly critical. However, in his attempts to accomplish this change in attitude, Priestley was not prepared to sacrifice the rights of students to make radical protests which he felt were fundamental to the life of any university of real value. Similarly, the media especially the newspapers, and mainly the *Argus* and the *Age*, needed to be persuaded to report on the more positive aspects of university life and its considerable benefits to the wider community, rather than concentrating, as hitherto, on the relative trivia of student behavior.

Coincidently with Priestley's appointment as the first vice-chancellor, the position of registrar was to become vacant imminently; based on his Cambridge experience, he considered this a post of vital importance to the smooth running of the university. He rated Joseph Bainbridge, the current incumbent who had held the post with distinction since 1909, very highly. Bainbridge's deputy, Alfred Greig, was penciled in as his natural successor and, while Priestley would have preferred his first choice, John Foster, who had been his assistant in the Overseas Survey, to be appointed immediately, he allowed Greig—with characteristic and well-judged diplomacy—to be given the job, as he would only hold this until his retirement in 1939. Thereafter, Foster was his natural successor and repaid Priestley's confidence by successfully filling the post until 1947.

Based yet again on his experience and, particularly, his personal and well documented success at Clare, he recognized the need to bring Melbourne into line with what was required and expected of a twentieth century university; a visit to Sydney University, for the purposes of comparative analysis, did nothing to advance his cause and, even at this early stage of his tenure,

8. Vice-Chancellor—Melbourne University

in July he was already considering a tour of overseas universities for fresh and proven initiatives. This, as we shall see, eventually took place in 1936, generously funded by the Carnegie Organization.

The University of Melbourne on his arrival was, by any measure, a relatively small institution with only 86 professors and teaching staff and less than 4,000 students, with the main governance of the university in the hands of its Professional Board, comprising 23 members headed by, prior to Priestley's appointment, the Chancellor Sir John MacFarland with whom Priestley felt he could work well. Unfortunately, his untimely death only five months into Priestley's tenure, and the appointment in August 1935 of Sir James Barrett as his successor, marked the beginning of an entirely unworkable relationship so far as Priestley was concerned. It was, as we shall see, highly influential in his subsequent decision to resign with his work only partially completed. The basic disagreement between them was unbridgeable, as Barrett simply would not accept the terms of the statute that appointed the vice-chancellor as chief executive of the university. The practical result was that Priestley had to fight, and waste considerable time and nervous energy, in trying to push through what were for him unquestionably essential reforms, with absolutely no guarantee he could achieve his program, which was quite often thwarted by university politics.

However, his strategy to make progress with his reforms, despite the total antipathy of Barrett towards them, was to make friends at all levels, both within the university and in the wider Melbourne community and, to this end, his membership of the influential Melbourne Club enabled him to win over many members to what had been, until his appointment as vice-chancellor, a much neglected area. In addition, his membership of the Rotary Club was also of value in a similar way, in gaining support for the university's cause, as was his election to the Boobooks Club. Priestley's diary of April 26, 1935, makes reference to the somewhat obscure Boobook bird after which the Club was named, and although it was mainly a dining club with a small membership and without specified rules, it included many who could be of great help to Priestley in achieving his long-term objectives.

Against the background of almost unremittingly hard work, in an atmosphere of increasing tension and often open hostility by those determined to undermine his proposed initiatives and reforms, the novelty of the scale and beauty of the Australian countryside was a great solace to him. This was especially the case during his initial camping trip to the Mornington Peninsula when he very much enjoyed the outdoor life and, not surprisingly with his Antarctic experience as a constant companion, the generous supply and quality of the food available.

In fact, without the strong support of the many friends that he made in the early days of his tenure, there seems little doubt that he would have found his situation entirely untenable. Among those singled out in his diaries for specific mention, Professor Harrison Moore and Dr. Gwyneth Buchanan were the foremost in making his early life at the university bearable. Equally, Professor Samuel Wadham, who held the seat for Agriculture at the university from 1926 until 1957, was one of Priestley's oldest and closest friends both at Cambridge and during his war service, and an ever present and reliable confidant.

In furtherance of his determination to make friends and influence people, Priestley, as he had on a much more limited budget at Cambridge, entertained on a fairly grand and quite lavish scale which, despite a generous salary and entertainment allowance, left him with so little to spare that he could not afford a car and relied on his aforementioned friends to transport him, amongst which Buchanan and Wadham were of the greatest support. Those entertained were an eclectic group including students, professors, local politicians and a wide cross-section of academics visiting by specific invitation, all with the aim of gaining support from those who could help him most in achieving the reforms which he held were inimitable to making Melbourne a university fit for the modern post-war era.

Overall, viewed in the context of those ranged against his strategy, 1935 was one of considerable achievement, amongst which the establishment of the Australian vice-chancellors' Committee, under Priestley's chairmanship, was a major initiative and force for progress on many of the issues that he held dear. Nonetheless, he remained convinced that Australian universities, and Melbourne in particular, had much to learn from overseas universities and especially those in the United States and Canada, which were gaining in reputation internationally.

Consequently, on February 19, 1936, thanks to the generosity of the Carnegie Organization, Priestley left Melbourne for Los Angeles via New Zealand and Hawaii, with a quick stop-over at the latter's university before arriving at his final destination in early March 1936. His first visit was to the California Institute of Technology, where he met and interviewed Dr. Millikan, the President of the Institute, himself a highly respected physicist and tutor to no less than six Nobel Prize winners, who provided him not only with his own educational philosophy as it applied to the Institute but also a brief history of the ways in which university education in the United States had developed through a system of both privately endowed and government funded institutions. It became quickly apparent to Priestley that, in the democratic system prevailing in the United States, the selection process in the state-funded universities had to guard against students being admitted whether they were fitted for higher education or not, without the rigorous selection process in place to ensure the highest standards were achieved.

This was a vitally important meeting as it provided him with an invaluable background for the remainder of his visit. This commenced with the University of California, Berkeley on March 24, 1936, followed by a whirlwind tour that included the universities of British Colombia, Alberta, Minnesota, Chicago, Michigan, Toronto, Princeton, John Hopkins, Yale, Harvard and McGill before sailing for England in early June 1936. Wherever he went, he received the best of hospitality which he compared favorably to that extended in England under similar circumstances. He was welcomed at the highest level and quickly made many new friends with his usual facility to do so. Furthermore, his considerable experience in academic administration at Cambridge enabled him to assimilate information across a wide spectrum of disciplines within the universities' curriculum.

With his customary enthusiasm and diligence, Priestley left no stone unturned in his desire to gain the greatest advantage from this unique opportunity, while trying to limit this to a perspective appropriate to the Australian environment in general, and Melbourne in particular. This included the terms and conditions of employment of both the academic and administrative staff, the breadth of the curriculum, the teaching methodologies and, a crucial issue for Priestley, the standard of facilities available to students and employment opportunities for graduates.

The influence of what he had seen and heard cannot be overestimated in its impact on what he regarded as the way forward for Melbourne. Amongst these, the way in which the universities in the United States fostered its alumni was a very powerful factor, not only in providing a continuity of generous financial support based on its graduates' success but also in the strength of its postgraduate programs and research. Of equally fundamental importance was the strong belief across the whole spectrum of the universities that he had visited that for a democracy to succeed to its full potential, the great mass of the population need to be properly educated, with the best reaching the highest standards achievable at its leading universities.

Individual universities contributed differing factors to his overall conclusions: California for the incredible strength of its alumni associations; student welfare at Minnesota; sporting facilities at Michigan; the scope of the archives at Toronto; the extensive library at John Hopkins, while both Princeton and Yale were most reminiscent of his Cambridge experience. His discussions, as always meticulously detailed in his diaries, covered a very wide range of topics ranging from, for example, the true purpose of education to serve both the intellect and the emotions at California, to the situation at Minnesota which he considered the best comparison with Melbourne, where the level of student grants was infinitely higher than those available to his Australian students.

From the tone of his diaries, there seems little doubt that he left the United States with some reluctance, having felt very much in tune with the general thrust of its university education programs and, indeed, would have been pleased to take up a high level administrative post there had he not made a strong five-year commitment to Melbourne. Nonetheless, in early June, he left for a brief stay in England, en route to Australia, for a combined holiday and business trip.

His first priority was to make an extensive program of visits to a wide cross-section of family members in England, including close relatives such as his brother and his wife then living in Leeds, and his two sisters, Joyce and Edith, the latter married to Charles Wright, a former colleague from Antarctic days. However, a significant period was spent at Cambridge, in fact most of July, where he felt immediately at home again, particularly as he took up residence at his old college, Clare. While at Cambridge, he took the opportunity of attending the Congress of universities of the British Empire where, not entirely to his liking, Sir James Barrett, the Melbourne Chancellor, also appeared.

During August, as well as attending the Centenary of London University and cricket at Lords, he renewed a number of Antarctic contacts, most notably with Aspley Cherry-Garrard from his days with Scott, as well as traveling to the Scott Polar Research Institute at Cambridge to meet other contemporaries. However, his main priorities were the arrangements for his daughter, Margaret, who had been left in England to continue her schooling, to return with him to Australia, which he organized with his customary attention to detail. Finally, on August 22, he and Margaret boarded the liner *Ceramic* at Liverpool for an uneventful but enjoyable forty days trip to Australia.

Immediately upon his return, he encountered three issues which were later at the center of his decision to resign his vice-chancellorship. The first was his view on the issue of freedom of speech which he considered to be at the heart of the ideals on which a university should be founded, indeed its inalienable right, and for which it had received extensive criticism because of its stance on the Spanish Civil War. The second, and by far the most influential, was his own position as vice-chancellor where, despite the new statutes passed to confirm his position as the first holder of the office, had not been properly implemented, making his situation virtually untenable. The third was the continual and almost total lack of interest in the university by either the state or municipal political establishments. Finally, however, 1936 ended with one major triumph with the laying of the foundation stone for the new Students' Union, a *sine qua non* for Priestley, though tempered by the necessity for his daughter, Margaret, to return to England to start her university education.

Another major priority for Priestley was to implement the reforms that had been held in abeyance during his American visit. Things started on some positive notes. First was his attendance at the Universities' Conference at

Adelaide, where he was correctly recognized as a pre-eminent universities' educationalist, based on his Cambridge experience and success. As importantly, the conference paved the way for the formation of the National Union of Australian University Students, an achievement very much in tune with Priestley's thinking and ambition. In addition, he attracted a number of new and highly regarded professors to lead departments: Max Crawford, an enthusiastic reformer, to history; Aubrey Burstell to engineering; and particularly, Fritz Loewe and Fritz Duras, both leaders in their fields, to Meteorology and Physical Education respectively. In amongst this hectic program, he still managed to fit in some cricket including the England tour of Australia, the latter including the legendary Don Bradman in its side.

However, these achievements could not disguise Priestley's great dissatisfaction in a number of continuing and major areas. The plans and finance for the new vice-chancellor's house were the subject of constant prevarication while the monies which Priestley had fully expected to be made available for the new Chemistry building were not forthcoming due to the combined inefficiency and parsimony of the state government. Nonetheless, by far the most disturbing and disruptive, was the attitude of Barrett, who tended to treat Priestley very much as a subordinate and had not, in any respect, accepted Priestley's new role as Chief Executive Officer of the university, although the University Council had begun to recognize this and provide him with limited support; not enough eventually, however, to persuade Priestley to remain at Melbourne.

Consequently, it is much to Priestley's credit and future reputation that he, nonetheless, pressed on with his extensive program for the university's reform, via a whole range of activities. He gave numerous speeches to political parties, the City Council and the Chamber of Manufacturers, all with the objective of raising the university's profile and to attract funding. He also traveled extensively, giving a host of lectures to schools, clubs and societies to publicize his planned building program and its future educational value to the wider community.

By June 1937, and despite the benefit derived from a much needed holiday, Priestley's long term future at Melbourne was heavily influenced, and put in doubt, by the knowledge that the University of Birmingham were actively interested in luring him to their vice-chancellorship: a very attractive prospect in so many ways, including its proximity to his family background in the Tewkesbury area. This prompted him to lay down some very specific conditions for his future at Melbourne, amongst which £25,000 of additional funding from the Victorian State Government was a non-negotiable requirement. Fortuitously, at this very moment, funding from other sources, including crucially the Chamber of Manufacturers, began to bear fruit and it appeared that his cherished aims of new buildings for both the Student Union and the Chemistry department would be realized.

He also took this opportunity to restate his strong and fundamental views on both the vital importance of free speech within the university community and, for him, the unarguable necessity to provide competitive salaries to fill the professorial appointments at Melbourne. Priestley augmented this with an exhausting tour, under the auspices of the New Education Fellowship, to Brisbane, Sydney, and Canberra, taking up the whole of August 1937.

However, while on tour, he received the entirely unacceptable news that the Victorian State Government would only provide £10,000 instead of the £25,000 that he had requested and anticipated. Immediately thereafter, in late August, he received a formal letter of invitation from the University of Birmingham to take up its vice-chancellorship and this coincidence of circumstances led to his instant acceptance and formal resignation from Melbourne, although this would not take place until June 1938.

With his customary diligence and sense of duty, Priestley did everything in his power not to leave Melbourne without achieving as many of his proposed reforms as possible and, by a happy coincidence, funds began to flow in from some unexpected sources, undoubtedly partly influenced by a reaction to his resignation; chief amongst these was the decision of the City Council to grant the university £50,000 over the ensuing ten years. Nevertheless, his major priority for the remainder of the year was to find a suitable successor, a more than difficult requirement in the light of his own disenchantment with the specific university politics at Melbourne.

Priestley's firm favorite to succeed him was Douglas Copland, currently the highly regarded Professor of Commerce, and, as it transpired, a role in which he would continue to serve with great distinction until 1945. While devoting considerable energy to Copland's cause, he was also heavily involved in important family affairs. His daughter, Jocelyn, who had accompanied him to Melbourne from the outset, announced her intention to take up permanent residence in Australia. In addition, he and his wife Phyllis faced the upheaval of moving house although this was mitigated, for Priestley at least, by the opportunity to watch some very good cricket. Eventually, at the beginning of 1938, Phyllis returned to England to prepare for their return.

By February 1938, Copland had been replaced by a good deal of political maneuver by John Medley of Tudor Hall, Sydney as the primary candidate to replace Priestley and, on March 21, he was formally appointed to succeed him. The appointment was, in itself, controversial and made much more so by a deliberately orchestrated campaign by Copland himself, who felt his disappointment acutely. Nonetheless by April two of Priestley's most cherished and fundamental ambitions came to fruition with the opening of the new Students' Union and the state government providing a grant of £75,000 for further university buildings, resulting in the laying of foundations for a new Chemistry facility, in May.

8. Vice-Chancellor—Melbourne University

With the arrival of Medley in early June, his time as vice-chancellor came to an end, his final day being June 30. He could look back on his tenure, in almost equal measure, as one of considerable achievement and frustrated ambition. Apart from his success in the establishment of a strong Students' Union and a much enhanced Chemistry facility, he had also improved relations between the students and staff immeasurably and the university's links with its graduate community with all that this would mean for future financial support, making it more comparable with its counterparts in the U.S. However, despite his best efforts, Priestley still felt something of a voice in the wilderness as far as both students' freedom of speech and the level of resources available for the salaries and research of its Professoriate were concerned. Moreover, his plan to establish the vice-chancellor's residence on campus was only in the early stages of development.

Finally, when Priestley boarded ship in Sydney on July 6, 1938, for a journey via New Zealand and the Panama Canal back to England and, as will be seen, a long and distinguished vice-chancellorship of the University of Birmingham, it is generally acknowledged that he was the most forward-looking high level academic administrator in Australia, and Melbourne's loss was most assuredly Birmingham's gain.

9

Vice-Chancellor— Birmingham University

Following his arrival in England in late August 1938, and due to take up his new post at Birmingham on October 3, 1938, the intervening period was taken up with a flurry of activity mainly involving his move to the university, preparing for his new responsibilities and resettling his family; the latter was his first priority.[1] He also took the greatest delight in renewing his close association with the area, including trips into the countryside surrounding the city with his wife Phyllis and his daughter Margaret, taking a tram to the Lickey Hills and visiting friends in his native heath of Bredon's Norton and Tewkesbury. However, above all, he was concerned that his daughter should be properly settled and happy in her studies at Royal Holloway College, London University. Finally, emphasizing the immediacy and significance of his new appointment, a vice-chancellor's gown was delivered to him that had been made for one of his predecessors, Sir Oliver Lodge (first vice-chancellor), and currently worn by the retiring incumbent, Charles Grant Robertson that, as Priestley records, "required considerable alteration."

He also took the opportunity of discussing the various problems facing the university with Robertson, the retiring Vice Chancellor, and, particularly, the effect of the apparent resolution of the Munich Crisis on October 1, 1938, which had engaged public opinion to fever pitch and, as Priestley records, was regarded by quite a large section of the population "as a climb down, if not a rout, but the predominant feeling is still relief that war has been avoided although not 'peace in our time,' in contrast to the Prime Minister's view." As a consequence, one of Priestley's first actions, during his takeover period with Robertson, was to organize first aid classes as part of the general air raid precautions that had already been set in train. In addition, he was immediately made aware of the full extent of his duties in having to deal with the unpleasant task of replacing a lecturer in French whose subsequent sentencing on a charge of gross indecency received great publicity in the widely read *Birmingham Post*.

9. Vice-Chancellor—Birmingham University 93

The remaining three months of 1938, part of a very steep learning curve, included an incredibly high level of demanding intellectual and physical activity on a day-to-day basis. Although this was without respite, it was nonetheless entirely rewarding and worthwhile in establishing a very firm knowledge base on which to develop his later plans for the university over his eventually long term tenure. During this initial period he had meetings with the Faculties and Boards of Studies, the Association for Education in Citizenship when he heard Anthony Eden, the future Foreign Secretary speak, the Midland Branch of the Geological Association, the Guild of Undergraduates and the Universities Bureau in London, when he took the opportunity of visiting his daughter at Holloway College.

At this time he also had some initial concerns amongst which the conditions at Chancellor's Hall, which he had hoped could be developed as a students' hostel, were at the forefront; in its present form he considered it, as he records, "very unsuitable." He had a strong desire to establish an "up-to-date" hostel, well endowed, on the Edgbaston site providing the best environment possible for students outside the Birmingham area while covering the costs associated with Chancellor's Hall. In addition, he had a meeting with the Prime Minister, Neville Chamberlain, to discuss how to use donations, including substantial gifts from Sir Charles Clyde, Lord Hurst and Lord Nuffield towards the expansion of the Science faculty and, in the interim, still found time to accept an invitation to tour the new facilities at the Scott Polar Research Institute and renew many old friendships there. During these early months he also made his first acquaintance with the Berber Institute of Fine Art when at a meeting of its Trustees, and also attended a Baldwin Night dinner in Chancellor's Hall that he records as "enjoyable apart from some stories told by the speakers, (unnamed!), which were very near the knuckle and felt it a pity that youth feels it necessary to be salacious in order to be witty."

In late November, Priestley was involved in the appointment of the crucial role of University Treasurer in the course of which he made his first detailed study of the audited accounts; at this stage they provided no immediate cause for concern although with his plans in the embryonic stage for developing various aspects of the university there would be, quite evidently, substantial limitations to bringing all of these to fruition. In addition, in early December, and in spite of a punishing schedule, he found time to lecture to the University Guild on "Antarctic Adventure with Scott and Shackleton." Finally, a very demanding year ended with Christmas festivities at the Guild of Graduates and a much needed holiday with his family.

On January 2, 1939, Priestley returned to the university for a year of intensive work and subsequent achievement and, during the same week, attended a lecture at University House on the "Economic Causes of War," a subject at the forefront of the nation's collective concern and a matter of continual debate in which he was often included. By mid-January, he was in London speaking to the Medical Research Council about its application to the Rockefeller Foundation for help with "a research side to the University's Medical School"; a matter of huge significance leading to the university's later reputation as a leader in medical research. At the same time, negotiations were concluded leading to the eventual appointment of Solly Zuckerman to the Chair of Anatomy, an inspired choice in the light of his later success and unassailable reputation. Later in the same month, and with some reluctance, he was persuaded to talk about his life, and especially his Antarctic experiences, on the BBC's Midland Region station. To conclude a very active and productive start to the New Year, the Duke of Devonshire was installed as chancellor, at which Stanley Baldwin was the guest speaker.

During February, one of his major concerns was to make progress with an extension to the Student's Union and although this had the backing of the university's senior personnel, Priestley suspected that their support was more readily forthcoming in order to secure better staff amenities. As Priestley puts it, "I can see trouble with the lads if they go too far. After all, the Union is primarily a student affair and it will not do to try to turn it into a Faculty Club." As at both Cambridge and Melbourne, he again demonstrates his overriding concern for his students' welfare. The month was also significant for his meeting with Alderman William Cadbury, a patron of the university's Geography department, and a member of the renowned Cadbury's chocolate family noted for its extensive philanthropy, particularly in Birmingham and the surrounding district. Priestley was disappointed, on the university's behalf, that a fine collection of maps which the Cadbury family had presented to the Birmingham Reference Library, might very easily and, in his view "much better" have come to the university's Geography department, had it been better established. With the threat of war now a major concern, the month ended with the establishment of Air Warden courses and, by no coincidence, a meeting of the Committee of Vice-Chancellors to discuss the "Place of the Universities in War."

The remainder of the spring of 1939 involved Priestley in an eclectic and intense program of work. Not least of these was the appointment of the Pro-Chancellor and Deputy Pro-Chancellor, their roles being crucial in meeting the growing demands of the expanding university and in supporting Priestley in his plans and high aspirations for its future development and reputation. Of equal importance was the expansion of the medical school and, consequently, he was delighted when King George VI and Queen Elizabeth visited its facilities during a tour of the university; while at the same time, to Priestley's great satisfaction, the recently appointed Solly Zuckerman was making good progress with the university's application for support from the Rocke-

9. Vice-Chancellor—Birmingham University

feller Foundation. However, with the increasing prospect of war, Priestley found himself very much at odds with the vast majority of the guests at a dinner given by the Bishop of Birmingham "who were against conflict even in defence of one's ideals which with Hitler's complete absorption of Czechoslovakia and his economic threat to Rumania were becoming unpleasantly near a burning question."

During April, with the likelihood of war an ever present preoccupation, Priestley authorized further expenditure on ARP shelters, while at the same time recognizing the importance of completing the Medical School's application to the Rockefeller Foundation for funding. With his family's welfare a constant concern, he agreed to his daughter's proposed journey to the Greek islands, commenting that "we have been a little doubtful about letting her go, but if we waited on the international situation we should have done nothing for the last year for there has been crisis after crisis since Hitler went in to Austria; we shall be bound to be rather on tenterhooks until she is back after Chamberlain's unequivocal declaration of British support for Poland in case of Germany's invasion of that country."

For the remainder of the spring term, Priestley continued a program of "look and learn," taking action as appropriate, so far as his university duties were concerned, interspersed with a variety of activities reflecting his wider interests. One example was a speech to the Baptist Union of Great Britain and Ireland Annual Assembly, acknowledging his non-conformist antecedents; another, a visit to the Lord's Test illustrating his abiding passion for cricket. Finally, at the end of term, he was able to enjoy his carefully planned and keenly anticipated holiday in Cornwall, with the added precaution "of taking an extra tin of petrol as a reserve to bring us back to Birmingham in case war breaks out while we are down there."

Priestley had just returned to prepare for the forthcoming term when, on September 3, war was declared. He was instantly confronted with the effects of the Conscription Bill, which would have profound implications for existing students at Birmingham, and university life in general; indeed, this would be the main and most urgent focus of his attention for the remainder of the year. Not least among his concerns were the implications of the Joint Recruiting Board's statement that men aged twenty should not return to university while, at the same time, the Queen Elizabeth Hospital was "attempting to seize University House for billeting purposes"; its loss could mean that a large number of potential students would not be able to take up a place at the university. Moreover, the urgent need to recruit officers for all three Services was becoming a drain on both university staff and undergraduates. By late autumn, however, because of the dispersal of some of the students from London University to Birmingham and the Government's agreement, indeed, stipulation, that engineers, chemists and physicists should be allowed to complete their courses, the numbers at the university, in fact, rose above previous levels.

Towards the end of the year, not surprisingly, Priestley found himself more and more involved in matters relating to the war at both a personal and university level. While on fire-watching duty, he almost fell into a pit outside the Union building, recording that "this is a peculiarly awkward time to have the local authorities digging up the streets." He also made visits to both an AA battery and its brigade HQ to deliver a lecture on his Antarctic experiences, designed as some light relief in the course of their normal duties. As this momentous year drew to a close, Priestley records his pessimism as to the progress of the war and the "present racial theories dominant in Germany." Finally, Christmas was spent in Devon with his wife and his daughter Margaret, although with very little news from, and some concern for, his other daughter, Jocelyn, who had remained in Australia when he left Melbourne.

Priestley was reminded of the war at an early stage and in a variety of ways, in 1940. At the cinema he watched a news feature on the scuttling of the *Graf Spee* by the German Navy, gave a lantern slide show to members of the 5th South Staffordshire Regiment, commented on the introduction of food rationing of bacon, ham, butter and sugar and described a lecture given to a company of the Worcester Regiment. However, these were all over and above his vice-chancellor's duties, on which the war was having a huge impact. Nonetheless, the usual and more prosaic aspects of university life continued when, for example, he was involved in deciding on the action to be taken against some medical students who had carried out "rags" against other students. He questions why "these youngsters cannot control themselves in times like these I don't know.... At the moment incidents like these leave a nasty taste when our men are being drowned right and left and their fellows are being reserved to become doctors after a six year course."

Emphasizing that he was now getting well into his stride, Priestley felt sufficiently confident to send copies of his first full Annual Report to academic colleagues both in Britain and Australia, together with a request for information concerning the representation of non-professional staff on the faculties and senate. However, the effects of the war continued to bear very heavily on his already extensive workload, as he gradually assimilated the full extent of the vice-chancellor's duties. Some were especially demanding as in the case of how conscientious objectors, particularly amongst the younger members of staff, should be dealt with. In another instance, based on both his Antarctic and First World War experiences, he was asked to lecture to the Canadian Signals Division at Aldershot that would be operating wireless stations in the Arctic regions.

In addition, he visited the Birmingham City Council House to hear what transpired to be Neville Chamberlain's final speech on the war, before his resignation and replacement by Winston Churchill as Prime Minister. Despite his very full schedule of official duties however, at no stage did these override his strong sense of commitment to his family.

During the Easter vacation, for example, he records his great pleasure at walking with his wife and daughter on the Clent Hills and their camping holiday in the New Forest. Nonetheless, the war was an ever present preoccupation and while on holiday he records his concern at hearing wireless broadcasts illustrating that "the war has started in earnest with the invasion of Norway and Denmark by the Germans and our consequent counter attacks in the North Sea."

As he approached the summer term, it is clearly evident from his meticulously maintained diaries that Priestley was becoming more comfortable with the varied demands placed upon him as vice-chancellor of one of Britain's major universities. However, the often extreme and entirely unpredictable pressure of events as a result of the war added greatly and disproportionately to his duties in terms of both time and concern; as a result, they increasingly take precedence to his record which, at the same time, becomes more curtailed.

It is, therefore, not the least surprising that his main concern at the commencement of the new term centered around world events and the German invasion of Belgium, Holland, and Luxemburg which "brings the war much nearer to us all"; nevertheless, the work of the university had to continue and adapt to the new and increasingly demanding circumstances. In a similar vein, he notes that "his diary seems trivial in the circumstances and that it is difficult to reconcile himself to being in civilian clothes ... if I use my head I know that I am more use here, but unfortunately one is ruled by emotions normally and not by one's brain." He contrasts his own confusion of emotions with that of many of his students, who tended to put their own priorities ahead of their willingness to help in the war effort. Consequently, he was delighted that his daughter Margaret was planning to spend a month on a "student harvesting scheme" that would be of direct assistance in releasing men for war service. On a personal level he records that he and his wife Phyllis had moved their beds away from the window in their flat to avoid splinters of glass, given the growing incidence of air raids, particularly around the Birmingham area, which was at the industrial heart of the British war effort.

Against this background, Priestley very much welcomed a brief respite during his holiday in Devon, once again, with his wife and daughter, in late August. Following immediately after this, it had been his intention to visit London with Phyllis to celebrate his daughter's twenty-first birthday but this had to be postponed as he had to attend a memorial service for Sir Oliver Lodge, a vice-chancellor at Birmingham before Priestley.

The beginning of the autumn term saw an intensification of air raids, on an almost nightly basis, increasing his "night vigils" as he describes them and placing a very considerable strain on the members of the university staff involved, as there was little if any opportunity to sleep during their spell of duty. University life suffered accordingly with damage to both the geography and anatomy departments and parts of the staff accommodation and the Guild. With the prospect of further indiscriminate damage almost a certainty, he decided that much of the university's valuable library should be moved to a safer but, as a consequence, less easily accessible location; these included the majority of the law school's books, which would have a particularly serious effect on students in this subject who required constant access as source material.

As the autumn term drew to a close, Priestley reflected on the impact of the war on university life over the past few months, including the general migration of university education to safer sites in the Edgbaston area of the city and the number of deaths already recorded amongst staff and students as a result of the continuing and intensifying air raids including one, paradoxically, who was a Polish refugee. The end of term and the Christmas festivities provided a brief respite from the increasing and often extreme challenges of retaining some sense of normality in university life under wartime conditions. However, in early January 1941, he received a reminder of the brutalities of the Nazi regime while watching a newsreel at the cinema in Cheltenham which he records "as being all the more harrowing because it gave the impression all the time of understatement rather than exaggeration."

By early February, he was receiving mostly positive responses to his second Annual Report although the effects of the war on university life continued to dominate his thoughts and actions. Of immediate concern was the effect on university recruitment of the proposal to call up nineteen year olds for military service; in this regard, Priestley thought that the RAF recruiting scheme "would strike at the heart of both the quality and quantity of the entry to the universities next year." Nonetheless, he fully recognized that his primary aim should be to do everything he could to assist in winning the war as quickly as possible and a return to peacetime conditions, and the establishment of a Senior Training Corps at the university and further discussions with the post-war Reconstruction Group are but two examples of his good intent.

In the late spring of the year, Priestley and his wife moved to a flat in Lawn House, some distance from the university, where an immediate concern was to build suitable air raid shelters for the residents "who also attempted to grow vegetables, especially radishes, to provide relishes to help with food restrictions." During the same period, he attended a reception at the Lord

9. Vice-Chancellor—Birmingham University

Mayor's Parlour in Birmingham to meet Australian Prime Minister, Robert Menzies, lectured to the Mathematical Society on "Antarctic Ice Formations" and attended a National Day of Prayer service where he read the lesson. Indeed, at this point, his working life comprised a highly varied and unremitting round of activities as he sought to satisfy the increasing demands on his time. However there is no indication that, despite the demands made upon him, he was not able to fulfill his duties to his own general satisfaction and, at the same time, plan constructively for the future of both the university and his family for the remainder of the war and its aftermath, despite his deep concern at the recent reverses suffered by the Allies in Greece and Libya.

Indeed, by the late spring of 1941, discussions were already taking place at a vice-chancellor's meeting that he attended concerning the insurance of university property under the War Damage Act, with night raids over industrial areas such as Birmingham bringing this into sharp focus. In another seemingly bizarre incident Priestley records, though without further comment, the flight of Rudolf Hess to Britain. However, on a lighter and more optimistic note towards the end of May, Priestley was delighted by the engagement of his elder daughter, Jocelyn, still living in Australia; moreover, in keeping with the times, he was pleased to receive a letter from her future husband, Ian, asking for his formal consent to their marriage. At this stage, although the war affected university life at all levels, Priestley was therefore very pleased that the most recent examination results illustrated they had been scarcely affected by the conflict. The same could not be said, however, at a personal level, where he had great difficulty in obtaining a new pair of trousers within the limits of his clothing allowance!

A major development with far reaching consequence towards the end of June was Germany's decision to invade Russia. Priestley supported the generally held view that this would lead to the almost inevitable defeat of Russia as he did not foresee, and therefore concluded, that with Germany's resources heavily overstretched, and with the U.S. becoming fully involved in the war firmly on the side of the Allies against the Axis powers, this would lead to its eventual defeat; indeed, even the release of German forces from the Eastern Front, following the Russian Revolution, merely prolonged the conflict as it progressed towards ultimate Allied victory.

On a more positive note, towards the end of the summer term during July, Priestley records, with some relish, his return to Tewkesbury for an Old Boys cricket match; it is not clear whether he played or not. By this time, the wedding of his elder daughter Jocelyn had also taken place, though neither he nor his wife had been able to travel to Australia in wartime circumstances to be present. However, by way of some compensation, they had received the welcome news of an excellent result by their younger daughter, Margaret, in her degree examinations. During the summer vacation that followed it is apparent that Priestley had very little university business demanding his attention and felt somewhat isolated "by not having a more direct connection with the war effort."

By the beginning of the winter term, Priestley was delighted that he had been able to establish a Theological lectureship at the university thanks, yet again, to the generosity of the Cadbury family. However, this was somewhat overshadowed by the continued campaign on behalf of the government to release undergraduates for National Service. Although he fully supported and recognized the need for this intervention he nevertheless felt that it should be tempered by allowing potential First Class Honors men to continue their studies until the full Honors Degree had been attained. Consequently, during October, his preoccupation with military affairs often demanded precedence over the more prosaic aspects of university life amongst which meetings with members of the Oxford University Air Squadron, the Military Education Committee and the Joint Recruitment Board provide examples from across a wide spectrum. Nevertheless, he still made it a priority to attend a vice-chancellor's committee meeting in early November although, not surprisingly, its main deliberations centered around wartime issues of which current negotiations over compulsory military registration, critically affecting large numbers of potential and existing students, was at the top of its agenda. Christmas festivities, both at the university and at home, provided a brief but welcome break before his early return to university duties shortly after the beginning of 1942, with the war at a highly critical stage but, as he records, "the considerable reassurance of America being absolutely solid against the Axis powers now."

As Priestley, and indeed the entire nation, returned to the harsh realities of the New Year of 1942 under wartime conditions, his first weekend was spent at a conference at the Adams Agricultural College in Shropshire, on Land Utilization in connection with the post-war Reconstruction schemes. This emphasized, yet again, that the distinction between the traditional functions of both public and business organizations had become inextricably linked to those of the war and its outcome. Against this background, it is not surprising that Priestley's greatest concern at this time was with the progress of the war, particularly the situation on the Russian Front, Japanese successes in the Far East, the ongoing Libyan campaign and the vital importance of Churchill as leader in these profoundly difficult circumstances.

This is not to infer in any way that university life did not impose its usual diversity of demands and problems, particularly those affecting its students who were experiencing their university education under exceptional circumstances. For example, an early decision for Priestley during the winter term was what disciplinary action should be taken against a group of students who had been stealing belisha beacons and lamp tops and concealing them

9. Vice-Chancellor—Birmingham University

in Chancellor's Hall; although certainly not without precedent as an example of the exuberant behavior of youth, and students in particular, it had to be regarded as more irresponsible and distracting under wartime circumstances. In a different and more serious category entirely was the action of some students who were buying spirits and wines on the black market which could result in direct action against the university.

The remainder of the term comprised a seemingly endless list of commitments commensurate with his vice-chancellor's office; including amongst these were frequent meetings with the Faculties, particularly the Faculty of Medicine which was expanding exponentially, in addition to attending meetings of the Joint Recruitment Board, speaking at a Workers' Educational Association Summer School, and being present at frequent social events in the Guild of Students; the latter he regarded as an absolute priority whatever the restrictions on his time. By the beginning of the spring term, Priestley records, not surprisingly, that "his personal life and feelings are becoming subordinated to the overwhelming drama of the international struggle" and his hope that "the war might really be broken by next winter." Nonetheless, despite the exigencies of the times, university life had to be maintained at the highest level possible and Priestley was unstinting in his efforts to achieve this, whatever the demands placed upon him from both within the university and the complementary commitments in the wider community. Of particular satisfaction in this regard was his appointment to the Council of the Royal Geographical Society with which he would become even more closely involved in later life and, ultimately, be appointed as its President.

Priestley's overriding concerns with the progress of the war remains clearly evident at the beginning of the final university term of 1942; amongst these were the increasing Allied air offensive over Germany, the abortive raid on Tobruk and Rommel's attempt to break through the lines at El Alamein. The military theme continues with his attendance at a reunion of colleagues from the Wireless Training Centre, reflecting his First World War service, a meeting of the Joint Recruitment Board at the Ministry of Labour in London, and visits to a Sea Cadets Headquarters at Wimbledon and an Army Physical Reconstruction Unit at Kingston. It was perhaps fortunate, therefore, that he views his vice-chancellor's principal role at this time as remaining one of "improvisation and does not provide a great deal of scope when Deans and officials, such as ours, are efficient as a whole." This undoubtedly reflects his success as vice-chancellor and although he claims no credit for it whatsoever, it was fundamentally important in allowing him the time and energy to carry out the myriad of additional and often arduous commitments, and the decision-making process associated with them, that the war imposed to an unprecedented degree. Finally, with the advent of Christmas, the term ended on a slightly lighter and more relaxed note when he enjoyed a carol service given by the Student Christian Movement, Christmas Eve spent with Home Guard duty section and, later, his own family celebrations.

By the beginning of the New Year of 1943, with the nation not surprisingly showing severe signs of war weariness, Priestley too was feeling the strain with the preparation of his Annual Report badly affected by the illness of his trusted secretary, Miss Taylor. The situation was exacerbated by the sudden death of the university treasurer, and the difficulty of his deputy's unpopularity with senior members of the academic staff. In addition, there were tensions between the University Council and the Senate; as Priestley records, "the Senate is about as unrepresentative of the University staff as it could be, with little representation of non-professional staff." He compares this very unfavorably with the more democratic constitution he had experienced at Cambridge. However, by contrast, he was delighted to receive a photograph of his new grandson, Edward, from his daughter Jocelyn in Australia, and also found the physical work on his allotment a great help in working out his frustrations over the course of recent developments at the university. Another welcome interlude in the increasingly difficult challenges of running a university in wartime conditions was his attendance at the Guild of Graduates Ball, with his daughter, Margaret.

The war, however, continued to give him constant cause for concern to the extent that he viewed the recent long distance meetings between Roosevelt and Churchill in both North Africa and at Casablanca as a real danger on the basis that "it would be a tragedy of the first order for the United Nations if anything serious happened to one or both of them." A visit to the University Air Squadron and an inspection of the Home Guard were further reminders of the ever present realities of the war. It was also at this time that he became more closely involved with the Canadian Migration Scheme, in this instance involving the evacuation of university staff family members to Canada with the proviso that boys of sixteen and over should return to Britain later if they were not intending to go to a Canadian university. Finally, during February, he attended an event in London at which Hugh Dalton, one of Churchill's principal aids, gave the address to pay tribute to the Soviet Army on Red Army Day.

By the late spring, with the war showing some encouraging signs of moving a little more in the Allies favor and taking up slightly less of his time in Birmingham, Priestley felt able to make a series of visits to London for committee meetings of vice-chancellors and the British Association. In addition, he attended a conference of the Joint Recruitment Board at the Ministry of Labour to discuss the way forward, as an end to the war could now be discussed with a marginally enhanced degree of confidence. While in London, he also took the opportunity of visiting an exhibition of photographs of the war, "some of which were rather horrible."

9. Vice-Chancellor—Birmingham University

It was, however, at his time that Priestley reached the fundamental conclusion, and not without much heart searching, that he should consider curtailing his diary to its more essential elements and that it should be maintained more as a record than a detailed, almost daily, account. As he puts it, "I fancy that the time is coming when I shall pack up this diary as little happens within the orbit of my life to incline me to write at any length." However, his reluctance to do so, at least for the duration of the conflict, is well illustrated by his follow-up remarks that "it would perhaps be a pity to close it down until the whole impact of the war on the family is told." The reality was that he continued with his diary until 1945 and the Allied victory and, thereafter, maintained a much reduced record, limited to significant events, until his retirement in 1952.

With the commencement of the summer term, Priestley was again heavily engaged in university affairs, reflecting his increasing involvement with a huge diversity of committees and other aspects of university life, and his growing confidence in his role as vice-chancellor clearly apparent. By way of illustration, amongst a multitude of examples, these included: a Planning Committee of the West Midland Reconstruction Group; discussions with the Faculties of Medicine concerning its continuing development; meetings with the Faculty of Science concerning the appointment of a new professor of Mining and schemes for developing Engineering; a Physical Education demonstration for members of the Senate and Council; and a lunchtime concert given by the Musical Society. He also found time, away from his immediate university duties, to inspect an aircraft factory making Spitfires in company with a group of ARP wardens and the Observer Corps. There are also constant and detailed accounts of the progress of his allotment, particularly his great satisfaction with the growth of his tomatoes, broccoli and spinach, quite evidently an essential element of maintaining some degree of normality in his life, as well as providing essential elements of his family's diet, in the uniquely difficult circumstances of wartime Britain.

Inevitably in his role as vice-chancellor, he had to deal with matters of university discipline amongst which a recent case brought to his attention by the University Disciplinary Committee caused him particular concern as it involved what he describes as "common thieving" and goes on to record that "I am afraid there is yet another admitted case in the offing and yet the epidemic of theft goes on unabated ... there is something really sinister about the situation." Fortunately disciplinary matters were not an overriding concern and, by late May, he was soon immersed in the inevitable round of his vice-chancellor's responsibilities as well as enjoying some extramural activities, including a visit to the Scott Polar Research Institute in Cambridge and attending the production of a play, *The Bird in Hand*, the first of the Plays in the Parks season in Birmingham, while even finding an opportunity to attend

Priestley's great granddaughter, after receiving her Doctor of Medicine degree at the University of Birmingham. Behind her is a portrait of Priestley, painted during his tenure as vice-chancellor (courtesy Ellen Scrivens).

a cricket match at Castle Bromwich watched by a rather bored audience of American soldiers from their Lichfield depot. Finally, as the term drew to a close, he was involved with the preparations of the Degree Congregations, to which he attached the greatest importance and established a tradition for excellence of which the university is proud to this day; indeed, his great-granddaughter received her medical doctorate at the university in 2012 and is pictured beneath the portrait of Priestley on the day of her congregation.[2]

During the summer vacation, Priestley was able to enjoy some time with his family, including cycling with his daughter Margaret, working in his garden, walking in the Tewkesbury area and, even, blackberry picking. However, the war was, understandably, never far from his thoughts and he returns to the theme of Churchill's constant trips abroad and expresses his concern that "it may be essential but it is dangerous, for he is as near irreplaceable as a man may be."

With the approach of the new academic year, Priestley was beginning, with some justification, to sound more upbeat about the progress of the war and, particularly, the signing of the armistice with Italy while recording that "we are well established in the toe of Italy, have now landed around Naples and have only the Germans to deal with."

His first priority was to raise professional staff salaries, which he felt had been falling well behind those of similar universities for some time; this was, of course, well before the establishment of national pay scales. Consequently, this item was at the top of the Finance Committee's next meeting when he not only successfully achieved his objective but also received its support for the launching of the university's Development Appeal, including special emphasis in its brochure on Engineering, a *sine qua non* for Birmingham's position at the heart of the United Kingdom's industrial base.

He was also launched immediately into a round of social events and visits. These included a meeting with the new public relations officer of the Salvation Army whose magnificent wartime work Priestley greatly admired and supported. In addition, he was at Birmingham Town Hall when Lady Mountbatten marked the occasion upon which the Lady Mayoress issued no less than her millionth item as the result of her "Comforts for the Troops Appeal." Later in the term, Priestley mentions particularly talking to a Freshers' meeting "when it was the first time since he came to Birmingham that he was able to say with some conviction that I thought it very likely that, unless they left the University prematurely, they were unlikely to see active fighting." Visits to London for Vice-Chancellors' and Royal Geographical Society Council meetings were also regular items in his schedule; indeed, at this point, he had to manage his commitments very carefully as, with the increasing passage of the years in his role as vice-chancellor, the demands on his time were growing exponentially.

This is demonstrated conclusively in October, when his diary included a plethora of activities both within and away from the university. Within short order, he had meetings with the Ph.D. Degree Committee, the Physical Education Committee, the Diocesan Council for Religious Education and a Senate meeting to discuss university development and finance, while in London he had lunch at the Savoy Grill to discuss the assistance ICI might give to the Metallurgy Department.

By November, and for the first time, Priestley records his first really optimistic forecast for the war in expressing the view that it might well be over by the end of 1944. At the same time he is immediately brought down to earth by the less agreeable aspects of university life in dealing with "a rather nasty case of ragging" in the Dental School, following a report by the Disciplinary Committee. He records that "the lads responsible would have been suspended, but suspension would have meant de-reservation and as the Country cannot get enough dentists we thought it better to give alternative penalties."

With the approach of the end of the winter term, Priestley received what would prove to be a highly significant invitation to join the Asquith Commission on Higher Education in the Colonies and to go to the West Indies at the end of January 1944, for three months; after Senate approval, he not only accepted the invitation with alacrity, but also recognized the opportunity that this would provide for him to have a real and lasting influence in a sphere of education in which he was keenly interested. Thereafter, the year ended with the now familiar round of Christmas celebrations, both at the university and at home, marked by "a very welcome present of chicken, eggs, honey and cream from my brother, Bert, in Bushey."

Priestley's New Year started with the recording of his radio broadcast to West Africa on university finance as part of a series to encourage discussion, in preparation for the visit of the Commission for Higher Education in the Colonies, to that area. This followed a trip to London for his first meeting of the Asquith Committee when he also learned that his visit to the West Indies would not now start until February 16. In the meantime, he was more heavily involved in university related affairs than ever as he tried to accomplish as much as possible in view of his forthcoming absence which would be, eventually, for four months rather than the predicted three. In the short period before his departure and amongst many others engagements, he attended a Nuffield Conference at Oxford on the future of industrial and university research; met the Chairman of British Thomson-Houston in Rugby to discuss possible funding for Birmingham's postwar engineering courses; received a visit from his brother-in-law and a fellow member of Scott's Terra Nova Expedition, Charles Wright, to meet some of his Physics researchers; visited the Wellcome Research Institution for his yellow fever vaccination, and met the secretary of the West Indies Committee to order his tropical kit, both preparatory to his forthcoming trip.

Before finally leaving for the West Indies, he displayed his usual concern for the progress of the war and comments on the Allied air offensive over Germany, concluding that "the destruction within Germany must be stupendous and, although one hates to see any system of gloating, there can be no question that the chance of another war will be considerably diminished by the fact that Germany has at last had brought home to her, on her own ground, the effect of war at its worst."

His work on the Asquith Commission is covered in the chapter following with his resumption of duties at Birmingham recommencing on June 11, 1944. Having returned to England bearing welcome gifts of lemons, oranges, chocolates, nuts and fabric for his family and his support staff at the university, he had to catch up immediately on developments during his absence. While drawing great comfort from the Allied landings in Normandy, this was somewhat overshadowed during a visit to London, by Germany's V1 bombing raids, when he was very distressed by the damage he saw and the raids he witnessed. As he records, "the things make quite a characteristic bumbling noise which some people have compared to a motor bus" and goes on to say that "I was awakened by an explosion which must have been from one fairly near but was not worried. I feel rather like I did in 1918 when shelling took place that was not obviously directed at me." Moreover, his continuing work on the Asquith Commission not only interrupted his university duties constantly, but also, because its meetings were held in London, meant his V1 experiences were repeated on a fairly regular basis.

By mid-July, Priestley was fascinated by the implications of the attempt to assassinate Hitler, despite attempts by Germany to suppress details of the plot. When taken in conjunction with the resignation of the entire Japanese cabinet after the American assault on Saipan, he drew considerable comfort from the fact that "an end to the war cannot be too much further delayed." In the light of these developments, it was of particular satisfaction to him that the University Development Appeal was achieving greater success in the more optimistic outlook prevailing.

The approach of the end of the summer term was marked by further success when Priestley was able to reach agreement on the long awaited increases in staff salaries. At the same time, and despite an incredibly wide range and increasing level of activities, he felt able to accept an invitation to become a member of the West Midland Regional Reconstruction Group (its work and conclusions are summarized later). He very much welcomed his inclusion, as its decisions would have considerable implications for the way in which the university should plan for the future.

The new academic year brought further challenges, some as a direct result of the war, one involving a scheme offering six month courses for American servicemen, once the active phase of the war in Europe was over, which Priestley fully supported. Equally, with a sense that victory could not be much longer delayed, Priestley records his attendance at a Red Cross Parade and "March Past" on the university grounds on a cold and windy day, followed by tea. With his customary compassionate view, he makes the point that "I should have been much happier, however, if the tea had been given instead to some of the children who took part in the parade, many of them without overcoats at all. They must have been starved with cold."

The remainder of the term continued with his vice-chancellor's duties which are worth summarizing for their incredible number and diversity. They included: the opening of a youth hostel on the outskirts of the city; an Education Committee meeting at Warwick; a meeting of the Guild Council; the appointment of a new commander for the Senior Training Corps; a conference of university representatives, Technical College Principals and Industrialists to discuss a National Scholarship scheme; meetings with potential university benefactors; the appointment of a new Professor of English; meetings in London of the Asquith Commission, with the Union of Education Institutions, with other vice-chancellors to discuss Technical Education and at the Ministry of Labour for discussions on demobilization as it will affect universities. While in London, these were often interspersed with brief interludes reflecting his personal interests amongst which lectures at the Royal Geographical Society allowed him some respite from his unremitting schedule of duties.

By the end of term and the approach of Christmas, Priestley was already looking forward to the New Year and the anticipated end to hostilities in Europe at least, when he repeats that "he is only continuing his diary until the end of the war, for the routine matters of everyday life will hardly justify it in normal peacetime." Not surprisingly, Priestley's main preoccupation at the beginning of 1945 was with the progress of the war, which had entered its final and critical stage with the American landings in Luzon and the opening of the Russian winter offensive. Nearer home, he was delighted by the substantial sums received as a result of the Development Appeal, particularly as the 1944 Education Act lacked any real provision for university grants.

Following on from time in the West Indies, he attended his first meeting of the newly established Colonial Advisory Education Committee, gave lectures in the local area at both Smethwick and Shirley on the work of the university and took great pleasure in attending a meeting of Coventry City Council to celebrate the six hundredth anniversary of the granting of the Charter of the city. By February his attention is focused, once again, on the progress of the war and, particularly, the Yalta Conference and the meeting between Churchill, Roosevelt and Stalin, the ongoing Russian offensive and

American attacks on Japan. This was especially relevant as he had been asked to undertake a lecture tour to the Royal Navy in both Italy and Malta from the middle of March until early May, focusing on the time when a period of adjustment and resettlement would be required for all arms of the services. The tour was, quite evidently, a great success and one he enjoyed immensely, as portrayed in the frequent letters that he wrote to his wife covering his journeys, transport difficulties, accommodation of varying standards, his diet, interaction with Naval Officers and the reaction of the sailors to his lectures, descriptions of the local scenery and facilities and his meeting with local officials including those at Malta University—all very much grist to the Priestley mill.

On returning to Birmingham in May, he was immediately confronted with an end to the war in Europe, the extensive celebrations that ensued and, above all, the administrative process of returning the university to peacetime conditions. He was also very saddened by the death of President Roosevelt and, as he records, "his death has removed the political personality with the most potentiality for good in what is going to be a very difficult post-war world." With his diary now giving way to a more or less summary record, his final detailed comments surround VJ Day in August and the dropping of the atomic bombs on Hiroshima and Nagasaki, "in which scientists of this University, notably Peierls, Oliphant and Haworth, in that order of importance, I should imagine have played a part that has been recently acknowledged, as has also Oliphant's radar work." He goes further by reflecting on the discovery of the practical use of nuclear fission, and "standing just outside a world war as we do we are at the moment inclined to be pessimistic. This is quite natural as we only beat the Germans to it by a few months, while I should have been equally anxious had our Russian allies been the Power to develop the bomb, for they are still inclined to play power politics hard." Although he was, to a degree, surprised by the election of a majority Labour Government that followed, he felt it would now retain power for next five years. He had also been very impressed by the King's speech at the end of the war and felt that "it was very reassuring for a rather shocked America and a rather startled world. There is no doubt that we live in stirring times with great potential both for evil and for good." As he looked back, with considerable satisfaction, over a momentous academic year before the summer vacation, he also looked forward to an increase in the general grant for the university to support an inevitable increase in student numbers following the end of the war. However, he felt that the Development Appeal Fund would almost certainly be adversely affected by "the shock of the prospective nationalisation of banks, coal and transport." With much to accomplish before the beginning of the new academic year he was not able to accompany his wife and daughter on a holiday to Anglesey, as he had additional responsibilities as a member of the committee appointed to oversee the reconstruction of the University of Hong Kong, and also because the Asquith Commission Report had been published, with considerable work to complete towards its acceptance and implementation.

It was at this point that, as heralded on a number of occasions in his diary, Priestley discontinued his almost daily record entirely, and thereafter merely accumulated an assortment of documents, press cuttings and, mainly, family photographs covering his activities between October 1945 and his retirement in July 1952. They cover the whole and very wide range of his vice-chancellor's responsibilities, in which his growing confidence is clearly apparent, but inevitably are repetitive as they follow the cycle of the academic year which, by its very nature, follows an ordered pattern of similar activities. For this reason, only those events that stand out as exceptional from amongst those that follow the natural rhythm of university and family life are included, by way of summary hereafter, together with a final assessment of the university's success during Priestley's tenure.

Following the Armistice in 1945, Anthony Eden was installed as Chancellor of the University in November of the same year; Priestley considered this a great coup in view of the high reputation Eden had gained as a result of his outstanding service to his country and invaluable support for Churchill during the war. Thereafter, in late 1946, to the great satisfaction of Priestley and his wife, Phyllis, some members of their family in Australia were now able to visit England following the end of hostilities. Although their son-in-law, Ian, and grandson, Edward, were not able to travel for reasons of business and schooling, they were delighted to see their daughter, Jocelyn, and for the first time, their granddaughter, Gillian, with whom they also enjoyed a holiday in Wales that included other family members, including Priestley's daughter, Margaret, and his sister, Edith. At the university, the appointment of Sydney Vernon as the new pro-chancellor was a highly significant event in view of his later longevity and success in this role.

By far the most important development in 1947 was the first steps towards the establishment of a University of the West Indies and an Inter-University Council for Higher Education in the Colonies, in January. This was followed by a visit to Jamaica by provisional members of the Council later in the year, among who Priestley was included, and received widespread and favorable coverage in the media. On a less agreeable but, nonetheless, successful note, Priestley had to undergo an operation for prostate cancer in November of the same year, a condition that had been troubling him for some time.

By 1948, the establishment of the University of the West Indies and developments elsewhere in the Colonies, following the Asquith Commission's Report, were taking up an ever-increasing amount of Priestley's time; fortunately, his growing confidence in Vernon as pro-chancellor allowed him to

9. Vice-Chancellor—Birmingham University

undertake extensive foreign travel towards the end of this year and well into 1949 in support of not only his considerable interest in these projects but also illustrating his determination that he should play a full part in their successful implementation. As a result, Princess Alice of Athlone was named as the first Chancellor of the University of The West Indies and it received its Royal Charter in 1949.

Priestley visited Trinidad and Jamaica, again, between December 1948 and January of the following year, spending Christmas at sea on board SS *Bayano*. During his voyage to Trinidad he visited St. Kitts and Antigua before returning to Jamaica for meetings of the Provisional Council, a tour of the university site, dealt with details of the installation of the new chancellor and visited local industry, returning home via the Bahamas and Canada, where he visited McGill University, then by plane from Newfoundland to Prestwick. During his absence, his knighthood was announced in the New Year's Honors List, specifically for his work on higher education in the Colonies, an accolade with which he would have been delighted as it recognized his contribution in an area of education very close to his heart. More extensive travel followed in the spring of 1949 when he left by plane for South Africa, via Tripoli, Khartoum and Nairobi to Johannesburg where he visited the University of Witwatersrand. Thereafter, he visited Maritzburg, Durban and the University of Natal where he was awarded an Honorary Degree and had meetings with some Zulu groups before flying on to Cape Town, a visit to its university, and finally the return journey home via Johannesburg, Victoria Falls, Kampala, Khartoum and Luxor, arriving in England in April 1949.

Within a very short time, in June 1949, he was travelling again, on this occasion to Canada, from Shannon Airport, to Halifax in Newfoundland where he visited Dalhousie University and was awarded a further Honorary Degree. From Halifax he went by train to Montreal, visited both McGill and Montreal universities before his onward journey to Toronto and eventual return to Shannon via Montreal and Newfoundland in late July. Following his return home, he very much welcomed the opportunity to spend some time on holiday in the Lake District with his family during the summer vacation before returning for the winter term when he was delighted to be appointed to the governing body of the Imperial College of Tropical Agriculture, in which he had a particular interest.

By March 1950, he was again engaged with the fast moving educational developments in the Colonies, specifically during another trip to visit Trinidad and Jamaica; on this occasion and to his great delight accompanied by his daughter, Margaret, and by sea on the SS *Cavina*, with Princess Alice of Athlone as a fellow passenger, prior to taking up her appointment as the first Chancellor of the University College of the West Indies. During the installation ceremony, at which Priestley and his daughter were present, she laid the foundation of the library, hall of residence and the hospital before attending a university service in Spanish Town Cathedral. Visits to Newcastle, Flamstead, the Hermitage Dam, Monymusk and the Imperial College of Tropical Agriculture followed, before their return home, on this occasion by plane, via Jamaica, the Bahamas, Bermuda, and Lisbon.

For the remainder of the year, and after a number of lengthy absences, Priestley was heavily engaged in not only his more routine duties but also with a number of special events, amongst which the University of Birmingham's Golden Jubilee was by far the most significant. He felt it particularly important to focus on the achievements of its first two vice-chancellors, Sir Oliver Lodge and Sir Charles Grant Robertson, and of Joseph Chamberlain as the first Chancellor. He felt strongly that their contribution in successfully establishing the first Civic University should be fully recognized, in which a University Jubilee Dinner and Honorary Degree ceremony played their part and, as important, received extensive and favorable media coverage. On a much smaller scale but of huge significance to Priestley, he was asked to give a eulogy for Scott at a memorial service at Scott's home church in Binton, Warwickshire, when a stained glass window was dedicated to his memory and those who died with him, on their return from the South Pole.

Shortly following the Jubilee, in July 1950, Priestley was travelling again, (although not before he had attended the Lord's test match!); with his possible retirement in mind, there appears to be every indication that he wished to consolidate his achievements and fully merited reputation as one of the leading educationalists of his generation. As a consequence, he was delighted to accept an invitation to visit universities in Singapore, Australia and New Zealand, travelling first by plane to Singapore via Rome, Cairo, Karachi and Calcutta. His Singapore program included a tour and conference at the Raffle College Medical School where he also attended a Malay Federation graduation ceremony and gave a lecture on Antarctic exploration. From Singapore he flew to Melbourne, travelling via Darwin and Sydney, where he was met, to his great delight, by his daughter, Jocelyn, together with her husband and grandchildren. An extensive program of engagements followed including a tour of the university of which he had, of course, been the first vice-chancellor, a radio broadcast on behalf of the Sydney University Appeal Fund, official and social engagements in the city as well as spending as much time with his family as his busy schedule allowed.

From Melbourne, he flew on to Canberra for a brief visit including meetings and a reception at University College and thereafter to Sydney for a similar round of engagements before flying on to New Zealand, arriving in Auckland towards the end of July. After meetings at the geological department of the university, a number of official receptions, and an Association of British Commonwealth Universities conference, he was relieved and delighted to be

9. Vice-Chancellor—Birmingham University

taken on a short sightseeing tour of the Wairakei Valley, although not before he had suffered a brief gastrointestinal illness which he attributed, without doubt accurately, to his hectic lifestyle. Flights to and engagements in Dunedin, Christchurch and Wellington quickly followed before his return to Prestwick, again with brief visits and official engagements, en route, via Fiji, Honolulu, San Francisco, Winnipeg, Toronto and Montreal, arriving home in August 1950.

For a man approaching retirement, this had been a very physically challenging tour but he was not finished yet. After briefly picking up the reins again at Birmingham, he was scheduled to make another visit to the University of the West Indies in early January 1951 that was, if anything, even more demanding. After flying to Jamaica via Bermuda and the Bahamas, he attended meetings at University College, before moving on to Trinidad where he very much enjoyed and valued an informative visit to a sugar plantation, the crop forming the backbone of the Trinidad economy. Thereafter, he returned to Jamaica, undertaking brief commitments in Barbados, Antigua, San Juan and Haiti before finally attending meetings of the University of the West Indies in Kingston. A return journey to England by sea, in extremely rough weather conditions, was a rather disappointing finale to what had been, in all other respects, a very fitting and rewarding conclusion to both his commitment and valuable contribution to the wider field of university education.

Although Priestley had been considering retirement for some time, he only arrived at his final decision to do so shortly after his return from the West Indies at the end of February, and made his intention known officially. While it cannot have been a complete surprise, in view of his age, there is every indication that both Anthony Eden, the Chancellor and Sydney Vernon, the Pro-Chancellor, for both of whom Priestley had huge respect, made efforts to persuade him to remain in post for a further two years, but he was firm in his resolve to do so and retired at the end of the winter term. At a reception held to acknowledge the event, in June 1952, extensive tributes were paid to Priestley from amongst the educational community and beyond. However, in reality, this marked only the beginning of another chapter of activities, covering a whole series of mainly unexpected challenges that he fully embraced, that he counted as some of the best experiences of his life and form the remainder of his biography.

Although Priestley's successes and achievements are largely self-evident from his record, all stemmed from his very basic educational philosophy which has been described as "both humane and liberal."[3] He was firmly against overspecialization and held strongly to the values of a wide breadth in university education that should not be merely vocational but promote the ability to think, read and make future critical judgements across industry, the professions and all aspects of a student's subsequent endeavors; indeed Anne Howarth, who had been a pupil, teacher and acting headmistress, respectively, of Edgbaston High School for Girls in Birmingham and of which Priestley was president, and Lady Priestley a member, of its governing Council, recollects meeting him later at the opening of the university's Physical Education Department at which he continued to take the greatest interest in all aspects of student life and he and Lady Priestley were described by the school's headmistress, during the period of his vice-chancellorship, as "very good friends to the School."[4] There is no doubt that, above all, he fully deserved and very much merited the sobriquet that was frequently applied to him as "the students' Vice-Chancellor"[5] which he would have regarded as the most satisfying and fitting epitaph to his long and distinguished career as an educationalist.

10

The Commission for Higher Education in the Colonies

It was during the relatively early years of his period as vice-chancellor of the University of Birmingham that Priestley was invited to be a member of a Commission for Higher Education in the Colonies, chaired by Sir Cyril Asquith, set up in 1943. His involvement was purely fortuitous and as the result of the resignation of A.V. Hill, a Fellow of the Cambridge Graduates Science Club, before the Commission began its detailed work; he was required to take up urgent duties in India. Priestley was immediately considered as his replacement, very much as the result of a radio broadcast he had made covering his experiences as the first vice-chancellor of Melbourne University and "although I had vowed not to make any public pronouncements in the foreseeable future," he was persuaded by a friend, working for the BBC Overseas Service, that his services would be invaluable and, in Priestley's words, "the fat was in the fire"; the official invitation arrived from the Secretary of State for the Colonies immediately thereafter.[1]

Enquiry by Commission was very much an established and valued part of the British Constitution; Priestley notes, wryly, that "it would be considered a waste of time in a Totalitarian State." Moreover, the situation in the Colonies was "over-ripe" and would certainly reward the effort involved provided that the Commission was set up based on a number of fundamental criteria. These included the appointment of a good Chairman with a legal background; an experienced and well regarded Civil Servant to carry out the detailed writing up of the Commission's conclusions and recommendations; an adequate period of time to carry out its investigations; and a Panel of Experts to advise the Commission. Priestley noted, not entirely ironically, that "if you want a quick result base the Commission in a major capital city in a time of war, subject to constant air attack then 1944 would be ideal!"

An essential element of the Commission's work was to study the situation on the ground, wherever possible, with West Africa and the West Indies as the most urgent priorities although its deliberations should cover the entire Colonial World; consequently, two sub-committees were appointed. The first and larger of the two, for West Africa, comprised twelve members while a smaller committee for the West Indies included Priestley amongst its number. This was completely in line with his wishes as he had always been fascinated by the Islands "from afar," he had distant family relations there and he had read a great deal of its turbulent history. He was of the firm opinion that to study any region "de novo" it was good for the committee to have amongst its members those who were entirely new to the area, free of preconceptions and able to take "a fresh and whole view."

The West Indies Committee, which comprised relevant experience amongst all its members, had as its Chairman Sir James Irvine, Vice-Chancellor and Principal of St. Andrew's University and was known hereafter as the Irvine Committee. In Priestley's view, "Sir James was the doyen of Vice-Chancellors—it seemed he had been at St. Andrew's since time began." The Committee was also very fortunate to have as its efficient secretary and Colonial specialist, Thomas Rowell and, in addition, two indigenous members whose future might be influenced by the findings of the Committee—Philip Sherlock of Jamaica and Hugh Springer of Barbados. Both brought with them distinct advantages and, utilized properly, they were the key to the Committee's success. They ensured that the Committee was welcome wherever it went, they helped to minimize suspicion of its motives and made its recommendations more readily acceptable. In the event, both proved excellent members of the Committee and made a major contribution towards its work.

The Committee determined at the outset that no existing type of political and social democracy was appropriate for Colonial government whether in the West Indies or, indeed, any of the Colonies; as Priestley puts it so aptly, "we come from a continent littered with the ruins of parliamentary democracy that has failed." However, there was universal support amongst the Committee's membership for a system of higher education as the essential prerequisite to an effective system of self-government which was inevitable at some early future date.

The Committee established as its primary aim the answer to three fundamental questions: does the West Indies at present justify the creation of an institution of higher education; what type of university would be best suited to its needs; and where should it be situated amongst scattered and disparate islands? Beyond doubt, in the almost inevitable circumstances that the answer to the first question would be yes, then immediately the answer to question three would be "a major headache."

The fact that the Committee's work took place during a World War of unprecedented geographical scope and intensity only increased the aim, now common to all political parties in Britain, towards devolution and self-determination throughout the Commonwealth; this could not have been more clearly illustrated than by the dangers of essential air travel to its outlying locations. Priestley records that a plane that he and Sir James Irvine had travelled home in from the West Indies had been shot down on its return journey and that the plane carrying the Royal Charter for University College, signed by King George VI, met a similar fate on its way to Jamaica.

Priestley and his fellow Committee members arrived in the West Indies in February 1944, flying by way of Brazil; they had an exhausting schedule planned during which "they resolved to see anybody who could help them." The first three weeks of their tour were to be spent in Trinidad, followed by a week in British Guiana, ten days in Puerto Rico (as guests of the United States), three weeks in Jamaica and four weeks in Barbados, of which the final two would be spent "in retreat," writing up the draft report. The ensuing weeks were of great value and full of interest although accompanied by "some weird experiences."

For example, almost immediately while in Trinidad, "we were faced with a very voluble person clutching a sheaf of notes, prepared to talk all day." After a first very lengthy sentence, and during a pause for breath, Sir James Irvine gave an early indication of his skill as a chairman with his intervention; "Mr. X, we are glad to hear you end on that note." Priestley records that "he sat down in some confusion and that was the end of him." During the Committee's early visits to schools and other educational institutions, its members gathered invaluable information in spite of some early antipathy. The first and anticipated reaction was that this was yet another government commission and "nothing much would come of it." However, as the Committee members became better known and benefiting from the inclusion of two indigenous participants, the impression spread that "they meant business" and the Committee's knowledge grew rapidly.

Undoubtedly, the Committee's greatest problem would be to overcome the wide geographical spread and cultural differences of the various islands comprising the West Indies; in this regard, the location of its first University College would be a major issue, in which the establishment of "an overall West Indies feel without splinter groups" would be the primary consideration. Against this background, the Committee would need to follow some well-focused lines of enquiry.

First and foremost, the Committee would need to establish that the situation was "ripe" for education of the university type; this was, by no means, a foregone conclusion in view of the high illiteracy rate. Indeed, many of those interviewed, with this in mind, felt that any money available could be spent to greater advantage on primary education. However, already over a thousand young people gained a good School Certificate each year, with at least one hundred going on to achieve a Higher Certificate; both were local qualifications of considerable merit, with the latter equating to the second year of a normal honors degree in the Britain.

Others interviewed thought that their brightest students should be directed towards British universities but the Committee members were aware that acceptance of overseas students at these institutions would lessen against the background of government plans to increase its indigenous student flow.

A further major consideration, one which would be crucial in gaining acceptance of the Committee's findings, was to decide if the West Indies would be able to absorb its own graduates; it was decided that this question could be answered "with a resounding yes." There was clear evidence that the West Indies economy would grow exponentially over the ensuing years and, with it, a growing demand for a better standard of living. In this regard, the provision of much improved health facilities would be a *sine qua non* in which the establishment of a Medical School would be the first priority. Furthermore, in the growing economy, scientists and engineers would be at a premium, amongst which the oil industry alone could absorb thirty good graduates every year.

Another fundamental question requiring immediate consideration was the type of university required for the situation specific to the West Indies in which a safe environment for its students was a key element. Of equal importance was the general opinion of all those consulted that a university that set low standards would be much worse that no university at all. The obvious solution was that, in its early days, the newly established university would receive huge benefits through tutelage from existing universities with established high standards in North American and Britain. To this end, McGill University of Canada was eventually chosen to mentor the new university's medical school.

In the early stages of its investigation, the Committee arrived at the conclusion that only one type of university would suit, specifically, the situation in the West Indies with its fragmented locations separated by immense distances between the islands. For example, travel by air between Jamaica and Trinidad involved a flight of between twelve to fifteen hundred miles; this alone had expensive implications. In addition, the university would need to be small but with scope for future development; it would need to be wholly residential and a high staff/student ratio would be essential with staff of proven ability recruited, initially from existing universities. The value of community life in a residential setting allowing interaction between men and women of intelligence and character would foster a West Indies' outlook and the attainment of high ethical and academic standards.

The critical question arising, therefore, was would the West Indies be able to afford what appeared to be the only style of university appropriate for its special circumstances; the Committee decided that it would, based on its growing trade surplus which was, after all, what made the provision of good higher education an urgent requirement. Moreover, the Committee would be able to make recommendations to mitigate the costs and to ensure that they were evenly spread across the West Indies as a whole. This required a triple response.

Firstly, the cost of travelling to and from the university should be borne centrally and provided free of charge to all students, and extra mural work would be more than ordinarily important, including local chapters and guilds of graduates. Secondly, a "Travelling Circus" of members of the university staff should tour the islands to select students, with consequent costs savings. Finally, and by far the most difficult area in which to arrive at an appropriate response, was where the university should be located. The eventual decision that this should be in Jamaica proved to be, by the course of events, the correct choice although not without huge political problems and wrangling, which were eventually overcome. The Committee made this vital decision while in Barbados when preparing its final report, and Priestley records that "an eruption of fruits from a mahogany tree under which the members were sitting signaled a similar eruption before this question was eventually answered." The Irvine report, with recommendations, was published in June 1945, and included in the wider-ranging Asquith Commission Report which was eventually approved by the governments of all of the ten Colonies concerned and by the Secretary of State for the Colonies.

From this point onwards, Priestley was involved purely and immediately in the arrangements for setting up the University of the West Indies, of which by far the most important was the appointment of a Principal. Here, as he describes it, "he nailed his colours to the mast" in supporting the crucially important appointment of Dr. W.J. Taylor of Brasenose College, Oxford, to the post. Priestley lists his qualities and background with his customary precision. He describes him as "a chemist of considerable though specialised university experience, with very sound ideas of university policy and practice and wide outside experience including his work with Lord Mountbatten in Ceylon." Temperamentally, he assesses him as "driving himself hard, often too hard, and consequently not always easy to live with if you fancy a quiet life." He adds, "he can be all things to all men if required, has no radical prejudices whatsoever, can be nice or brusque as the situation demands, and easy to quarrel with without rancour." In support of Priestley's judgement, the Secretary of State for the Colonies had no hesitation in subsequently renewing Dr. Taylor's appointment for a further five years; as Priestley was later to express his opinion, "if he left it would be a minor tragedy, 'T' would not be easy to replace and has done a wonderful and worthwhile job."

The next equally key and, as it proved, successful appointment was that of Philip Sherlock as Director of Extra-Mural Studies, later the obvious choice as the university's first vice-chancellor. A local man of marked urbanity, he had a wide knowledge of, and interest in, the indigenous people, as well as being a cultured individual with a fine intellect and an outstanding public speaker. After establishing the first Extra-Mural Centre in Kingston, he went on to create similar institutions in many other parts of the West Indies, all of which flourished. This followed on from his excellent work as a member of the Commission, and, in his role as director, he was instrumental in establishing a cadre of future politicians who would exercise tolerance and self-control with the power to weigh evidence and objective judgement that are crucial to successful democratic government.

Thus, in October 1946, as Priestley records, "the good ship UCWI was launched." This was preceded, during the early months of the year, by the creation of an Inter-University Council covering all the Colonies together with a Colonial University Grant's Advisory Committee with a budget of six million pounds covering the period 1946–56 to provide for capital expenditure, of which the West Indies was apportioned one-and-a-half million pounds, confirming the advantage of the participation of ten Colonies and not only one. Priestley remarks that "this illustrated much goodwill in giving, in a World not noticeably altruistic"—it is not clear from his diaries if he had taken account of the extremely fragile world economy following the recent cessation of hostilities.

What is clear, however, is that there was real interest from men of proven ability and status, as is illustrated by the appointment to the first Chair of Surgery at UCWI of one of the King's surgeons who put his name forward with enthusiasm and commitment. An additional benefit was that his progress was monitored by "men who count" for later application. Priestley records that while McGill did not, in the event, develop the School of Medicine, good relations were maintained, nonetheless, between the universities in Canada and the West Indies. Indeed, medicine continued to take priority because of the pressing need for improvements in the West Indies and despite its economy "working on a shoestring," conditions at this time were looking more hopeful than ever before. Nevertheless, despite the development of oil in Trinidad and bauxite in British Guiana, the West Indies remained a mainly agriculture-dependent economy, using the tropical sun for its past success, and the establishment of a School of Agriculture through collaboration between UCWI and Imperial College, London University, with its highly regarded reputation in tropical agriculture, was also a priority. Furthermore, the Committee had not overlooked the crucial importance of research as a vital element in the development of the new university from the very beginning. This was seen as an essential prerequisite to sustaining high levels of

10. The Commission for Higher Education in the Colonies 121

teaching and standards, leading to academic excellence and commensurately outstanding results.

The following two years were spent in the strenuous activity needed to prepare for the new university's first intake of students, including the provision of teaching facilities and staff, and student applications, accommodation and administration. In October 1948, a first class of thirty-four medical students was admitted, with twenty-five more the following year together with fifteen reading pure science. By 1950, the university had a Department of Fine Arts and a student population totaling one hundred forty-three. Its future growth would proceed very much on an incremental scale because the relatively low standard of living in the West Indies meant that higher education was not a practical proposition for most families who, despite the provision of a limited number of fee scholarships, could not afford to lose a potential breadwinner in the family to higher education; the few that could afford the luxury of university education still looked to the better perceived alternatives in the U.S. and the U.K. Indeed, previously, any educational funds that were made available for scholarships had been aimed, mainly, towards Oxford and Cambridge with their perception as "high prestige" universities.

However, based on his Melbourne experience, Priestley felt that West Indies first degrees should be regarded as a desirable steppingstone towards postgraduate study, attracting funding more readily, and acting as a good advertisement for its university. He considered that "they will return better balanced, less prejudiced and with more mature judgement." This proposition was also endorsed by the thirteen years he had spent in high level academic administration at Cambridge where he had studied this happening at first hand, especially when working with students on Ph.D. research degrees.

Overall, the new venture went well, despite the lack of resources being an ever present handicap, and the appointment of Princess Alice as its Principal proved an inspired choice. She had long experience as Principal of Royal Holloway College, London, and her husband, who had been Governor General of Canada and also knew the West Indies well, was Chancellor of London University. She immediately took charge and officiated at the First University Council and the opening of its six hundred eighty acre site.

By the time that Priestley's official interest was completed in 1951, the university had a staff of sixty from eight different countries, with Hugh Stringer, the other indigenous member of the Irvine Committee, as its registrar and a student body representing all the islands, highly selected for intellect regardless of race or creed, with its campus ideally situated on high ground above Kingston to alleviate the humid heat in summer. The first hall of residence, Irvine Hall, was complete and occupied. All major departments were under construction with openings planned from 1952 onwards. Priestley was of the view that very firm foundations had been laid for a successful university. As he records, "let us hope that this is one good thing that has come out of the West as its motto is Oriens ex Occidente Lux!"

Although there is no record that Priestley was Sir James Irvine's deputy on the Committee, it was he and Sir James who "signed on the dotted line of its charter" with recognition by London as its degree-conferring university. Indeed, Princess Alice referred to "London University as its Alma Mater and to Sir James and Priestley as its midwives; Mother had some subsequent qualms about her new children but midwives have seldom taken such a sustained interest in their growing children."

11

Acting Director— Falkland Islands Dependencies Survey

A short history of the Falkland Islands Dependencies Survey (FIDS) is essential to an understanding of the organization of which Priestley became Acting Director; responsibilities he assumed in the absence of its Director, Sir Vivian Fuchs, during his leadership of the Trans-Antarctic Expedition in which Sir Edmund Hillary who, with Tensing Norgay, had first reached the summit of Mount Everest, was also a major contributor towards its eventual success.[1]

On January 28, 1943, under the code name of Operation Taberin, the Government War Cabinet approved an expedition to the Falkland Island Dependencies with two major objectives; to strengthen British title in the face of Argentine and Chilean claims and to deny the use of harbors and stocks of shipping oil to enemy forces. For no immediately apparent reason, the code name "Taberin" was selected after a famous London nightclub!

Initially, Tabarin was a naval operation under the Admiralty for administrative control and was a secret venture until its existence was released to the press in April 1944. An Expedition Committee was established for its planning and organization with a wide ranging multi-disciplinary membership including, amongst others, representatives from the Admiralty, the Colonial Office, the Foreign Office and the Ministry for War. The Committee also benefited considerably from logistics advice from experienced Polar hands such as J. Wordie and N.A. Mackintosh, survivors of the Heroic Age with Scott and Shackleton.

Although central administrative control was exercised from London, while the expedition was in the field the Governor of the Falkland Islands assumed responsibility as the representative of the Secretary of State for the Colonies with Commander J.W.S. Marr, RNVR, as the Expedition Leader. By

February 1944, two initial bases had been established at Port Lockroy and Deception Island, designated A and B respectively, initiating a sequence of alphabetical distinction for future locations. At the same time, the Admiralty released HMS *William Scoresby* for permanent assignment as the expedition ship while J.W.S. Marr was replaced, due to ill health, by Captain A. Taylor RCE, as Expedition Leader.

On July 17, 1945, with a reduced requirement for secrecy following the press release, the codename Tabarin was replaced by that of the Falkland Islands Dependencies Survey and the Colonial Office assumed responsibility from the Admiralty, although the War Cabinet continued to attach great importance to the operation and still attempted to keep base locations as secret as possible. At the same time, Surgeon-Commander E.W. Bingham was appointed Expedition Leader. By January/February 1946, bases C and E had been established at Laurie Island and Stonington Island respectively while base D, at Hope Bay, was already operational, unaccountably out of alphabetical sequence, by February 1945. Furthermore, the base commanders had considerable legal powers as resident Magistrate, Coroner, Deputy Receiver of Wrecks, Deputy Collector of Customs and Deputy Postmaster under the Governor's delegated responsibilities. By 1946/7 both dogs and a light aircraft were available to FIDS in addition to a support ship although HMS *Scoresby* was proving inadequate due to lack of storage space and a replacement was being sort.

By March 1949, as the scope of FIDS activities increased, the need for a Scientific Bureau was recognized and, after much deliberation, was finally established on June 19, 1950, with Sir Vivian Fuchs appointed as its Principal Scientific Officer; his initial responsibilities were both demanding and wide-ranging. From his offices in Queen Anne's Chambers in Dean Farrar Street, London, he was responsible for the FIDS Scientific Bureau under the Secretary of State for the Colonies; the custodianship of specimens, documents and photographs; the supervision of contracts of employment for scientists employed by the Bureau; the writing up and analysis of data; the publication of FIDS reports; attendance at FIDS meetings and, as time allowed, his own research. Thereafter, the work of the Bureau increased exponentially and, in April 1953, Fuchs was designated as Director of FIDS Scientific Bureau with overall responsibility for its entire operation under the Governor of the Falkland Islands and, ultimately, the Secretary of State for the Colonies.

It was to these responsibilities that Priestley was appointed on November 1, 1955, although, at his insistence, only as Acting Director, when Fuchs embarked on his Trans-Antarctic Expedition. By this point the Survey had a growing number of bases established across a wide geographical area and owned two ships, registered in the Falklands Islands, the *John Biscoe* and the *Shackleton*.

11. Acting Director

In addition, the scope and size of the organization had grown very considerably since its inception and, by the time Priestley assumed control, had an administrative structure of increasing complexity which the distance from the London office tended only to exacerbate. Although Priestley's term of office would, by the very nature of Fuchs' expedition, be only of relatively short duration, he recognized an immediate need for some rationalization during which he would need to overcome some inherent resistance by those already heavily committed to, and involved in, the running of the organization in its current form.

The main areas for consideration in any proposed organization structure were the provision of a ship (or ships) more appropriate to the Survey's requirements; finance and a reorganization of the Accounts Section; communications involving a complete reappraisal of the Wireless Section[2]; Rear Base in London which was in urgent need of more adequate accommodation[3]; and recruitment at a time when there were increasing difficulties in finding suitable candidates.[4] With Priestley's inherent ability and unique position, he was able to bring a fresh approach to an organization that had grown incrementally with an almost inevitable fragmentation of duties and responsibilities that now required a fundamental reappraisal. In addition, at this time he was already aware that he would be accompanying His Royal Highness, the Duke of Edinburgh, on RY *Britannia*, to West Antarctica in late 1956 and early 1957 and also that 1957/58 had been designated as International Geophysical Years in which FIDS scientists would be very actively involved and for which detailed planning would be required.

However, the voyage with His Royal Highness would provide a unique opportunity to visit the majority of FIDS bases, often in company with the governor of the Falkland Islands. Such visits are covered, comprehensively, in the chapter that follows, as are other issues requiring Priestley's unremitting attention during his absence and, consequently, should be read against the background of what he immediately perceived as an urgent necessity, in order to place FIDS in the best possible administrative framework for its increasingly complex array of activities.

In doing so, he did not regard this as an implied criticism either of his predecessors or those entrusted with the day-to-day management of FIDS but, much more, as the need for some rationalization to meet the anticipated demands that would be placed upon it.

In Priestley's view, a merger between Rear Base and the Scientific Bureau to provide a single FIDS London Office was a *sine qua non*; this would require the acquiescence of not only staff at key levels but, ultimately, Fuchs himself who, despite his long but nonetheless temporary absence, would need to be consulted. As a result, Priestley put forward initial proposals to the Colonial Office in early July 1956. After a great deal of discussion and an intervention and, indeed some disagreement by Fuchs at the outset, final agreement to a revised organizational structure was arrived at by the end of 1956, prior to Priestley's departure on RY *Britannia*.[5] The overall result of the changes meant that, effectively, the Director was now the implied head of all FIDS affairs, not something Priestley had envisaged or necessarily intended originally, but the logical outcome of sensible deliberations. FIDS would now have only one London office with three departments; the Scientific Bureau; Supplies and Establishments; and Liaison and Publicity, with Priestley as (Acting) Director responsible to the governor and, ultimately, the Colonial Office.

The overall result was that by the time he handed back his responsibilities to Fuchs at the end of end of 1958,[6] the London office was fully functional in all departments under the new arrangements, and Priestley was able to take up his role as the British Observer on Operation Deep Freeze IV, opening up yet another, and totally unexpected, chapter in his life. Characteristically for Priestley, the challenge was irresistible, despite his advancing years, and one that he ultimately valued very highly even when set against an array of competing and often life-changing experiences.

12

West Antarctica on the RY *Britannia*

During 1956/7 the Royal Yacht was engaged in a world tour, involving various members of the royal family at different stages in the voyage, covering a wide variety of duties and events. From October 16, 1956, His Royal Highness Prince Philip, the Duke of Edinburgh, was on board, joining the ship at Mombasa for a voyage to Australia and New Zealand via, amongst other destinations, the Seychelles, Colombo and Penang, prior to visiting the Falkland Islands, South Georgia and Antarctica as part of his itinerary, and following his opening of the Olympic Games in Melbourne.

It was decided that Prince Philip and his staff would derive considerable benefit from the inclusion of someone with proven expertise, both geographically and historically, so far as Antarctica was concerned. After due consultation, Sir Harold Hartley, a former president of the British Association and a prominent Fellow of the Royal Society, recommended Priestley, who was at that time Acting Director of the Falkland Islands Dependencies Survey (FIDS—later, the British Antarctic Survey), as the obvious choice; his profound experiences with both Scott and Shackleton, his involvement in the establishment of the Scott Polar Research Institute in Cambridge, his current position with FIDS and, at age seventy, a lifetime's interest in the region made him eminently qualified for the role, one he accepted with great enthusiasm though some trepidation.[1]

Consequently, while in FIDS London office on November 20, 1956, he received his tickets to enable him to join the Royal Yacht in Melbourne, initially scheduled for December 2; the timetable would allow him a brief stay with members of his family in Melbourne, as well as an opportunity to visit the university of which he had been vice-chancellor—not necessarily the happiest of associations, as previously described—and many old friends.

The following day, while back at home in Tewkesbury, he was greatly saddened to hear of the death, at age eighty-one, of Victor Campbell, leader of Scott's Northern Party, in which Priestley's crucial involvement at a very young age was indelibly stamped on his memory.

Over the ensuing few days, he wrote a thousand-word appreciation of Campbell, which was later published, attended a meeting of the Research Committee of the Royal Geographical Society in London and enjoyed an early Christmas dinner with his family before embarking on his journey on November 27, 1956, flying via Rome, Istanbul and Karachi before arriving in Melbourne on December 1, 1956.

In Melbourne, while Prince Philip was opening the Olympic Games, he attended the Melbourne Antarctic Conference, where he met Douglas Mawson who had been one of the party that successfully reached and located the South Magnetic Pole as part of the Nimrod Expedition in which Priestley had served. Mawson had also led his own Australian Expedition, following on from the *Nimrod* but prior to Scott's Terra Nova Expedition, during which he had survived an epic return journey, alone, from the South, after his two companions had perished.[2] Also in attendance was John King Davis, who had been First Officer on the *Nimrod* and Master of SY *Aurora*, Mawson's expedition ship, as well as being his Second-in-Command. For Priestley, as he records, this was a poignant reminder of his past association with Antarctica and the men with whom he had served.

While at home with his family in Melbourne, he listened to the cathedral service at which "Prince Philip read the lesson well," and was also asked to comment on the speech that Prince Philip was due to deliver to the Antarctic Symposium; he attended the Symposium at the Royal Society at which Mawson also spoke, on the following day where "the Duke made use of all his suggestions and everyone liked his speech." On the same occasion, Prince Philip conferred the Polar Medal on thirty of the Australian Antarctic Research Expedition. At the same time, he heard from Prince Philip and Lieutenant-Commander Mike Parker, his Private Secretary, that he need not now report for duty until December 10.

However, in advance of reporting for his official duties, he was consulted by Vice-Admiral Sir Connolly Abel Smith, Flag Officer Royal Yachts, of the *Britannia*, as to the ship's likely position on Christmas Day, with particular reference to a BBC broadcast that the Duke would be making. In turning to John King Davis for advice, Priestley received merely the rather unhelpful reply that "the *Britannia* was a toy and oughtn't to be allowed in the Southern Ocean on its own"—which, in fact, would not be the case. In bidding Davis farewell, he told him "it would be a good time to die as I am insured for £5,000 and worth more to my family in death than in life!"

Before joining *Britannia* permanently, he welcomed the opportunity of a short visit to the ship where he was shown not only his cabin but also the Royal Chartroom, with which he was greatly impressed. However, he was somewhat overwhelmed when leaving the ship "to go down the gangway with a Vice-Admiral and two Commanders at the salute."

The few remaining days before his departure were spent in a flurry of activity. On a visit to Melbourne University, he was reunited with the sledging flag he had used when with both Shackleton and Scott, which had been embroidered by one of his sisters prior to his first expedition in 1907. On another occasion, while travelling by train to the opening of a new gasification plant by Prince Philip, he shared a compartment with the Archbishop of Melbourne and his wife, both old friends. On what he describes as "another strenuous day," he visited the Antarctic Division of the Department of External Affairs, where he was able to provide assistance by arranging for copies of Heap's Ice Observation Instructions to be made available for the survey ship, the *Krista Dan* (a ship later used by Sir Ranulph Fiennes during his Trans-Global Expedition) which would be leaving shortly. Finally, at a farewell dinner at the university, he was surprised to be presented with a check for £1,400; as he was to record later, with entirely good humor, "they seemed to be prepared to pay any price to get rid of me!"

On December 10 he was taken by a Commonwealth driver to join the *Britannia* and installed in his "wonderful en-suite cabin" (that was almost twice the size of his bedroom at home in Bredon's Norton) with which he was most impressed, particularly by comparison with his experiences on board ship with Scott and Shackleton. Immediately he was invited to a party that was already under way at which he "passed the time of day with Prince Philip" and met many old friends including the Governor, the Chief Justice and, even, the Prime Minister, Robert Menzies.

The day following, while a few miles down Port Phillip Bay, he met the artist Edward Seago for the first time, an association that would flourish during his time on board. Priestley records that the ships the *Britannia* passed were all dressed with ensigns dipped, and farewell signals included one message, "you'll be lucky!" In addition, and to his great delight, he spotted his Melbourne family, Jocelyn, Ian and their children, "waving furiously" from the shoreline.

After lunch with the Admiral, Parker and Seago, he spent the late evening after dinner listening, with great fascination, to the reminiscences of Lord Cilcennin, a guest of Prince Philip's, on politics and people; Cilcennin had followed Churchill as First Lord of the Admiralty. Cilcennin also told him that, apart from doctors, the color of naval sleeve rings no longer distinguished individual functions; this had led one naval lady to declare at a function that it was no longer possible to know at a glance who were executives and you were always meeting "these dreadful people." The following day, he had a long discussion with Seago concerning "the iniquities of the Arts Council." In the course of the discussion he learned that one of its members, Lady

Munnings, still carried around her deceased Pekinese, Black Night, stuffed, in her handbag! On retiring for the evening, he started to read Baldwin's *Life of my Father* lent to him by Lord Cilcennin.

Now en route for Wellington, and at the first formal dinner, Priestley learned two of the finer points of life on board *Britannia*: the first, that officers stood to drink the Queen's health, contrary to usual naval practice; the second, that officers should refrain from wearing a button to hold the sides of the mess jacket together. The latter was decreed by Edward VII, who was "too fat" to do one up and so this should become naval custom for all officers on the Royal Yacht.

As the *Britannia* headed towards New Zealand, the Admiral ordered an increase in speed to twenty knots so that the ship could steam around Wellington Harbour that night, to show it to best effect, to the people of Christchurch. This was, in fact, Priestley's fifth journey through the Tasman Sea, but never in what he describes as "such Royal weather."

On the way towards Wellington, Seago told Priestley that the increased motion of the ship was affecting his painting technique; Priestley's response was that if they encountered really strong westerlies between Chatham and Deception Islands, then he may yet qualify for that Contemporary British School which Seago disliked so much and Priestley failed to appreciate. Priestley further suggested that he should attribute these paintings to his "Seagoing Period." Before finally arriving in Wellington at 9:00 p.m. on December 14, Commander Mitchell had advised him of strong gales in the harbor. Priestley countered by telling Mitchell that "you could always recognise a citizen of Wellington, because he always held his hat by the hand when going round a corner."

While in Wellington Harbour, Priestley was grateful for an early opportunity to gain an insight into the general layout and capabilities of the Royal Yacht, while accompanying the Admiral on a general inspection of the ship. On the bridge he was shown the gyrocompass, the echo-sounding apparatus and the radar and, elsewhere, the Evaporator that was capable of creating drinkable water from the sea at a cost of £1 per ton, at a rate of 120 tons per day; all standard equipment, in contrast to some newspaper criticism which had inferred special treatment for the Royal Yacht. Throughout the inspection, Priestley arrived at the conclusion at this early stage in the voyage that the ship's morale was very high, reflecting the Admiral's outstanding qualities; he found him "a delightful companion."

Later in the day, the *Britannia* left Wellington Harbour where the illuminated Christmas tree "was a magnificent sight" and Priestley was able to interpret a message from an amateur signaler, on shore, as "Goodbye *Britannia*," which he was pleased that he could still read easily so that "his eyes had not entirely lost their cunning." As the ship sailed down the west coast of

12. West Antarctica on the RY Britannia 131

South Island, he worked on an introductory lecture he was to deliver to the crew, almost none of whom had sailed in Antarctic waters previously. At dinner in the Wardroom, he was pleased to receive twelve *Britannia* Christmas cards, which he would be allowed to send off to England on arrival in Christchurch in the Buckingham Palace mail. On the same occasion he was invited to take snuff, from a golden box, which he declined but records "that it would not induce Lord Cilcennin to sneeze."

On December 15, *Britannia* entered Lyttelton Harbour and, while refueling, gave the jetty "a tremendous bump" causing damage to one side of the ship and the luggage doors; damage that would later require quite extensive repairs, and gaining some immediate coverage in the New Zealand press. The *Britannia* band had played the ship into harbor "strophe and antistrophe" with a band on shore, including some hymns by the latter, "which startled him and Seago." He was also surprised to see the SS *Runic* leaving harbor, the ship on which he had arrived in Australia as far back as 1907.

In Lyttelton, he and Seago took the opportunity to go ashore but as the banks were closed, it being Saturday, they had to resort to borrowing £4 between them from the Royal Cook. Ashore, they visited the Art Gallery, the Botanical Gardens and Canterbury College and at the railway station Priestley records clear signs of the welfare state in New Zealand where there was a notice "all about what passengers are not to do." Back on board, Priestley was given a pamphlet on *Britannia* illustrating some interesting information and statistics. Drawing 4,715 tons, the engines created 12,000 brake horsepower, her maximum speed was 22.75 knots and she had a range of 2,000 miles on 490 tons of fuel and 20 tons of diesel oil. Additionally, she had 4 motor boats, including the Royal Barge, 2 saluting guns and the Shelter deck was reinforced to take a helicopter. In times of war, she assumed the role of a hospital ship, for which she was well suited, having stabilizers, air-conditioning, a large laundry facility and a comparatively high speed.

Back on board, he very much appreciated and enjoyed a Gilbert and Sullivan concert on "gramophone" in the Royal Salon, where he was now on Christian name terms with all but, of course, Prince Philip and "gets on well with all of them." Furthermore, he was advised that it was in order to bring friends onto the ship when Prince Philip was not on board and, also, that he had qualified for a Royal Yacht tie as he had been at sea with the Royal Standard flying. His only concern was for the Admiral who was somewhat depressed by the damage to the ship, which had only been repaired temporarily.

The following day, being Sunday, Divine Service was held on the mess deck, conducted by a local Presbyterian minister with the Admiral reading the lesson and, even, the Banns of Marriage read on behalf of one of the ship's crew. Sunday also marked the arrival of a number of visitors on board, one of whom was Jean Cottrell (whose sister was Dolla Bowden—"the Almighty Dolla and the Dolla Princess") and who had been a friend of Priestley's wife, Phyllis, in her youth. Another visitor was one McLeod, known to Priestley as a former Supervisor of Trinity Hall. Lord and Lady Lansdowne were also amongst the visitors, not known to Priestley personally, who stayed for the night on board; Priestley found them "a delightful couple." At dinner, Priestley sat alongside Prince Philip and had a prolonged conversation on Antarctica until the Duke retired to record his Christmas Message, which was later played back to Priestley and which he notes as being "superb."

It was also at this time that some disconcerting news concerning the *Britannia*'s Antarctic escort, the *John Biscoe*, was received; it appeared that water had penetrated the hold and some stores destined for the Royal Yacht had been ruined. It was also while in Lyttelton Harbour that Priestley toured the *Endeavor* with Prince Philip; the ship was due to pick up some dogs from Dunedin and deliver them to the Bluff, the real starting point of their Antarctic voyage. Priestley also met Sir Edmund Hillary, of the conquest of Everest fame, bearing a letter for him from his erstwhile expedition leader, Lord Hunt; Hillary would not be joining the Antarctic voyage on the *John Biscoe* until it reached the Bluff, but an early incident is worthy of note. Eight Christmas trees had been ordered, of which three were destined for the *John Biscoe* which Hillary declined. The order was reinstated, by whom is not recorded, with the accompanying comment, "it's time he realised that the *Biscoe* belongs to the New Zealand navy and not to him!"

Another visitor was R.A. Allen, a geologist who had done six months' work on Chatham Island and provided Priestley with some very useful photographs and good samples of schists, volcanics and many interesting fossils. At lunch with Allen, but while sitting alongside Seago, he learned that the latter had been a camouflage expert during the Second World War and had also lectured with, somewhat bizarrely, a ventriloquist's dummy, on photographic interpretation. He had also camouflaged both the *Illustrious* and the *Pluto*, two veterans of the war.

Finally, late on December 17, the *Britannia* left Lyttelton Harbour after what Priestley records as "a tremendous evening" given by Prince Philip for both the ship and shore parties, which opened with the band playing *Cockleshell Heroes*. At dinner one of the guests, the New Zealand Prime Minister, Holland, told him how he had witnessed *Nimrod* leaving in 1908 "and had never forgotten the occasion." Also on a very personal and heartfelt note, Priestley records that "all the lads I met were much appreciative of my presence and this was warming in its effect."

The following day as the *Britannia* headed towards Chatham Island accompanied by two frigates, *F422* and *F424*, he enjoyed a short walk on deck with Prince Philip, who allayed his fears, to some extent, about landing

12. West Antarctica on the RY Britannia

in small boats; as Priestley puts it, " I told him I do not fold up as well as I used to do." Later in the evening, Prince Philip showed Seago and Priestley over his quarters and those of the Queen, during which he recounted how a Norfolk Island lady said to him, "Philip is looking very beautiful tonight." He was somewhat startled by the remark until he realized that she was referring to Prince Philip Island, on the horizon. On another occasion, at dinner, Prince Philip said he was somewhat taken aback when his neighbor said, tartly, "Philip, you are talking nonsense," only to discover that she was talking to one Philip Walker, another guest.

At this point in his personal diary, Priestley, as always meticulous on points of detail, had to contend with crossing the International Date Line, so that December 19 appears twice! Both "days" were extremely active as he completed a "wonderful" tour of Chatham Island. He landed in the Royal Barge and after an official reception at which Prince Philip was presented with a carved wooden ornament for the Queen, he visited the hospital and also Patterson, the Resident Commissioner, who provided him with some interesting statistics. At that time, no less than 80,000 live sheep and 3,000 bales of wool were exported from Chatham Island every year. With his interest in growing vegetables, Priestley also observed peas, spinach, potatoes, cabbages, chives, parsnips, carrots, strawberries and various currants in the Resident's kitchen garden. During the tour, and in his honor, Prince Philip and his Party were also given a traditional and very tender Māori roast of meat cooked underground on pebbles for four hours, much enjoyed by Priestley.

After leaving Chatham Island, when the two accompanying frigates also departed, Commander Adams' birthday party was celebrated, with an obligation to stand drinks again on the following day, which would also be December 19! It was also at this point that he learned of Prince Philip's intention to grow a beard next month, as would some of his party, but Priestley "did not think that I had better," for reasons unspecified in his diary although his grandson recollects that this was because he feared that it would be "too white."

At this stage, he was involved in a planning session for the Antarctic section of the cruise. The intention was to meet with the *Southern Harvester* (for refueling) and the *Protector* (one of the ship's official escorts for this part of the voyage) at seventy degrees south and to transfer to either *Protector* or the *John Biscoe* for a visit to the first of the Falkland Islands Dependencies Survey bases, coded W, before proceeding to F, N, A and B. Priestley had hoped, in addition, to visit base D, but time limits were constrained by the requirement for *Britannia* to be in Portugal in time for a later visit by the Queen.

Back on board, Prince Philip and Priestley watched Seago painting a picture of the former winning the second race at a meeting which had been held while the party was on Chatham Island, followed by the fortuitous second celebration of Adams' birthday and a showing of the film, *The Baby and the Battleship*, which Priestley found "hilarious."

The few days remaining before Christmas, starting with the shortest day (in England), December 21, when Priestley "hoped his shallots would be going in," were filled with a variety of shipboard activities. Prince Philip was painting a portrait of Priestley, which he felt "has the head outline just right but the purple nose is as usual giving trouble"; while sitting he took the opportunity to put in a plea for Prince Philip to be the guest speaker at the Antarctic Club Dinner in 1958, Priestley being a past president. He also learned from Mike Parker of some farewell remarks, much favored by Princess Margaret, as alternatives to the "see you later alligator" theme such as "Toodle-oo, Kangaroo" and "Ooh! la! la!, Koala." All this was very much grist to the mill of his diary and as he puts it, "so the days pass, and I pinch myself every now and then to convince myself that I am really here."

With the *Wave Chief*, another of their refueling ships, in sight, Priestley was delighted to be photographed alongside the *Britannia*'s very handsome bell, presented by the Corporation of Trinity House, in 1953. He also gave a lecture on his Antarctic experiences to the crew, although was a little unhappy that it had to be rushed as it preceded a deck hockey match, at which "incipient beards were now very much in evidence." Mike Parker had also helped him to brush up on pidgin English, which the cruise members had encountered at an earlier stage; for example, when Prince Philip asked a New Guinea chief where the church was, the reply came "Bugger-up, finish." In similar circumstances, Prince Philip was known as "Number One Fella, belong Mrs Queen!"

Sitting on deck at fifty-two degrees south in bright sunshine and no wind, with the band playing "There's a Tavern in the Town," Priestley found the refueling process fascinating and fully approved the transfer of a bottle of beer for each man on the *Wave Chief* as a gesture of thanks. At the time he was engaged with Prince Philip in a discussion about public speaking, arising from Priestley's proposed lecture to the Stewards Mess. He recounted to the Prince his experiences relating to his part in a lecture to the Royal Geographical Society about Scott's Northern Party. The then President, Lord Curzon, advised him to take three glasses of champagne before speaking; Priestley, although not a drinker, complied, and said the lecture went "swimmingly!"

At the same time, Prince Philip recommended the extent and quality of the ship's library to him but Priestley advised him that, at the moment, he was at one with the village idiot who said, "sometimes I sits and thinks and sometimes I just sits." He also outlined for the Prince the extremely bizarre process by which he had been selected for his first Antarctic expedition with

Shackleton (detailed previously) which was not unlike his appointment as Secretary to the body to oversee the introduction of the New Statutes on Education Policy at Cambridge in 1926 where he had, flippantly, suggested himself and to his immense surprise, been appointed. As he records, apart from his election to a Clare Fellowship, "it was the best thing that ever happened to me at Cambridge." In similar vein, he had been seconded by General Boyd, GOC 46th (North Midlands) Division, to write its Official History during the final Hundred Days of the First World War merely because he had written a book on Antarctica, *Antarctic Adventure*, when he would much preferred to have returned to Cambridge to resume his studies that the war had interrupted; all instances of "happenchance and turning points in his life."

Priestley continued to enjoy life on board *Britannia* to the full, with many references to his "expanding waistline," including afternoon tea at 4:00 p.m. sharp consisting of "three-layered cakes and superfine sandwiches" which, on December 22, preceded his scheduled talk to the Stewards Mess, which was well received, and included intelligent questions surrounding the issue of sovereignty vis-à-vis Argentina. On the same day he learned that a bulletin was being sent to the BBC advertising the Carol Concert on board *Britannia* "as being accompanied by a portable harmonium powered by an electric vacuum cleaner."

By December 23, preparations were well advanced for Prince Philip's Christmas broadcast to be filmed, while at the same time the dining room was made ready for Sunday Service which Priestley appears to record with some regret was "now voluntary in the Navy"; at the service the Admiral read the wrong collect for the day which did not go unremarked by Lieutenant-Commander Mike Parker. The *Britannia* was also refueled again, in much colder weather conditions, although this had not prevented some of the crew being entertained to a "good alcoholic dinner" on board the *Wave Chief*. Priestley spent the remainder of Sunday writing out memories of his youth "which became more vivid every day."

Christmas Eve was another busy day. Prince Philip and Seago had completed Antarctic Certificates for all those on board, for which Priestley had in jest suggested the wording "A.B., having squared the circle, is entitled once every year to be up the pole." At breakfast, Seago had told a story concerning the poet John Masefield, who was apparently a close personal friend. It appears that a "huddle" of ladies who were to present a Women's Institute Charade wanted to illustrate Masefield's poem "I must go down to the sea again" and were doubtful about the appropriate costume. Seago promised to consult Masefield who, after due thought, wrote, "Dear Madam, I have given the matter serious consideration and have decided that a bathing dress is the most appropriate costume!"

In the morning, while sitting out on deck, Priestley compared the weather to "a Mediterranean day in April" and had to retreat to his cabin to collect his red and blue handkerchief because his head was tender where it had peeled. He also recorded that for the Carol Service program, Seago had devised some rather flippant angels—"non angli, sed angeli." He was also delighted, though somewhat embarrassed because he could not reciprocate, to receive a set of cufflinks from Prince Philip and books from both Lord Cilcennin and Mike Parker.

Christmas Day he enjoyed immensely. After listening to Prince Philip's broadcast and the Queen's Speech, he was able to telephone home to speak to his daughter Margaret, who also reported that his wife Phyllis, who was at that time suffering from Parkinson's disease was, nonetheless, quite well and "excited by his call." After Christmas morning service, followed by lunch and drinks in the Wardroom, Father Christmas paid a short visit with presents, Priestley's being a mechanical penguin of which his grandsons Mark and Tim "would have approved." More food followed—"we are all swelling visibly"—with tea which included a huge Christmas cake and yule log. This had been preceded by the inevitable game of deck hockey, which had been more vigorous and unpredictable than ever as the ship "bounced a good deal in a confused sea." Indeed, prior to the game, O'Brien, the Principal Medical Officer, had confided to him at lunch that he had never had a Christmas at sea without operating on someone. Priestley records that "there might be a simple explanation for this, when he saw O'Brien knock Mike Parker head over heels during the game." Later, he walked a measured mile around the ship and, indeed, might have been a casualty himself, when "he fell headlong" on the wet deck.

Later, a dinner party followed for both the Household and the mess deck and "it was one of the nicest he had ever attended." The games played in the saloon drawing room afterwards, however, were either too vigorous or mind testing for Priestley, who retired early, tired but extremely happy with the day's events.

The remaining days of December were relatively quiet by comparison with the Christmas festivities. He spent some time watching Seago painting, on this occasion icebergs, which was, as usual, accompanied by interesting discussion and comment. With reference to Masefield again, Seago related how he had remonstrated with him, as poet laureate, for not writing anything about the last war. Masefield had replied, "what can I write," merely "to fight for freedom is our happy fate, unsupported—unarmed—and too late." Priestley himself commented "that he had gone to war to save Poland and ended the war allowing her to be absorbed by Russia."

By the turn of the year, as the ship proceeded south, it began to roll more in heavier seas but Priestley was delighted that he "had nearly got my sea legs." In addition, the production line for Antarctic Circle Certificates was in full swing; Prince Philip inked the linocut, Squadron Leader Henry Chinnery (the Duke of Edinburgh's Equerry-in-Waiting) and Commander Adams manipulated the press, Mike put in the red noses, with Priestley named as foreman.

Nicknames had also been ascribed to many of the Household based on what Priestley denotes as "Avifauna Britannia Antarctica." Prince Philip was the Royal Crested Philip, Seago the Greater Bearded Seago, Priestley the Lesser (later Greater) Polar Backchat, Mike Parker the Yellow Billed Tuff-Mike, Lord Cilcennin the Barefaced Electrotherapic Firstlord, Chinnery the Brokenbacked Longchinned Equerry, and the Admiral, the Fiercer Ill-Oil Admiral. All owed their derivation to personal characteristics and/or events observed on board and, undoubtedly, illustrated a great degree of comradeship and good humor throughout the ship, reflecting Prince Philip's highly effective leadership style.

On December 30, Priestley records an "hilarious" dinner, sitting next to the Admiral, when he learned that he had been a member of the first Naval Flying Course, later flying helicopters, and that the Queen Mother had been converted to this mode of travel quite late on in life. He also heard, from Prince Philip, that Edward VII had invented the dinner jacket in order to bring him and his civilian guests into line with serving officers wearing Mess Jackets, with black bow ties. Finally, before retiring for the night he notes, with exquisite attention to detail, that he finds some difficulty having his pajamas starched even though it is only the front of the coat and the waistband of the trousers.

New Year's Eve found the Royal Yacht moving steadily south east at twelve knots with a southerly gale blowing and a lumpy swell. He had risen early to witness the crossing of the Antarctic Circle, wearing woolen underclothing for the first time in forty-three years, since his life-changing experience with Scott's Northern Party. At this point the *Protector* was exchanging signals with the *Britannia* while the *Southern Harvester* with the *John Biscoe* and three whale catchers were now close at hand, comprising overall a sizeable fleet. The day marked the first of a number of transfers to other vessels that were more suited to the landings and excursions that those on board *Britannia* would be involved in on the ensuing days. Priestley completed a transfer to the *Southern Harvester* using one of the whale catchers, *Sandra*, as an intermediary, dressed for the first time on the tour in semi-Antarctic kit of flannels over pajama trousers, thick socks over trouser-ends, woolen vest, shirt and jumper under tweed jacket, cap with ear muffs and woolen gloves; a far cry from the more sophisticated cold weather clothing available today. He very much enjoyed the experience, apart from the smell of a three days dead sperm whale alongside the *Sandra*, used as a buffer, and which exploded when squeezed "with a gust of quite mephitic odour."

With the *Britannia* now only one hundred twenty miles from the first of the Falkland Islands Dependencies Survey (FIDS) bases to be visited, Base "W," Prince Philip and the Admiral were making detailed plans, on which Priestley was consulted in his duel capacity as both Acting Director of FIDS and Antarctic advisor. This was followed by New Year's Eve celebrations but Priestley retired early after a strenuous day which had included a basket transfer between ships which he had found "innocuous" though, in view of his age, "it had enhanced his reputation."

On New Year's Day 1957, Prince Philip with members from among his Party moved to the *John Biscoe* which, with its capacity to penetrate light pack ice, would enable them to visit the FIDS bases as planned. With Cape Rae and Graham Land in the middle distance, Captain Johnson welcomed the Party on board in the fine wood paneled wardroom, and the ship traversed ten miles before entering the pack. After penetrating thirty miles of new pack ice, which was intensely interesting to newcomers, Base "W" was sighted with its dogs, the hut, stores and tents clearly visible and members of the base personnel "streaming down to the beach." From the shore, Priestley identified snowy and Antarctic petrels, Cape pigeons and Weddell and Crabeater seals and some small but rather spectacular icebergs. He met the resident geologist, Wright, who, "sporting a fine red beard," was unhappy with some aspects of FIDS administration, of which the provision of a geological hammer head which did not fit its ironbound handle and some Canadian footwear, so-called mukluks, that wore out in only three weeks' usage, were just two examples; nonetheless, he acknowledged that some good geological progress had been made.

Within the limits of a tight schedule, the visit lasted only two hours but was sufficient for Priestley to form a good impression of its personnel and the work being accomplished. Priestley notes that Mike Parker was responsible for the "canard" reported to him by Prince Philip that the first penguin seen today said to his chums, "My God, boys, here's that bloody chap Priestley back again!" After a somewhat wakeful night, due to the throb of the ship's engines and "excitement," he rose early at 4:00 a.m. and went onto the bridge where he was provided with cocoa and cold roast turkey, reminding him of the days, nearly fifty years ago, when the preparation of cocoa for the Officer of the Watch, with Scott's party, had been part of his duties. From the bridge, he could see Graham Land clearly to starboard with the Argentine Islands and Base "F" only six miles away.

After an approach at right angles to a narrow channel, which reminded Priestley of the *Terra Nova*'s approach to McMurdo Sound, the party arrived at Base "F," which comprised Non-Magnetic, Balloon and Survey huts, the latter with a special second stage for ozone work and a radio room which was of special interest to him. The base had been particularly successful in experimenting with a full-time chef, which had proved popular. In addition, from the peak balloon height achieved of over 80,000 feet, signals were still clearly relayed to ground instruments; valuable information for Priestley and FIDS H.Q.

On leaving Base "F," the *John Biscoe* entered the Lemaire Channel (known to later cruise ships as "Kodak Alley") where it brushed some "growler" ice, which was not visible above the surface of the sea. Priestley was captivated by the view of "black rugged rocks and mountains with glacier caps and ... valley glaciers." Small avalanches and some spectacular icebergs completed coastal scenery that he found much finer than anything he had seen in East Antarctica. Indeed, he goes so far as to suggest that "there can be little scenery as grand in the world and I would not have missed it for anything."

At the southern end of the Lemaire Channel, Priestley encountered equally beautiful scenery at Cape Renard, including two mountain peaks known colloquially to FIDS personnel as "Una's Tits," reflecting their anatomical similarity to an erstwhile Falkland's governor's wife! At lunch on the same day, Prince Philip asked him, referring to cooked penguins, "Do you have to hang them?" Priestley replied, without thinking, "Well Sir, we usually preferred to club them." He was promoted immediately from Lesser to Greater Polar Backchat.

The *John Biscoe* arrived at Base "N" shortly thereafter where Priestley had a discussion with the base geologist, who was also its leader, and rated outstandingly successful by the governor. A party from the base staged a man-hauling demonstration for the visitors as well as showing them a very good collection of geological specimens. Later, Priestley relayed a story to Prince Philip that he had picked up during the visit. It appeared that the base party had spent the last three weeks teaching each other not to call a recently born pup, called Duke, a bastard!

The next port of call was Base "A" at Port Lockroy; on the way there, Priestley had packed everything except his current diary, preparatory to returning to the *Britannia* the next day. While sailing, he also took the opportunity of telling Prince Philip "how much I appreciated his giving me what was almost certainly the last outstanding experience of my life." In doing so, he could not have envisaged another Antarctic adventure, the America Deep Freeze IV Expedition, quite soon thereafter. During the tour of the base, the governor told Priestley that this was the first time he had seen Copper Peak on Anvers Island, as on all previous visits it was shrouded in mist. Priestley also met a detachment of marines living on the base and remarked that their accommodation distinguished itself from that of other bases visited "by the number of nude studies in the bedroom."

After steaming back through the Lemaire Channel, the *John Biscoe* reached the small Base "O," with a complement of only three men. Everything was "in apple pie order," with a notice on the hut door suggesting "it is not necessary to be scruffy to be tough." After a short inspection, the Party transferred back to the *Britannia* on January 3, and were heading towards their next destination, Deception Island, where the whaling station hut was known as "Biscoe," but later renamed "Priestley." Priestley found the place "altogether a rather decrepit whaling and maritime museum" where he had the opportunity to examine an old whaling boat, as he records, "fortunately not too roughly, as it was found out later to be full of dynamite." During lunch he sat next to a naval lieutenant named Erskine and was most interested to discover that he had the distinction of being an equerry to both King George V and King George VI. It is also at this point that Priestley records, with gratitude, that "I must have been helped into more boats by more people with greater goodwill than any other southern traveler in the history of the world."

During the visit, the governor had related a story to him concerning the ghostly possibilities of discarded whaling stations. Apparently, one evening at dinner, when the occupants thought they were alone, they heard ghostly footsteps approaching followed by the door opening slowly and a large Norwegian entering and saying solemnly, "My arse is vet!"

On January 4, the *Britannia* was heading for Base "Q," located at Admiralty Bay on King George's Island. While sailing, Priestley, in his role as Acting Director of FIDS, was able to agree, with the governor, a short statement safeguarding the size and status of the Falkland Islands' Scientific Bureau as part of a general reorganization of FIDS. He also learned that, at Deception Island, while he had lost the end of his Birmingham University Air Squadron tie to the base trophy board, Mike Parker had lost the end of his shirt tail in addition to his tie-end, while Lord Cilcennin's Royal Yacht tie had suffered a similar fate. He also records, relating to the two secretaries and the only two ladies on the cruise, "I saw Anne Stevenson (now Dame Anne Griffiths, Archivist to the Duke of Edinburgh) deprived of at least two locks of hair with a penknife and a rather blunt one at that. In addition, both she and Ione Eadie (who later married Commander Adams, Commander of the Royal Yacht in 1956/57) contributed a scarf each."

As the Royal Party entered Admiralty Bay, Priestley reflected that it must have been an abnormal season of good weather as, when he had met Captain Johnson of the *John Biscoe* at Paisley in the previous July, he had "scoffed" at the idea of reaching Deception Island in early January, and had certainly felt that they would be lucky if they were able to visit more than one or two bases at best. Having been fortunate to complete a full program so far, he realized the added value the tour would have for his tenure as Acting Director of FIDS, as he would be able to visualize both the people and places with which he was dealing, at long range.

At Base "Q," the Royal Launch landed to the sound of pipes and drums with the men parading for inspection by Prince Philip in full naval uniform, while the helicopters from *Protector* cruised around overhead. Priestley, with his keen horticultural eye, was surprised that no attempt had been made to acclimatize such plants as Kerguelen cabbage and Tussock grass, in view of the high summer temperatures.

During the tour of inspection, with some time to spare, he picked up three from the governor's seemingly endless list of stories. The first concerned the Falkland Island's Alcoholic Black List to which people could volunteer to be added. A certain Mr. "Thirsty" Allen and his wife decided to add their names for reasons of economy, with just one proviso; "There ain't no more loyal man in these islands than wot I am. I must have two days off when 'Is Royal 'Ighness is 'ere." The second related to a notorious "soaker" named Biggs who was found dead on a hillside with a bottle of rum in his hand. A comrade was heard to remark, "Poor old Ernie, the call must have come pretty sudden for 'im to leave all that rum." Finally, a local skipper, one Harrison Jansen, was washed overboard from his ship. In relating the story to Prince Philip, one of the residents remarked, "Poor old chap, he must have just gone up on the bridge with his *saxophone* to take his readings and a wave must 'a come and took 'im."

After lunch, the *Britannia* steamed along the South Shetlands, passing Livingston Island which, as it came into view, presented a fine sight with its precipitate black mountain ridges, some with triangular faces and heavily interspersed with crevassed glaciers ending in vertical cliffs; plans were already well advanced to put a base on the island. While sailing, in discussion, Priestley and Prince Philip differed on the derivation of the naming of Adélie penguins, which were much in evidence. While Priestley favored Dumont d'Urville, who named Adélie Land after his wife, Prince Philip attributed it to Adélie, the wife of Bellingshausen, an earlier explorer.

The next destination was at the South Shetland's Base "Q," a difficult landing during which Priestley felt "I was walking the plank and due for my fourth Antarctic immersion." For reasons unspecified, Mike Parker landed wearing a top hat while Priestley was likened, by Prince Philip, to a German prisoner in his outfit of peaked cap and camouflage trousers; he and Parker linked arms and were photographed by Prince Philip as "the Marx Brothers." The base had a very good hut with a proper bathroom, electric light, a storeroom "resembling a grocers shop" and a library, where he spotted Aspley Cherry-Garrard's book, *The Worst Journey in the World*, covering his five week ordeal in a mid-winter journey, as part of Scott's final expedition, to the site of the nesting Emperor penguin colony at Cape Crozier.[3] As the base hut had not been named, Prince Philip suggested Backchat House. The day ended with the best sunset Priestley had witnessed so far.

On the following day, January 5, the governor was again "in good form" at breakfast relating that a Falkland's sandwich was a piece of hot mutton between two pieces of cold mutton, lamb is served as the traditional Christmas Dinner, and that his host at a farm thought he had lost his appetite when he could not eat more than three eggs for breakfast as well as two mutton chops. He also described the unpopularity of his predecessor, Max Clifford, who, when receiving the reply to his question about the pay of a captain of a whale-catcher, remarked, "Good Lord, he earns more than I do." The grim rejoinder was "but he earns it."

The next day, January 6, a Sunday, Priestley had further discussions with the governor about future plans for a new *John Biscoe* which, being better equipped for ice penetration, would enable survey work further south and the reopening of Base "E," helped by support from the air. After another fall "in his Sunday shoes," Priestley nonetheless enjoyed Divine Service which included "*Jerusalem*—the W.I. song." Later in the day, those on board received the news of the Suez Crisis and Priestley was infuriated by what he saw as " America double-crossing us in Egypt and then moving in, in force, in Middle East affairs; but all of a piece with the way America's oil interests have acted, first in Persia [Iran] and then Saudi Arabia." A clay pigeon shoot followed in the afternoon and, later, a much enjoyed film showing of *To Paris with Love*. Before retiring, Prince Philip related his best New Zealand pun; when he said to Prime Minister Holland, "what a pity the Moa is extinct," he replied, "Oh, I don't know, I've got a mower on my lawn."

By January 7, the ship was lying off East Falkland, where a three-day visit was planned, with Priestley suffering from a cough and sore throat. Alongside, the *Protector*, like the *Britannia*, was "dressed over all" while the *John Biscoe* was moored nearby. Ashore, a keenly contested hockey match took place between the Household and the Marines, with further challenges put down to almost anything, including, even, a beer drinking contest. The governor mentioned to Priestley that, as the Queen's representative, he could claim precedence over Prince Philip, but indicating that "it was a right most Governors would not wish to exercise." He also mentioned that the Falkland's National Anthem was "Woo-oo-oo-oo-oo … the Wind!" He was also delighted to be presented with a sheep's skin which would be sent home for him (later used on a settee at Barn's Hill, Breden's Norton).

Of particular interest to Priestley, because of past experience, was a visit to the Wireless Station where he met Tyson, the Chief Wireless Officer—as he notes, no relation to Frank "Typhoon" Tyson, the cricketer.

Of even greater interest and significance was his visit to Government House, where he was shown the Shackleton room and FIDS Headquarters, followed by dinner with Stanley "notables."

On the day following, he relished a seaplane flight over Port Louis, the original seat of Falkland's government, San Salvador, Teal Inlet, Wickham Heights, Fitzroy Camp, and witnessed a Sonde balloon ascent.

12. West Antarctica on the RY Britannia

Later, he had been astonished by the very warm welcome given to him personally at both the town hall and racetrack. Prior to dinner, a reception was given on *Britannia* for two hundred guests in the dining salon where Priestley was delighted to meet a number of people who had known Frank Wild, Shackleton's "right-hand man" and his comrade from the Nimrod Expedition. Overall, the Falkland Islands visit had been judged "a great success," as the *Britannia* departed en route to South Georgia on January 9. At dinner that evening, Priestley heard of the resignation of Anthony Eden as Prime Minister, following the Suez Crisis, as he expresses it "ostensibly on the grounds of ill health"; a dinner at which Seago appeared, unaccountably, in a magnificent poncho and cap given him by the governor.

On arrival in South Georgia, their first port of call was Gritviken, where Priestley visited the magistrate's house for tea, near to the site of Shackleton's startling reappearance after a first and incredibly difficult crossing of the island, bringing to a successful though unbelievably arduous conclusion, his escape from his icebound ship the *Endurance*, months spent drifting on the pack ice, reaching and then leaving the majority of his crew on Elephant Island and undertaking a perilous sea crossing of over eight hundred miles in a small and virtually open boat, over some of the worst ocean conditions in the world.[4] During his short stay, he visited both the Shackleton Memorial and his grave, and although his diary does not dwell unduly on the poignancy of the occasion, photographs taken at the time of him standing, alone, beside both, illustrate most clearly what must have been a very emotional moment for him. On the same day he heard that Harold MacMillan had been become Prime Minister, following Eden's resignation.

The 15th of January marked a new phase in the Tour in many ways, as the *Britannia* approached Tristan da Cunha, warmer climes and, effectively, the end of Priestley's official role as Antarctic expert and advisor. A telegram was received from the *News Chronicle* congratulating Mike Parker on the "breeziness" of his bulletins, to which he replied, "that they had been the joint effort of a team of loquacious, truculent, observant, but ill-disciplined enthusiasts with a lively but perverted sense of humour," or as Priestley adds, "words to that effect!" This was also the appropriate moment for Priestley to prepare some headings for a Mansion House speech, covering the tour, to be delivered by Prince Philip on his return to London.

Of historical significance, it was the day when, at 10:30 a.m., four blasts were given on the ship's siren to mark the crossing of the fifteen degrees west meridian, making the completion of *Britannia's* world tour, east to west, since she passed down the west coast of Africa on the way to Mombasa on Princess Margaret's leg of the tour. The round-the-world trip had taken 135 days and the ship's crew had established a record, as they had all been on board since Mombasa.

Priestley beside the Shackleton Memorial on South Georgia in early 1957, during the voyage with His Royal Highness, the Duke of Edinburgh, on the RY *Britannia* (Crown copyright reserved).

Priestley enjoyed a "terrific" day on Tristan da Cunha on January 17, coincidentally the identical day that Scott reached the South Pole in 1912, and Priestley records that he himself should have been attending the Antarctic Dining Club dinner on this day. Thereafter, from January 19 onwards, and crossing the equator on January 26, the *Britannia* made a series of visits including St. Helena, the Ascension Islands, and the Gambia before arriving in Gibraltar Harbour on February 6, 1957, at the end of the tour. Here, Priestley boarded a Dakota en route to Madrid, a Viscount to London Airport (pre–Heathrow) and then a train to his home in Tewkesbury. As he finally records, "so the great trek ends with rain beating down on the window and myself warm in bed, and very little the worse for wear."

13

American Deep Freeze IV Expedition

Operation Deep Freeze (ODF) was the code name given to a series of United States missions to Antarctica, beginning with "Operation Deep Freeze I" in 1955-56, followed by ODF II and III, with ODF IV taking place in 1958-59, in which Priestley was invited to take part, not only as the United Kingdom's observer, but also because of a lifetime's experience in the region, including its earliest exploration; he exercised his responsibilities alongside observers from Argentina and Chile who, like the British, had longstanding interests in Antarctica. Given the continuing and constant U.S. presence in Antarctica since ODF IV, Deep Freeze has come to be used as a general term for U.S. operations on the continent and in particular for the regular missions to re-supply U.S. Antarctic bases, coordinated by the United States Navy, using a series of ships including freighters, icebreakers and fuel tankers.[1]

Against this background, Priestley found himself "safely and comfortably installed" on the freighter USS *Wyandot*, on December 14, 1958, in Lyttelton Harbour, New Zealand, sharing a fifteen by twelve feet cabin with Richard Newman, a scientist en route to Antarctica who, he surmised, "should prove a good companion as he was more concerned for my welfare than his own." At the same time, he learned that he would be messing with, amongst other officers, Rear Admiral Tyree, in overall charge of the flotilla assigned to ODF IV and Captain Irving commanding USS *Wyandot*, with Priestley anticipating "good food and a threat to his waistline."[2]

Consequently, on December 15, 1958, as Priestley took his first Avamine tablet, his trusted remedy against Southern Ocean seasickness, the USS *Wyandot* left Lyttelton Harbour in company with the icebreaker USS *North Wind* and the fuel tanker USS *Nespolen*; he watched its departure with Commander May, the Chilean observer, and Lieutenant Gonzales, his Argentine counterpart. Early weather reports from Antarctica indicated that the areas around both Scott's and Shackleton's former bases, two of the expedition's objectives and both scenes of former glory and poignant memories for Priestley, illustrated some surrounding ice although the approach through McMurdo Sound was clear.

Two early encounters were with his travelling companions Stewart and Russell, two glaciologists bound for Scott Base, to whom he imparted some of his earlier Antarctic experiences including, in written form, some of the research material he had compiled following his experiences with both Scott and Shackleton, "which was well received." He was also struck immediately by the differences between life with the U.S. Navy compared with his recent voyage on RY *Britannia*; principally the informality and relaxed approach of the former, with "O.K. much in use and sailors smoking whilst on guard duty," or, as he expresses it, "Autre Terres, Autre Mœurs." It was also at this early stage of the expedition that he was invited by Admiral Tyree to provide some basic geological instruction to the officers assembled over dinner in the wardroom.

December 17 found the *Wyandot* at forty-six degrees south proceeding at ten knots in dense fog with the accompanying ships, though invisible, very much in evidence by the noise of their fog horns, "which hindered conversation." Later in the day, Priestley discussed the employment of dogs in Antarctica with Admiral Tyree, based on his experiences with both Scott and Shackleton, which inevitably touched on the advantages that Amundsen had enjoyed through their successful use. During a conversation with some of the U.S. sailors he also gained the impression that Captain Irving was both respected and popular as being "hard but fair" and that the *Wyandot* was a happy ship.

Over the next few days, Priestley began to feel very much an integral part of Deep Freeze IV's mission as the result of a myriad of opportunities to talk to those involved and to use and impart his unique knowledge and perspective. During a meeting with Gonzalez, the Argentine observer, he learned that, although he had not over-wintered in Antarctica, he had made eight voyages to the region, had crossed the Antarctic Circle six times and was well versed in the history of its exploration. He also gave his first talk to "a well filled" wardroom about Scott's Northern Party accompanied by, as a novelty in his experience, a short film which had been specially prepared for him prior to the voyage.

Though Priestley was generally enjoying life aboard *Wyandot* and getting on well with his cabin mate, Newman, he was occasionally disturbed by him in the night "as he had clearly not had his prostate dealt with!" This observation may have been prompted by a previous discussion with the Admiral and Captain Irving about the decrease in the numbers applying for Antarctica service, more especially scientists, almost certainly because of the more stringent physical and psychological examinations increasingly being insisted upon, and despite the incentive of guarantees of high level posts being awarded to those returning from Antarctica and the award of prestigious polar medals to those who had over-wintered; he concludes that "this was not now considered a glamorous posting."

By December 19, *Wyandot* had reached fifty-nine degrees south and Priestley, whose previous experience had accustomed him to isolation in Antarctica, was surprised to see packing cases and other debris passing the ship as well as some oil pollution in the sea. In addition, icebergs now began to appear on the ship's radar, which he noted during a tour of the Communications Room, having been given the freedom of the Bridge Deck, which he much appreciated. He was also enjoying life in the wardroom and, particularly, the company of Captain Irving who had a wealth of good anecdotes, being a widely experienced and observant traveler. He knew Jamaica particularly well and produced, as a trophy, an "Article"—a Victorian synonym for a chamber pot—which he had acquired as a souvenir from the Myrtle Bank Hotel, on the island, and which he had carried with him ever since. Priestley was able to counter with his own experience of the same hotel where he had his haircut and on protesting at paying a dollar for the privilege, the barber had remarked, "I'm not charging you for cutting it, Sir, I'm charging you for fin'ing it!"

With the ship now approaching the Antarctic Circle, and a crossing anticipated on the afternoon of December 20, many more sea birds, seals and whales were in evidence on and around the occasional tabular icebergs encountered. Priestley also took an opportunity, over dinner, to discuss Anglo-Chilean relations with LeMay, the Chilean observer, and the way in which these had been enhanced by the visit of Prince Philip to the Chilean Base, as part of the RY *Britannia*'s tour. Furthermore, to illustrate the differences for the people "on the ground" compared with the diplomatic climate at home, LeMay cited the example of the football match between the British, Argentine and Chilean Bases, where the winner exercised the sovereignty of Deception Island for one year, an ephemeral but nonetheless significant illustration of goodwill amongst the Antarctic community.

By December 21 and hereafter, as the *Wyandot* approached scattered pack ice and occasional icebergs, Priestley was called upon more and more to exercise his previous Antarctic experience, often being called for "duty" in the early hours of the morning. As he describes it, he was "labelled by my winter clothing as very much, and clearly, U.S. Army, in gold letters." At Divine Service on the mess deck, it being Sunday, his thoughts turned to home and Barn Hill where, with Christmas approaching, preparations would be in full swing and, having sung "Rock of Ages" to an unfamiliar tune, he would have preferred "Eternal Father, Strong to Save," particularly as the singing generally "did not do justice to the hymns as they had in the cave with Scott's Northern Party."

It was at this point that news filtered through from the USS *Staten Island*, with which the *Wyandot* would later rendezvous, that it was working on the ice in McMurdo Sound, where Captain Irving estimated they should arrive by Christmas Eve. Consequently, over lunch, the Admiral asked Priestley what locations he would like to visit on their arrival. Priestley's expressed preferences were the huts at his old Headquarters, as well as Marble Point and Beardsmore Station, while indicating that he was "not especially interested in going to the Pole."

In very close ice, the ship was following the icebreaker *North Wind*, which also carried two helicopters, likened to "great red birds" by Priestley. On occasions, *Wyandot* required help from the icebreaker if it did not follow precisely in its wake, and Priestley was able to brush up on his Morse code when signals from the ship's lamps were required. Indeed, by December 22, the ship was brought to a complete standstill by a pressure field of ice, three feet thick, with the *Nespelen* lagging further behind, though not in Priestley's view "a complete lame duck." With the Admiralty Range in sight through binoculars, and the approach to Cape Adare showing clear lanes of water on the radar, Priestley took the opportunity to give a lecture in the wardroom on Antarctic geology, including paleomagnetism and the wandering of the continents. He also touched on any future economic prospects for the Continent, bearing in mind the Japanese unsubstantiated claim to have discovered uranium.

Later, on the bridge with the Admiral, during what he describes as "an hour and a half he would not have missed for anything," he watched the ships' convoy, in close column, culling through quite heavy ice with the *Wyandot* controlled magnificently by Captain Irving, for whom his growing admiration was clearly apparent. Indeed, Priestley, somewhat unusually, waxed poetical with a reference to "the black water of the polnia [sic] crawling with serpentine patterns as the new ice forms in the night frost." The day following, some four hundred ninety-five miles from McMurdo, he was surprised to learn that, despite generally very high morale on board ship, most of the crew were nonetheless looking forward to the end of their service and grateful not be over-wintering in Antarctica, very much more a reflection of Priestley's general approach to life than anything that should be considered unusual in the attitude of the crew. Towards evening, and in Priestley's words, "this must be recorded, Cape Adare could be seen in its whole black length by the naked eye"; for him it was a moment not only of historic significance but also some emotion, as he had last seen it in very different circumstances, almost fifty years previously, with a close knit group of young companions, many of whom had since died.

The following day, Christmas Eve, awakened by the bosun's call and pipe of "Rally, Rally, Rally, Rouse out and Tie up," a reminder of the days when hammocks were used, he found the ship stopped opposite Cape Adare at seventy-two degrees south. While watching with LeMay from the bridge, the latter mentioned, *en passant*, that his watch had only lost seventeen seconds since leaving Valparaiso; Priestley's instant response was that "if he picked him out of a helicopter crash, that would be his share of the loot!" Later in the day, an exciting if alarming situation occurred when the *North Wind* suddenly swerved from her course on the port side as if she was making a landing. As a result, *Wyandot* had to go "Hard Astern," and although disaster was averted she came very close to losing her propeller. Finally, before turning in and being Christmas Eve, Priestley's thoughts were very much with his family in Breden's Norton and "his hopes that the hamper and York ham had arrived"; as he records in his diary, "a Happy Christmas to everyone."

On Christmas Day, he was presented with a certificate illustrating his status as an honorary member of the *Wyandot's* crew and, to his embarrassment, a leather notebook and key-holder from his cabin mate, Newman, with nothing to give in return; he attributes this to the small baggage allowance on his flights to New Zealand coupled with the five-day week that had prevented him from shopping on his arrival at a weekend. However, he admits to having previous form on this issue, having found himself similarly embarrassed on RY *Britannia*! Nonetheless, these is no doubt that Priestley was very much enjoying life and, as he records, "I have been treated like a prince on *Wynadot* and will never forget it." He goes so far as to say that in many respects it matched his trip on *Britannia*, "except no Prince Phillip."

Still some three hundred twenty-five miles from McMurdo and behind Captain Irving's estimated date of arrival, it was anticipated that the Sound would be reached on Boxing Day. This allowed Priestley time to reflect on previous Antarctic Christmases: 1907 in New Zealand; 1908 spent with his companions Armitage and Brocklehurst in Windy Gully on the Ferrar Glacier when, "if my memory served me right, we had with us a small Christmas pudding which we cooked in our tea water and then went back to pemmican with some relief"; 1909 in Sydney, with his mentor Edgeworth David; 1910 in the *Terra Nova* in the Ross Sea amongst the pack ice and in the company of his two future brothers-in-law, Charles (later Sir Charles) Wright and Griffith Taylor, "both of whom like Brocklehurst still flourish and I hope they too remember these Christmases in Canada, Australia and Swithamley Park respectively"; 1911, a never-to-be-forgotten Christmas with Campbell, Levick, Abbott, Browning and Dickason in the snow cave as part of Scott's Northern Party and, 1912, at Cape Royds with, amongst others, Frank Debenham (who he later helped to found the Scott Polar Research Institute at Cambridge) when they had discovered a bottle of whisky in Frank Wild's locker which, after considerable imbibing, encouraged Debenham to relate his life story to Priestley for over four hours, much of which he had forgotten "but wished I had remembered for use in our occasional occupational encounters nowadays"; and finally, and more recently in 1956, with Prince Philip in the Antarctic Ocean. Overall, it was a unique record.

During the morning of Christmas Day, he received a telegram from Captain MacDonald, commander of USS *Staten Island*, to which Priestley would transfer on arrival in McMurdo Sound, illustrating a warm reception in prospect and worth quoting in full as an example of the unfailing generosity of the U.S. Navy towards him during the whole of his involvement with Deep Freeze IV: "*Wyandot* pass RADM Tyree and Sir Raymond Priestley welcome to the Antarctic. Ships should soon be in open water and well on the way to McMurdo Sound. Plan have *Staten Island* as welcoming committee meet ships vicinity of Beaufort Island and escort to designated berths in bay ice. Two deadmen are installed each for *Wyandot* and *Nespolen*. Merry Christmas to all."

At midday, a traditional Christmas Lunch was served of turkey with cranberry sauce, mince pies, ice cream and all the trimmings. In addition, and to his surprise, he had received two identical Red Cross parcels, as he puts it, "very much like a POW." At lunch, he sat next to Lieutenants Krull and Cross and witnessed a "pseudo-hot" argument about Rebels versus Yanks when he heard the one from the state of Georgia declare that "we are about to get rid of the last carpet-baggers this year."

Later in the day he found that he could read the signals from *North Wind* "much better than our signalman Moffett," announcing that it had broken through into open water at last, which was celebrated at an egg-nog party in the wardroom; Priestley apparently "outlasted the Admiral but on one glass of lime juice." During the celebration, both the Admiral and the Captain offered him the alternative of a slightly longer stay in the area, which would allow him to do some collecting at both Hut Point and Cape Royds, and involve a later return to Sydney rather than New Zealand "unless the authorities dispose otherwise."

At dinner, at which an excellent steak and kidney pudding was served, Priestley was delighted to be seated next to Captain Irving, who told him of his appearance, in a pageant, as Captain John Smith, to mark the 350th Anniversary of his landing in Jamestown, held in 1957. Both the Queen and Prince Philip were there and on being presented, Prince Philip looked at his beard with appreciation and said, "Good show," having just returned from his tour to Antarctica on the Royal Yacht. Priestley remarked "that I must remind him of that some time."

Feeling that he had very little to contribute to the conversation, generally, in lieu of this and his known obsession with watching his calorie intake, he related the story of his friend Henry Thirkill at Cambridge and the weighing machine that, when faced with his seventeen stone, made a loud whirring noise and said, "One at a time please!"

13. American Deep Freeze IV Expedition

Boxing Day, by contrast, and not unreasonably considering the extensive celebration of the previous day, he spent quietly but, nonetheless, with great satisfaction as the ships had reached open water at last, at seventy-five degrees south. His diary notes for the day were uncharacteristically brief, merely noting of interest concerning public relations in the Navy that the *Wyandot* carries a journalist apprentice seaman, a graduate of one of the lesser universities, who has responsibilities for this.

On the day following, the *Wyandot*'s sojourn in open water was short-lived as the ships attempted to pass between Beaufort and Bird Islands in heavy though close packed ice with tabular icebergs ahead. The atmosphere on the Bridge was tense, with helicopters scouting ahead, but eventually *Staten Island* was sighted, carrying a huge WELCOME balloon in bright red letters and helped them into McMurdo Sound, where they arrived at 8:25 a.m.; a truly wonderful and overwhelming moment for Priestley.

He records that Cape Bird was clear as was Mount Erebus and its "Old Fang" in evidence, with a plume of steam. Immediately in view were Cape Royds, Cape Barne, Cape Evans, Razorback and Little Razorback, Tent Island, Inaccessible Island, Glacier Tongue, Castle Rock, Observation Hill, Mount Lister, Ferrar Glacier, Knot Head, Butter Point and Dry Valley, each and every one with poignant memories for Priestley; in his words, "It is almost too much." He was acting as guide to the Admiral and the Argentine and Chilean observers, Stewart and LeMay, together with others assembled on the upper deck, and recounted Edgeworth David's leadership of the first ascent of Mount Erebus.

He goes on to describe this "as the most exciting hour of the voyage," not only because of his return to places of such huge significance to him after such a long interval but also because *Wyandot* became "properly wedged" in the narrow channel left by the icebreaker. In helping to extract the ship, *Staten Island* charged towards the *Wyandot*'s bows, but was deflected by the ice and hit the ship. Fortunately, although "collision quarters" was sounded, there was no damage and the *Wyandot* was eventually released. With the *Staten Island* alongside, Priestley noticed, with his customary eye for unusual detail, among the luggage awaiting unloading, one piece marked, "Do not sit upon, post no posteriors, un-ass it."

This was followed by a session of general visiting between the two ships and although Priestley met so many people that he could remember very few names he, nonetheless, felt that "the omens were favourable." Still wearing his U.S. Army "uniform," enquiries were made as to whether he should be saluted, to which he replied, "No, I am only a private; but that after ten days on *Wyandot* I feel very much a private." Later, important guests from *Staten Island* were invited to dine on board *Wynadot* including Captain MacDonald, Commander Price-Lewis and Commander Cadwallader, the Operations

Officer at McMurdo Base. Earlier, Admiral Tyree had transferred to McMurdo Base by helicopter, preparatory to flying on to the South Pole, and although Priestley was again offered a similar opportunity, he declined on the basis that "it would not be wise for me to attempt a flight above 10,000 feet in an un-pressurised plane without oxygen and that the South Pole was not one of my ambitions." His day ended with a movie entitled *Lust for Life* about Vincent van Gogh which, although sad, was the best that he had seen so far in relation to "acting, presentation and content."

On December 28 with the year's end approaching, an early morning sighting of Mount Discovery, free of cloud, looked as beautiful as he had described it in his book, *Antarctic Adventure*.[3] It being Sunday, Divine Service followed which included, unusually, a film depicting the Birth of Christ "which was beautiful and moving." Later in the day, one of the seamen asked his advice on climbing Mount Erebus, which he hoped to receive permission to attempt. Priestley was happy to provide this, while emphasizing strongly that at least one person with mountaineering experience as well as one with knowledge of Antarctic travel were essential for the safety and chances of success of any party. In the evening he was invited to dinner on *Staten Island*, during which Priestley, as always interested in detail, learned from Commander Price-Lewis that the ship was fitted with an auto-cut-out for her propellers which reacts if they start chopping ice, and while this prevented damage it could be very disconcerting for the navigator relying on the particular propeller affected.

After dinner, back on board *Wyandot*, he was shown a chart by Captain Irving of the 1912 ascent of Mount Erebus, which the latter was determined to attempt. Priestley also discussed yet another change to his program which included visits to Cape Royds, Marble Point and Dry Valley by helicopter, then, after transferring to *Staten Island*, visits to Hallett and Little America bases before reverting to his original schedule and returning to New Zealand on the freighter *Arneb*. Meanwhile he agreed to talk to the biologists and the press, and give a talk based on his Antarctic experiences, together with his film, on a proposed visit to McMurdo Base. In addition, Cape Evans, Hut Point and Pram Point were also included in his program, with the prospect of further additions if conditions and time allowed.

The following day, with the ship anchored opposite Cape Royds, he was, not unsurprisingly, "thinking of the old days" and his reminiscences are certainly worth recording in full as, despite a fairly restrained diary entry, this must have been a moment of very strong emotion for him; specifically, he recalled the day when he was exercising the pony for which he had responsibility, Quan, who reared up, burst his halter and rushed straight up to Flagstaff Point. Shackleton, who was close by, heard the clatter of hooves and saw "25 percent of his chance of getting to the Pole" (pony numbers had been severely depleted by a series of disasters) apparently heading for total destruction; he turned to Priestley "with a face like thunder and his mouth opened to shout." However, seeing that Priestley still had the head rope in his hand and realizing that the fault was not his, Shackleton said, "Raymond, come along, we'll catch the blighter yet." In the chase that followed, he outdistanced Priestley easily and caught hold of the pony's mane just a few yards before a hundred-foot drop to the sea ice at the end of the Point. Priestley goes on to record that "he never heard any more about the matter except in jest; that was Shackleton through and through." To add additional poignancy to his memories, his afternoon tea included toast spread from a jar of Hartley's marmalade left over from his visit in 1907, which apparently tasted "very good."

Still later in the day he visited Hut Point, Cape Evans and Cape Royds, by helicopter, flying over many of the features with which he had become very familiar so many years ago, one after another, albeit from a very different viewpoint; these included Razorback looking "really knife edged," Glacier Tongue "unchanged since 1913," Mount Discovery, the Dailey Islands and the foothills of the Royal Society range. He described the flight on his return to the ship as "a great experience, no words of mine can could do justice to the kindness I have received."

During the flight, he observed a telephone cable parallel to a snow-road that had been created for the use of Weasels, "the Antarctic taxi," that was a far cry from the bare-wire communications from Cape Evans to Hut Point during his expedition with Scott. On landing, he was struck by the brightly colored inflatable hut at Cape Evans and given a tin of golden syrup left over from the Terra Nova Expedition, in addition to a couple of pages from a 1912 edition of the *Royal Magazine* and a 1908 copy of *Windsor*, which he remembered reading all those years ago.

Later, he was taken on "a windswept journey over the sea ice," to Cape Royds and found the hut from the Shackleton Expedition in much better condition than the Scott Hut at Cape Evans. He entered Shackleton's cabin, now very bare, and although Priestley's bed of packing cases was gone, there were four bedsteads and sleeping bags still in place and the photograph of King Edward VII and Queen Alexandra above the door. As a final gesture, Priestley added his signature to the visitors' book, certainly a moment of great personal satisfaction and historical significance.

He noticed, particularly, that the area around the hut was almost devoid of snow and records that "in 1908, Bernard Day would have had no difficulty in reaching Hut Point in the Arrol Johnson car on its ordinary wheels," during its experimental use. On returning to Hut Point, Priestley, as arranged, held a press conference followed by a lecture in the crowded mess hall at the base, "with people sitting and lying on the floor." During the conference, the question was raised of the Scott/Shackleton controversy surrounding Scott's supposed territorial priority in an attempt on the Pole, which he considered Shackleton had usurped; Priestley hoped "that I had been discreet in his answer." Also, while enjoying a walk through the penguin colony at Cape Royds, he appreciated being in a position to say to one of the penguins, "I knew your great, great grandfather; he was a very upstanding chap!" Finally, back on *Wyandot* at the end of a very busy and emotionally demanding day, he merely records, "This was bound to be the highlight of his sentimental Journey."

On the penultimate day of the year, yet another alteration to his travel plans was discussed, with an offer of returning to Melbourne after visiting Hallett and Wilkes bases, the only drawback being that all his "civilised stuff" was in Christchurch, New Zealand. He decided, eventually, to adopt the new proposal and to ask for his Christchurch luggage to be sent on so that his voyage would not be curtailed by returning direct to New Zealand on *Wyandot*; in his words, "the die is cast." Later, on the same day, the convoy was on the move again with *Staten Island* in the lead and Priestley was reminded of the day he left the snow cave on Inexpressible Island, with Scott's Northern Party, singing their sledging song:

> We're on the march, we're on the march,
> We can't afford to pay the rent,
> So we packed up our traps and away we went,
> All we left for the broker was a pound of stock.
> At two in the morning, without any warning, we're on the march.

On New Year's Eve, Priestley records with some feeling that "the Old Year is on the way out a good deal faster than we are moving," as *Staten Island* and *Wyandot* struggled through ice floes two feet above the water line from which they escaped eventually, with great difficulty. During the day, he received a cable from the *Birmingham Mail* asking for an article on his return to Antarctica. At the same time, he heard that his last cable home had cost $38.32 and, with his customary anxiety about money, "hoped that the Colonial Office would cover this in his official role as Observer." With this on his mind, "worrying about the $38," he hit his head, while bowed, on a steel girder on the way to dinner but observed that "luckily the old cranium, although un-upholstered, is still pretty thick." Finally, before seeing in the New Year, he packed his gear ready for transfer to the *Staten Island* the following day preparatory to his visit to Little America.

On January 1, 1959, Priestley packed early in the morning in anticipation of transfer to *Staten Island* on the following day, prior to a busy day ahead thanks to Captain Irving, who took him by jeep to Hut Point, Castle Rock, Crater Hill and Observation Hill en route passing an aircraft runway with red beacons and a number of parked planes. Also much in evidence were large piles of both oxygen and helium cylinders, "impressive evidence of the way in which things had changed since my day."

From Hut Point he was driven to Scott Base, "a very different affair," with the living quarters and most of the laboratories connected by covered passageways, all remarkably well maintained. On Priestley's arrival, New Year celebrations were already underway with pink champagne, burgundy, South African lager and home fermented beer. The Base also boasted a lavishly equipped kitchen and bathroom, underlining, for him, the comparative luxury of polar exploration in contrast to his day; however, as he passed the dog lines, this was a more familiar reminder of his past endeavors. In the living quarters, Priestley spotted a copy of Aspley Cherry-Garrard's book, *The Worst Journey in the World*, and he "impressed the occupants by a very specific page reference."[4]

By January 2, Priestley was more or less settled in *Staten Island* with a very small two-berth cabin, for his single use, but every inch of spare space was covered with his books and accumulated luggage. In order to board the ship he had to climb a Jacob's Ladder, "helped by a rope round his middle, with heart pumping and hauled ignominiously up the side." The late evening on board he describes, more lyrically than usual, as "unforgettable, as the sun makes a path of silver across the water and to starboard, the panorama of Mount Erebus, followed by the convex snow clad slopes of Mount Bird and the black rocks Cape Bird festooned with ribbon-like wall-sided glaciers."

The following day, with the ship still crashing through ice at around eight knots, he met one of the older scientists on board, a German named Neumann who, he was interested to learn, had served as a pilot during the First World War and knew Baron von Richthofen (the Red Baron) "who used to frighten me with his big red plane in the Ypres Sector in 1918." He was also fascinated to watch the launch of a helium balloon, used to register temperature, pressure and relative humidity between heights of 65,000 and 70,000 feet.

By January 4, with the ship in sight of clearer water and passing alongside the Ross Ice Shelf, with its face measuring 600 feet above sea level and covering an area the size of California, visits to all five of the Little America bases, past and present, were proposed. The sites of Little America I, II and III were no longer occupied, but still of great historical interest. At Little America I, for example, a large mound of snow covered what was obviously a submerged hut which, when uncovered, revealed a trap door leading to a square wood-lined well leading to a further door. Captain Lewis of *Staten Island* ventured down but Priestley did not, "feeling it a bit much for me"; souvenirs collected included a tin of Hershey's Hot Cocoa, a hurricane lamp and a slab of ice crystals that the helicopter pilot intended to keep in the ship's fridge. On arrival at the active base of Little America V, the ship took on board four officers and sixteen men who had reached the end of their tour of duty, from whom Priestley was surprised, and a little disappointed, to hear that they felt that the glamor had gone off polar work, which was now generally regarded merely as normal work carried out in a slightly different environment.

On the following day, cruising alongside Ross Island, adjacent to Cape Crozier, Priestley was fully appreciative of his surroundings; as he expresses it, "many a millionaire would pay a thousand dollars for a day like this and I am being paid for doing it, I hope!" He was also involved in a discussion about the value of bright colors in fostering morale in this generally monochrome environment and quoted his own preference for bright jerseys when man-hauling. On a note of less satisfaction, he records his disappointment that the Emperor penguins had left Cape Crozier; this was tempered, however, by his pleasure at seeing a population of 200,000 Adélie penguins still in residence.

As the *Staten Island* progressed northwards, the next few days marking Priestley's final departure from McMurdo Sound and his arrival at Hallett Harbour were full of interest. He heard that Captain Irving had almost climbed Mount Erebus, sacrificing his opportunity to achieve his long held ambition by remaining with an American reporter suffering from altitude sickness 700 feet below the summit, and eventually being airlifted off by helicopter. He also heard that the first plane to land at the Pole, the *Que sera, sera* had been loaded onto *Wyandot* for its final journey to the U.S. National War Museum. On rising at 5:00 a.m. to witness what would be his final departure from McMurdo, he expressed his feelings thus; "Who wouldn't sell a farm and go to sea? Why remain to suffer the rigours of a Florida winter where, we understand, the grapefruit crop has just been halved by frost—when one can summer in Antarctica instead!"

Hallett Harbour and its Base of red huts were reached, eventually, on January 10, with the icebreaker *North Wind* joining forces with *Staten Island* to break through the surrounding ice. While watching stores for the Base being unloaded, Priestley met Dr. Millar, the ichthyologist, who asked him to autograph a copy of *Antarctic Adventure*[5] which pleased him greatly. Later, he enjoyed the novel experience of being driven on a smaller version of the Snowcat, logically named the Snowkitten, which required him to wear a helmet telephonically connected to the driver through which he was "deafened by conversation not intended for me" but which, nonetheless, he found exhilarating.

Another task assigned to the *North Wind* had been to assist another accompanying freighter, *Arneb*, to break free of the ice, which was eventually completed with extreme caution as, some two years before, the freighter had been holed beneath the water line and almost sunk during a similar maneuver while, at the same time, the assisting icebreaker had suffered a stack-fire. In the midst of this furor, one marine biologist had calmly carried on collecting specimens between the ships. At that time, a cook was heard to remark, "Where else in the world could you see one of the American Navy's biggest ships sinking on the one hand, another on fire on the other, and a great hulking so-and-so son-of-a-bitch sitting fishing on a piece of ice in between."

While at Hallett Base, Priestley was involved in an interesting discussion on the difficulty of maintaining efficient administration where the majority of people are specialist scientists. He felt that it could not be as difficult as the position of a vice-chancellor at a university, based on both his Melbourne and Birmingham experiences, where he had to contend with up to fifty Heads of Departments, all thinking of their personal relationship with the vice-chancellor in terms of "Primus inter-pares, but not too much of the Bloody Pares!" At the same base, he picked up a useful piece of bamboo, "which made a good staff and saved wear and tear to the old nether limbs." This prompted him to record that "my Antarctic brothers-in-law have always claimed that I am dead from the neck up. I am now practically dead from the knees down as well and not a great deal of use in between"; this from a man aged seventy-four, still capable of both the physical and mental facility required to make a valuable contribution to a serious scientific and exploratory undertaking, in one of the most challenging and remote locations on Earth.

Suddenly, in mid-January, his proposed schedule was thrown entirely into disarray, as the *Staten Island* was now required to move some personnel from Hallett to McMurdo Base. Priestley appears quite unconcerned by the changed arrangements and, indeed, it revived his hopes of visiting Cape Adare. Consequently, this provided him with a couple of spare days at sea before reaching McMurdo Sound, which were not wasted. On board he had a useful discussion on a proposal to introduce some mature scientists into Antarctica, which he felt was a good idea and one he should mention to Sir Vivian Fuchs on his return.

This caused him to reflect on the huge differences between life in the Antarctic at the time of this journey compared with his experiences of fifty years ago. He provides three examples. The first was prompted by a Ship's Routine Order warning that "more than 11,000 gallons of water had been used on Thursday and therefore rationing would come into force forthwith," a very far cry from the very limited water supply available on the ships carrying his earlier expeditions; the second, the sight of a discolored blotch on a snow covered hillside where a Globemaster aircraft had crashed on its way to land at Hallett Base; and the third, a discussion about the safety of a helicopter being ultimately dependent on the strength of a single nut and bolt which hold the rotor arms in their proper place. He concludes that "circumstances change but the hazards remain."

On January 20, the *Staten Island* was again approaching McMurdo Sound against a stiff southerly breeze and over the next few days Priestley had the opportunity to make further unanticipated visits to his old haunts, including Hut Point and Scott Base where he was photographed continually as "the sole survivor." With this in mind, on January 24/25, he realized that it was exactly fifty years ago on these two fateful days that he was afloat on the ice off Butter Point but was unaware that it had separated from the main floe attached to the land. By the luckiest of chances in a change of wind direction, his party had managed, with extreme effort, to regain the safety of the main floe and shortly thereafter, at noon, spotted the *Nimrod* off Butter Point at fourteen miles distance. Using his shaving mirror directed over an ice axe 50 yards ahead aligned on the ship, he had signaled her and four hours later the party was picked up.

After leaving McMurdo, in very rough weather, with the ship rolling badly and his cabin "in a shambles with books and papers all over the place," Priestley answered a call for all passengers and crew to assemble in the wardroom. When they had gathered, Priestley records that the Captain said "he wished to read a message concerning one of the younger members; then I did cock my ear." He then announced that the Royal Geographical Society's Founder's Medal had been presented to Priestley "for services to Antarctic exploration." Priestley describes this "as an honour of which he had never dreamt and a very moving occasion." He dispatched an immediate reply as follows: "From *U.S. STATEN ISLAND* to President, RGS, London, England. *U.S STATEN ISLAND* proceeding through pack ice off Balleny Islands, Antarctica. Sir Raymond Priestley sends thanks to Lord Nathan and asks him to convey to her Majesty Loyal Greetings and Respectful Thanks for Award and Congratulations."[6]

On December 27, heading north, Priestley's first landing was on Sabrina Island, where he collected some very good rock specimens and describes it as "the best excursion yet" in this regard. In his view, the landing "illustrated what could be done by a combination of helicopters, keen scientists, and an icebreaker under an interested commander." Nonetheless, he noted some heart searching in the wardroom about making additional and unplanned landings which resulted in delays to the ship's return to port. Priestley's only comment, once again, was very much a reflection of his own highly focused and dedicated approach to life when he expresses it thus: "Good God, surely it is difficult to believe these young officers are not interested in what they are doing."

Over the ensuing days, the ship made steady progress north through, at times, some quite heavy pack ice but without the diversion of further landings

13. American Deep Freeze IV Expedition

The Founder's Medal of the Royal Geographical Society. Priestley received notice of the award during the American Deep Freeze IV Expedition (courtesy John Hubert, Priestley's grandson).

until anchoring off Walker Station on Clark Island. Priestley was taken on a short helicopter ride over the Base and later, by the ship's launch, to Peterson, Bailey, Midley, Hall and Wilkes Islands. With a change of some of the personnel at Wilkes Base, at the handing-over ceremony he had to compete with the full dress blue uniforms and medals of the naval crew so "settled for a check shirt, Antarctic Club tie and tweed jacket" in which he was likened by the ship's captain to "an English squire just going partridge shooting" which Priestley considered "exact!"

Over the next few days, the ship made rapid progress towards Australia at a good speed and, emphasizing the crew's state of mind, the Chief Engineer advising Priestley that even though the engines were capable of achieving 120 rpm the Captain had settled for only 100 rpm. Consequently, by February 13, the *Staten Island* was on its way into Melbourne Bay, when the pilot was taken on board bringing with him the daily newspapers; of great interest to Priestley particularly as the first Ashes Test was due to start on this day. One of his fellow passengers had been at school with the England captain,

Peter May, and mentioned that he was going to telephone for seats in the Pavilion. Priestley suggested a codicil to the effect that "a former Treasurer of Cambridge University Cricket Club had arrived in *Staten Island* and would like one too." Later in the day, he heard that the ship would be departing for New Zealand much earlier than expected and, although he was well prepared for disembarkation, he felt everyone on board would be very sorry to leave *Staten Island*.

The following day, he "enjoyed his last breakfast" before disembarking and travelling to his family's home in Melbourne, where he watched the Test Match on television "with England getting the worse of the exchange." He notes that his daughter, Jocelyn, was looking rather thin "as she has a man-sized job looking after the children, if you will excuse the misnomer" while his son-in-law, Ian, was also busy mowing lawns. For Priestley, this marked a definite return to normality and while he records that he was missing his companions on *Staten Island*, he was pleased not to be going to New Zealand. Later in the day, he received an invitation to a symposium organized by the Federal Meteorological Department, at which he had been asked to act as an advisor and, as he notes with some satisfaction, he can claim expenses of £4.10 per day. Finally, he distributed all the souvenirs he had brought for his family from both *Wyandot* and *Staten Island*, noting that his grandson, Tim, had "acquired his penguin shirt—this I did not intend!" Thus, his role on Deep Freeze IV concluded.

The remainder of February and March 1959, including Easter, he spent quietly enjoying time with his family, taking a fairly active part in the Federal Meteorological Department Symposium, visiting the University and meeting many old friends and colleagues, and taking a number of excursions, including one to the Blue Mountains, which was particularly memorable. Thereafter, be boarded the *Oronsay* at Adelaide on April 9, returning home, with a number of short breaks en route, via Colombo, the Suez Canal, Marseille, Barcelona and the Bay of Biscay, arriving in England on May 2, 1959.

This had been a remarkable journey for Priestley in many ways. It marked his first return to East Antarctica, the scene of his youthful and truly historic (in the proper meaning of the word) exploits with both Shackleton and Scott; indeed, it is clearly evident from his dairies, even for a man of his understatement, that it had had a profound effect on him. Furthermore, although he must have realized that this would almost certainly be his last visit to the place which had been at the center of his thinking and activities for much of his lifetime he had, nonetheless, come through the experience with great credit, having played a significant role on the expedition, and still fit and ready to contribute towards other aspects of public life.

14

President, Royal Geographical Society

After many invitations and continued pressure from those Fellows of the Royal Geographical Society (RGS) familiar with his life-long commitment to and achievements in Antarctic affairs, Priestley finally accepted the Presidency of the RGS in 1961, although with considerable reservations. His reluctance was based almost entirely on his extreme dislike, bordering on hatred, of public speaking (previously mentioned) in which he continued, though with no perceived justification, to feel at best inadequate and which he felt, and certainly overestimated, would form a major aspect of his duties. Indeed, in his first Presidential Address at the Society's Annual Dinner in 1962, he recollected the first occasion when he was invited to speak at the RGS, at the same event some forty-nine years earlier without any previous experience of public speaking. He was seated next to Lord Curzon, the President, who had the Italian Ambassador on his other side; after he had barely spoken for most of the dinner, as he recalls, Lord Curzon turned to him and said, "What in Heaven is the matter with you Priestley"? When Priestley advised him that he was "petrified with fright," Lord Curzon advised him "to take three glasses of champagne, neither more or less, and you will be alright." Priestley records that "I took his prescription and it worked even for a, more or less, teetotaller brought up in a strictly nonconformist home."[1]

It was partly for this reason he would only commit himself to one year at a time, subject to review, with of course a limitation of three years being the maximum laid down by the RGS's constitution. Furthermore, he was concerned that he would be able to meet this additional responsibility together with those of his family and his other still extensive commitments, as well as his awareness of the limitations, probably more imagined than real, imposed by his advancing years. In accepting the nomination he was also very mindful that a two year term would span an unprecedented number of historic anniversaries and events of huge geographical and exploratory significance.

Included in these would be the centenary of the discovery of the source of the Nile and the consequent opening up of Africa in which the RGS was heavily involved; the Golden Jubilee of Scott's last expedition; the anniversary of the death of Sir James Clark Ross, who first journeyed to the North Magnetic Pole, in addition to his Antarctic discoveries which included a first sighting of Mount Erebus and reaching seventy-eight degrees south before being stopped by the pack ice; the 150th anniversary of David Livingstone's death; and the tenth anniversary of the first ascent of Everest.

As a consequence, Priestley set himself a number of priorities, among which Exploration and Expeditions, Education and Research, Archives and Publications and, foremost, Finance were key, although his term of office covered a multitude of other matters of which the one of greatest moment was a scheme to place the Society's financial affairs on a more secure future by a long term property investment, whose rental income would cover the Society's future overheads; in fact, something way beyond the Society's ability to plan, finance, or manage but which, nonetheless, was not abandoned without a huge amount of heart searching and not before a great deal of time had been devoted to its consideration.

From the very beginning of his period of office, Priestley recognized the need for a more discriminatory approach to supporting expeditions. To this end, and with the agreement of the Expeditions Committee, following much lively but constructive discussion, a carefully considered statement of long term policy was prepared and criteria were laid down by which future decision-making to provide aid would be governed. As a result, the previous system of mere "approval" for expeditions, where no material support had been provided by the RGS, would cease. Consequently, the Society would not be regarded as an "umpire of credit worthiness" in encouraging other sources to provide aid whether in equipment or finance in cases where the RGS had not helped by way of either a grant or a loan, itself.

Among the most fundamental of the new criteria was the need to make it perfectly clear that support would only be provided where an expedition had a clearly defined geographical objective. This was not as restrictive as it might at first appear as it recognized that biological, geological, anthropological and archaeological expeditions could all have a geographical component without meeting the narrower confines of the subject as defined and taught in universities. Nonetheless, Priestley held strongly to the view that, as a geographical society, the RGS had to draw the line somewhere and expeditions intended primarily to further medical or zoological research or, for example, archaeological excavations had sources of finance available from within their own disciplines. The end result of the new criteria was that the Society's scarce resources would be applied to meet truly geographical needs first and foremost.

14. President, Royal Geographical Society

In an even more thorough application of the Expeditions Committee's new approach, three areas where expedition support had been in some doubt in the past relating to, specifically, research into water, speleological and ornithological matters were very carefully examined. As Priestley records, "many of the two former are just adventures undertaken for the thrill they afford and admirable as tests of initiative and grit" so that the Committee decided that, more often than not, such expeditions did not exploit new scientific techniques and added little if anything to the body of already established research, then support could not be justified on this basis alone. This in no way inferred that support would not be provided *per se*, as during Priestley's tenure, for example, help was given, wholeheartedly, to an underwater expedition that fulfilled the Society's new criteria and was duly recognized by one of the RGS's major awards for its pioneering geographical work.

Ornithology was regarded as a more difficult problem as, in the Committee's view, it rarely had much direct geographical significance. As a consequence, it was decided that ornithology would only be supported where it was merely a side issue within an expedition of undoubted geographical significance. Priestley expresses it succinctly; "bird watchers are legion in number and in this field I feel our help will not be missed!"

Priestley also records that even space research was not outside the scope of the Committee's review and that "although, so far, we have kept our eyes and feet on the ground, there is every reason why we should encourage and recognise voyages in space if such flights lead to better knowledge of the surface of the Earth."

As confirmation of the effectiveness of the new policy, during Priestley's presidency more than half of all applications for exploratory support were provided with aid; during 1963 alone, forty-two from seventy-five applications were sanctioned and, most importantly from Priestley's perspective, analysis showed that at least half of the expeditions helped included graduate members. In his view, a nucleus of more experienced, well qualified and mature participants should result in a higher quality of research and also provide the potential for them to react more wisely and effectively in difficult situations that were bound to arise in pioneering work.

There is no doubt that Priestley was very well supported by an Expeditions Committee, throughout the whole of his term of office, under the strong and imaginative leadership of Lord Shackleton, its Chairman. In addition, the Survey and Instruments Committee under General Brown had also been very actively involved in providing instruments to a large number of expeditions, especially those visiting mountainous regions, often in partnership with both the Alpine Club and the Mount Everest Foundation.

Priestley next turned his attention to the Archives, specifically the Library and the Map Room where, once again, a number of important and clearly defined projects were brought to a successful conclusion during his period of office, under what Priestley regarded as the inspirational leadership of its Chairman, Professor Darby, and which he considered would be welcomed by students particularly. The author catalogue of pre-1910 books was completed; a great achievement as the result of a project of four years' duration, with assistance from the Pilgrim Trust. Another constant preoccupation was the continuing problem of space with, for example, twenty-three thousand maps requiring not only cataloguing but being provided with accommodation in extra map chests in the Society's basement. This problem had now been largely overcome by a long-awaited extension to the Map Room.

His next priorities were the Society's role in the related fields of both education and research. So far as the former was concerned, a major breakthrough was achieved in the admittance of geographical societies and university exploration clubs to educational corporate membership of the RGS; in Priestley's opinion, the Education Committee under Dr. Briault had taken a leading and imaginative approach and, as a result, received enthusiastic support from the Society's Council. In relation to Research, its Committee Chairman, Dr. Dudley-Stamp, together with the RGS's Director, had been giving evidence to the Slater Committee, specifically formed to consider national planning of land use. When providing evidence, Priestley was particularly concerned that greater use should be made of work carried out by the geography departments of universities on this subject, coupled with the need to establish a Social Science Research Council "to coordinate research and disseminate information in this field."

Priestley had also overseen a very busy program by the Publications Committee during which the department under its supervision had been involved in a series of groundbreaking initiatives, leading to the publication of Hallett's *History of the African Association*[2] and Howe's *National Atlas of Disease Mortality*[3]—both seminal works in their field. A revised edition of *Hints for Travellers* was also published in addition to *Medical Hints for Travellers*, of which Lieutenant-Colonel J.M. Adams of the Royal Army Medical Corps was, appropriately, the editor. The final publication resulted from an extraordinarily successful Symposium on Exploration Medicine arranged by the RGS in collaboration with the Medical Research Council and the three Armed Services. Held at the Royal Medical College, the symposium included many experienced travelers together with aspirant explorers to whom this would be of inestimable value. Future plans for a forthcoming memoir on the *Roman Fenland* and a volume of *Explorers Maps of East Africa* were also well advanced and would add to the Society's already well established reputation in this area of publication.

Although the *Geographical Journal* continued as the Society's leading and most widely read publication, another gaining greater attention was *New*

14. President, Royal Geographical Society

Geographical Literature and Maps, particularly as a new section listing recently completed theses for M.A. and Ph.D. degrees had added markedly to its appeal and for its demand.

Inevitably, it was Finance and the committee involved in its governance that received a major share of Priestley's attention and subsequent concern. Not least of the issues under discussion on a continuing basis had been the proposal to demolish Lowther Lodge, the Society's headquarters and a building of huge historical significance in London's history; a building that, nonetheless, was undoubtedly expensive in relation to both general running and maintenance. The proposed plan, which had been under discussion prior to Priestley's presidency and continued thereafter, was to replace this with a combined development of business and residential facilities, the income from which would not only provide a continuing source of finance for the Society's future needs, but also make provision for a purpose built headquarters for the RGS adjoining the new premises. In the end, as previously mentioned and not surprisingly, the project never went much beyond the embryonic stage despite an entirely disproportionate expenditure of time, effort and deep concern.

In many other aspects, the Society's finances were in a reasonably stable position during Priestley's term of office, with Fellowship and Membership numbers, the basis of the Society's funding, rising to well over seven thousand together with a regular flow of income from a number of significant legacies. However, Priestley records, with uncharacteristic venom, that "the new high level of rates is an innovation that, unless offset by grants, will bear hardly on the cultural vitality of a nation already obsessed with the more material aspects of life."

Overall, Priestley looked back over two years as president with a good deal of his customarily modest satisfaction during which he had been, ex officio, a member of all the standing committees referred to as well as Chairman of the General Purposes Committee and had attended all of them on many occasions. This involved constant trips to London from his home in Breden's Norton via Pershore railway station, from which he almost certainly became its most regular and, possibly, its most distinguished traveler, in addition to often requiring overnight accommodation in London; all this by a man approaching his seventy-seventh birthday at the end of two years of his presidency. He cites his age as one of his principal reasons for not seeking a third annual term of office together with his feeling that, as he records, "he now felt one of an outmoded Victorian Age." In his second and last annual address he concludes, referring to his sometimes slightly flippant approach, "I must plead the need for some light relief as a safety valve in our world of increasing complexity and unpredictability, where the individual citizen becomes less and less the master of his destiny and the captain of his Soul." It would be interesting to hear his views of the world today.

15

Along the Way

The Antarctic Dining Club

What is widely regarded and known as "the Heroic Age of Antarctic Exploration" that was set in train by Borchgrevink's Southern Cross Expedition of 1898–1900 ended, effectively, with Shackleton's Trans-Antarctic Expedition of 1914–16. The survival of all its members, under Shackleton's inspirational leadership, during which the expedition's ship, the *Endurance*, had to be abandoned after being beset by ice, followed by an incredibly perilous journey over ice and sea via Elephant Island to, eventually, South Georgia, is undoubtedly among the great epics of Antarctic exploration. However, the members of the later British Graham Land Expedition of 1920–22 are also generally regarded as worthy of inclusion among this select band of scientists and explorers.

Against this background, it appears almost inevitable that for some who had shared in this life-changing experience that included, in addition to many groundbreaking scientific achievements, Amundsen's priority over Scott in the attainment of the Geographical South Pole, would wish to gather together periodically "to chew over old times, to set the world to rights and to despair for the future as they saw it developing."[1] As a result, the first Annual Dinner and Reunion with thirty-four prospective members attending was held at the Café Royal in Regent Street, London, on January 17, 1929, the day coinciding with Scott's Party's arrival at the South Pole in 1912. Vice-Admiral Reginald Skelton presided and it was proposed that an "Antarctic Club" be formed and a committee appointed.[2]

The first official Club Committee meeting took place in London, at which John Mather was appointed as Honorary Secretary; an inspired choice in the light of the Club's future prestige and success. Amongst the most important conclusions reached, and established as a set of rules for consideration, was that the Club would hold a reunion dinner annually and "membership should be restricted to those who had visited the Antarctic continent whilst engaged on expedition work."[3] The latter became a matter of continual debate, disagreement and contention, an almost inevitable outcome as the number, style and composition of later scientific and exploration work in Antarctica developed. Moreover, the first lady was not admitted until Lady Virginia Fiennes was accepted as a member of the Trans-Globe Expedition (1980–81).[4]

So far as Priestley is concerned, he was a founding member of the Club, presided at its Annual Dinner and Reunion in both 1955 and 1962 and was present at the 41st anniversary reunion, commemorating the 60th anniversary of the return of Shackleton's Nimrod Expedition (1906–09) when the Duke of Edinburgh, an Honorary Member, paid a special tribute to him. In what is recorded as "a witty speech"[5] in reply to the Loyal Toast, HRH praised Priestley not only for his inclusion in both the Nimrod and Terra Nova expeditions but also for his later encouragement of Polar exploration and, particularly, his highly valued participation in His Royal Highness's visit to Antarctica on the RY *Britannia* in 1957.

While the Club has experienced the inevitable disruption which the passage of time and the changing nature of Polar exploration have imposed upon it, nonetheless it still seeks to include members from among the dwindling number of privately funded expeditions with largely exploratory aims. However, inevitably, those from the scientific community predominate, particularly from publicly funded and proactive organizations such as the British Antarctic Survey.

The Post-War Planning Survey: West Midlands Group

The Group was founded in January 1941 under Priestley's chairmanship during his tenure as vice-chancellor of the University of Birmingham; its purpose was to carry out the type of research advocated by the Barlow Commission Report that had been published in the preceding December. Sir Montague Barlow's remit had covered a very wide range of Town and Country Planning, taking a long term view of the type of post-war reconstruction and development that would be required, covering all aspects including agriculture and industry. The establishment of the Group was facilitated by the Bourneville Village Trust which, at the time, was seeking an opportunity to widen its planning interests; in support of this, the Trustees had considerable experience in this area and offered to finance the Group and to place at its disposal office accommodation and administrative staff, including Paul Cadbury as its Honorary Secretary.

Geographically, the Group concentrated its initial research, in which Priestley was very actively involved, in two areas. Birmingham and the Black Country was chosen as one and the county of Herefordshire as the other, although the Group's overall responsibilities also covered Shropshire, Staffordshire, Warwickshire and Worcestershire. However, it was soon realized that a full survey covering such a wide area would be impossible to complete within any reasonable timeframe given the resources available. Consequently, the two areas were chosen for reasons of their almost complete contrast in relation to the comparative predominance regarding industry and agriculture.

The Group's widely accepted proposals were published in two reports[6] under the headings of: Land and its use; Cities, Towns and Urban Centers; Regional Communications; Social Services; Land Classification and Planning. Priestley's contribution and involvement had been considered as crucial in his role as vice-chancellor of the University of Birmingham as this had enabled the Group to draw upon resources of information which would not otherwise have been available.

The Royal Commission on the Civil Service

Immediately following his retirement as vice-chancellor of the University of Birmingham in 1952, Priestley was asked to become chairman of a Royal Commission, with a very wide ranging brief, to look into all aspects of the Civil Service; in support, Priestley had a multi-disciplined Commission membership and strong secretarial support.

The final report of the Commission's Conclusions and Recommendations was published on November 10, 1955,[7] and, although the degree to which its findings were implemented is unclear, there is every indication that the Commission's detailed and comprehensive work demanded respect if not, as would be expected, unquestioned and ready compliance. The areas covered were: Hours, Leave and Allied Matters; Rates of Pay; the Higher Civil Service; the Administrative Staff; the Executive Staff; the Clerical and Allied Staff; the Specialist Staff; the Post Office Classes and, overall, Superannuation.

Bearing in mind that immediately following the publication of the Commission's Conclusions and Recommendations, Priestley became Acting Director of the Falkland Islands Dependencies Survey, and in the course of these duties accompanied His Royal Highness, the Duke of Edinburgh, to Antarctica on the RY *Britannia*, he illustrated very considerable physical and mental resilience for a man not only well into retirement but also quite evidently ready for any new and demanding challenges that presented themselves.

Other Interests

Priestley was also a well-respected and longstanding member of both the British Association for the Advancement of Science and the Royal Society as well as a variety of other prestigious scientific institutions; the almost inevitable consequence of the distinction of his long, committed and very active life.

16

Later Life

It is important to remember that following the completion of his presidency of the Royal Geographical Society (RGS) in 1963, Priestley was approaching his seventy-seventh birthday and had suffered the loss of his wife, Phyllis, after a long illness, at the beginning of his two year term of office. Furthermore, not long after his official retirement from the vice-chancellorship of the University of Birmingham in 1952, he had accompanied His Royal Highness, the Duke of Edinburgh, on the RY *Britannia* as his Antarctic expert and advisor, closely followed by his role as British Observer on Operation U.S. Deep Freeze IV, prior to accepting the RGS Presidency.

As a consequence, it was not until 1964 that he was free to enjoy the accepted benefits of retirement, in any recognized meaning of the word, had he wished to do so. Indeed, it is clearly evident from his prolific diaries, which he maintained assiduously until less than two years before his death, that his life continued as one in which his commitment to service and sense of duty never faltered.

By 1964, he was living with his daughter, Margaret, and her husband together with his grandson, John, and granddaughter, Ellen, at Barn Hill, Bredon's Norton, Gloucester, and, as clearly evidenced in his diaries, he took a keen and constructive interest in his family's affairs including those, as distance allowed, of his other daughter, Jocelyn, and her family in Australia.

In fact, his first year of retirement very much set the pattern for the remainder of his life hereafter. For example, in March 1964 he attended a reunion, hosted by His Royal Highness, the Duke of Edinburgh, at Buckingham Palace for members of the party with which he had visited Antarctica on the RY *Britannia* where he was particularly pleased to meet Ted Seago and Mike Parker again. He felt that "I started out on the right foot with The Duke of Edinburgh by telling him that there was nothing artificial about me, even false teeth." During the same year, he made another trip to the West Indies where he was delighted to find the new university well established and thriving while, on his return, he attended a lecture at the Royal Geographical Society, given by Sir Vivien Fuchs, "where I sat on the front row with Dudley-Stamp" (later to a become a very well-known and highly regarded writer of school geography text books). He also took the opportunity to attend the Edgbaston Test against the Australians "where I was well entertained, including lunch."

The following year was equally busy. In January, he received a visit from Wally Herbert, who later became something of a Polar legend, but who, at this stage, was seeking Priestley's advice concerning his proposed intention to sledge across the Arctic Ocean. He also attended an Antarctic Club Dinner "where I met some of my old friends from RY *Britannia* days." On a more somber note and with feelings of deep regret, he records the news of the death of Sir Winston Churchill, whom he had always regarded as inimitable to our victory during the Second World War. Later in the year he attended dinners of both the Royal Geographical Society in London and the British Antarctic Survey in Cambridge. However, the year ended on a very sad and poignant note for Priestley with the news of the death of Frank Debenham, with whom he had helped to establish the Scott Polar Research Institute and who had been its first and long-term director. As he records, "Cambridge will never be quite the same now he is gone."

During the year 1966, the pace of events and commitments, if anything, increased. In the early part of 1966, he attended a degree ceremony at the University of the West Indies, where he was awarded an Honorary Doctorate of Science, attended by Her Majesty the Queen and His Royal Highness, the Duke of Edinburgh. During the same period, he was delighted to agree that both the new Clubs and Societies House at Melbourne University and the Base House on Deception Island, off the Antarctic Peninsula, should to be named after him. With equal pleasure, he was pleased and honored that the Royal Geographical Society arranged a party to celebrate his 80th birthday on July 20, 1966. However, and perhaps inevitably in view of the sustained and unremitting nature of his incredibly active and demanding life, he records, without further comment, that he suffered a slight heart attack during the latter part of the year.

Although there is no indication that he regarded this, particularly, as a health warning it may well have influenced his decision, in January 1967, amongst other things, to discontinue public speaking and giving lectures. In any event, public speaking in particular was something that he had always disliked and which he avoided whenever he could although, paradoxically, it had been an inescapable aspect of many of the appointments that he had held. It is also possible to discern a slightly more measured approach to his commitments hereafter, but still maintained at a much higher level than would normally be expected for a man of his age at this period in time.

Priestley's medals, including his Military Cross and his two Polar Medals in recognition of his expeditions with both Shackleton and Scott to Antarctica during the "Heroic Age" of its exploration—a rare distinction (courtesy John Hubert, Priestley's grandson).

Furthermore, in March, he was suffering more acutely with knee problems, partly as a result of injuries he had sustained in his early days in the Antarctic, and for which he was receiving treatment. Consequently, he had a relatively quieter summer than hitherto and it was not until October that he became more actively involved when he attended the opening, by Peter Scott, of the Fitzroy Arts Centre in Tewkesbury when he was delighted to record that "Peter said my presence had made his evening."

During the early months of 1968, he was involved in a series of events very close to his heart; indeed, the main focus of his life despite his considerable achievements in other fields of endeavor. These included a British Antarctic Survey Reunion Dinner at the Criterion in Piccadilly when "The Silent Toast" was proposed to those who had visited Antarctica and not returned; another, a meeting of the National Committee for Antarctic Research at The Royal Society in Charter House Terrace. However, health problems intervened again when he suffered from gout and complained of "the pressure of bed-clothes on my gouty foot."

In July of the same year he records, with some relish, that he had reached speeds of up to one hundred and fifteen miles an hour when being driven home by "Bunny" Fuchs on a journey from London! In November, he was back in London again for an art exhibition, at a gallery in Old Bedford Street, of pictures by Edward Seago, his friend and companion from his RY *Britannia* days and later, in the same month, attended a Vice-Chancellors' Dinner in the City.

By 1969 as, inevitably, he was travelling far less at the age of eighty-three while sustaining the usual meticulous care in completing his diaries, he instead received either visits or correspondence from a variety of those with interests in Antarctic affairs and research, including the media. Indeed, it is quite evident that he was regarded as the foremost living authority on the history of Antarctic exploration and science, most especially of the Heroic Age involving Scott, Shackleton and Amundsen with which he had been so acutely involved and committed.

His final diaries up until 1972 reflect this pattern. By way of example, he received a letter of thanks from Wally Herbert who, as previously mentioned, was to become something of a Polar legend in his own right, thanking him for all his past help. Similarly, he was delighted to receive a photograph from a recent expedition, illustrating the position of Scott's Northern Party's Snow Cave on Inexpressible Island where, while the snow cave had disappeared, a plaque had been erected to mark its site. Then, in early 1972, His Royal Highness, the Duke of Edinburgh, sent him a portrait which Edward Seago had painted of Priestley while on the RY *Britannia*, and later in the year he received a visit from his brother-in-law, Charles Wright, one of the last survivors, with Priestley, of Scott's final expedition.

Shortly following his eighty-sixth birthday, he records with considerable regret that he had to decline an invitation, due to ill health, to open the Dr. Edward Wilson Centenary Exhibition at Cheltenham—Dr. Wilson was an accomplished watercolor artist who had, of course, been one of Scott's party that had perished on its return from the South Pole. Finally, his last diary entry, on December 11, 1972 reflects, most appropriately, the news of the first Apollo landing on the Moon; indeed, an achievement that he might well have regarded as the pinnacle and triumph of human exploration and science to which he had been so fully committed throughout his whole life.

For the short period between the end of his diary record and his death, Priestley was suffering from an accumulation of illnesses, in part as a result of his early and near fatal experiences in the Antarctic with Shackleton and Scott. As a consequence, the last months of his life were, inevitably, spent more quietly at the family home in Bredon's Norton until he suffered a ruptured aorta and, very shortly thereafter, died at the Nuffield Nursing Home in Cheltenham on June 24, 1974.

It is entirely appropriate to leave to others the final words on his long, incredibly active and distinguished life, which the biography supports without reservation and in full measure.

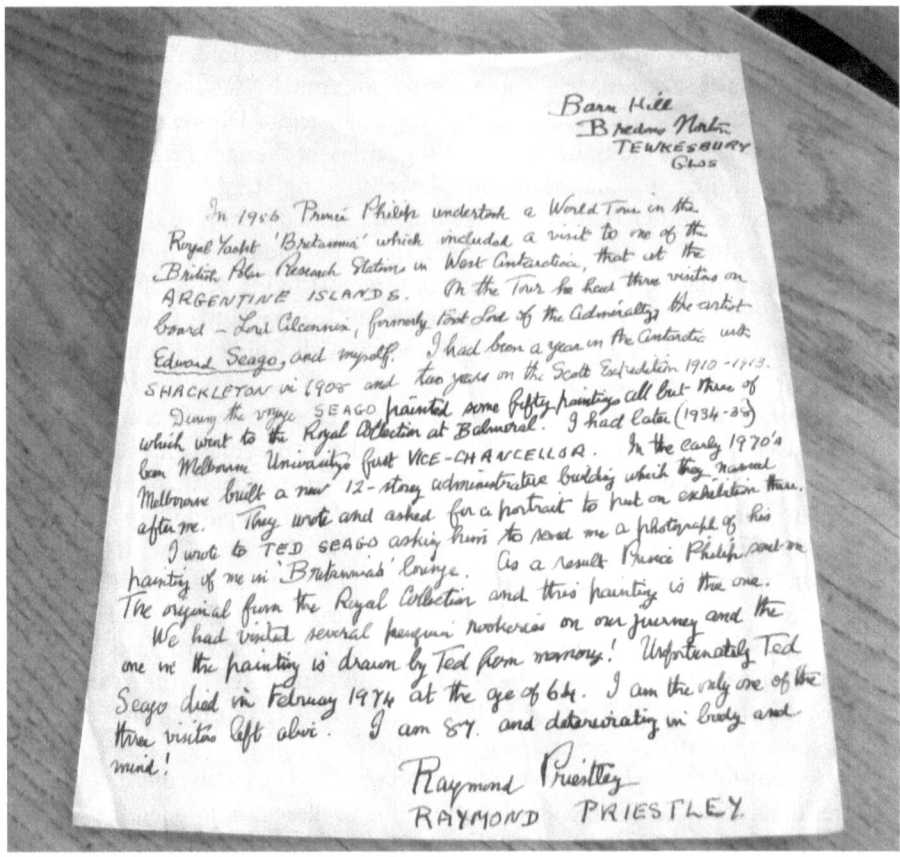

A letter written at age 87, recipient unknown, shortly before his death, referring to his voyage on the RY *Britannia* (courtesy Ellen Scrivens, Priestley's granddaughter).

Shortly following his death in 1974, H.G.R. King of the Scott Polar Research Institute in Cambridge wrote a profile in which he ends with Priestley's most quoted epigram. "For a leader of a scientific expedition give me Scott; for fast and efficient travel Amundsen; but if things go wrong and there isn't even the slightest chance of getting through, go down on your knees and pray for Shackleton. One might add that, failing Shackleton, one could hardly have bettered Raymond Priestley himself."[1]

Sir Charles Wright, his Antarctic companion and brother-in-law, in an appreciation of Priestley, strongly supports this view in emphasizing his "fortitude and adaptability, coupled with his generosity for which many of his friends throughout the world have reason to be grateful."[2]

Finally, at Priestley's Memorial Service in Tewkesbury Abbey on July 3,

1974, the Reverend L.J. Birch summed him up, with pinpoint accuracy, "as a man of humility, patience, quiet humour and patent security," concluding with the view which would have attracted strong local support that "he was undoubtedly the greatest man that this town has produced in our age and generation."³

Appendix I:
46th (North Midland) Division During the Hundred Days

Summary

At the division's first involvement in the Hundred Days, at the opening of the Battle of Bellenglise on September 29, 1918, and commanded by Major-General G. F. Boyd, C.M.G., D.S.O., D.C.M., it comprised[1]:

230th Brigade, R.F.A.
465th, 466th, 467th Field Company, R.E.
46th Divisional Signal Company, R.E.
(*2nd-in-Command, Captain R. E. Priestley, M.C.*)
137th Infantry Brigade comprising:
    1/5th Battalion South Staffordshire Regiment
    1/6th Battalion South Staffordshire Regiment
    1/6th Battalion North Staffordshire Regiment
138th Infantry Brigade comprising:
    1/5th Battalion Lincolnshire Regiment
    1/4th Battalion Leicestershire Regiment
    1/5th Battalion Leicestershire Regiment
139th Infantry Brigade comprising:
    1/5th Battalion Sherwood Foresters
    1/6th Battalion Sherwood Foresters
    1/8th Battalion Sherwood Foresters
    1/1st Battalion Monmouth Regiment
46th Battalion Machine Gun Corps

The Battle of Bellenglise[2]

The preliminary order for the Battle, issued by the General Staff on September 25, 1918, read "At an hour and date to be notified later, the 46th Division, as part of a major operation, will cross the St. Quentin Canal, capture the Hindenburg Line, and advance...." The order begged the question that had been the focus of Allied attention up to this point of the War: Would the Hindenburg Line hold back the now almost irresistible flow of the Allied advance? The question was now about to be answered, definitively, during an action in which the division would play a heroic and decisive part.

In the event, by the night of the September 29, 1918, the division had achieved all of the objectives set out in the General Staff Order, in the course of which it captured four thousand, two hundred prisoners and seventy guns at the remarkably low cost of eight hundred casualties. The breaking of the Hindenburg Line opened the way for the final advance to victory in which the division had yet a major part to play.

The Battle of Ramicourt[3]

To continue its advance, as set out in the General Staff Order, and following its almost miraculous victory at Belenglise, the division was now called upon to confront superior enemy forces in straightforward infantry fighting, in which all ranks acquitted themselves with great distinction, and during which Priestley's gallantry was recognized by the award of his Military Cross.

The Battle was fought and won on October 3, 1918, against no less than four Divisions of the German Army without, on this occasion, the providential fog that had been such a crucial factor in the division's successful breaching of the Hindenburg Line at Bellenglise. Furthermore, in this instance, the enemy's morale was much improved, compared with Bellenglise, as it now had greater machine gun and artillery support and, consequently, its infantry fought with greater confidence and determination. Moreover, the enemy forces were only too aware of the dire consequences should its line be broken and the quantities of military materiel that would have to be abandoned, must have given an added spur to its fighting spirit.

Nonetheless, the breakthrough against stubborn enemy resistance was achieved and, thereafter, the advance continued until, on October 10, the strategically important town of Bohain was relieved amidst an overwhelmingly enthusiastic reception by its two thousand French inhabitants.

The Battle of Andigny[4]

With the Divisional Headquarters now established at Fresney, its leading troops pushed forward to the Bois de Riqueval, a wood on the edge of the Forest of Andigny. There they met stiff enemy resistance, in strongly constructed defensive positions comprising machine guns, strong points, and deep trenches.

The 46th Division was allocated the task of a flanking attack on Andigny-les-Fermes Wood, while bypassing Riqueval Wood. In a hard-fought battle, in which all units and supporting sections of the Division were heavily involved sustaining substantial numbers of casualties, final success was eventually achieved on October 18 when its task of clearing Andigny Forest and its surrounding woods was completed. The measure of the resistance it had faced was exemplified by the number of hand-picked enemy troops captured from seventeen different Regiments from six separate divisions. At this point, a slight pause in the advance was essential for the division to regroup and rest.

The Final Advance to Sains du Nord[5]

On November 1, 1918, following its brief spell to recuperate, the division was again involved in a huge offensive, comprising the British First, Third and Fourth Armies, and elements of the French Army, in one final and decisive attack against the German's thinly held line, which quickly gave way to retreat and the first real return to mobile warfare since the early days of the War.

Eventually, and despite some setbacks in the face of heroic enemy resistance, the approach to the banks of the Rhine was completed on November 8, 1918, and the division along with other units and their supporting artillery crossed the river, using a bridge constructed by the Royal Engineers, on November 9, 1918.

The Armistice November 11, 1918

The war was won and the division had played a significant part during its final days and its successful conclusion. It had acquitted itself with great distinction and conspicuous gallantry with six Victoria Crosses awarded in the division during the Hundred Days alone. Furthermore, its contribution to the entire war effort is nowhere better, though sadly, illustrated than by reference to its total losses between February 1915, when it first arrived in France, and the Armistice on November 11, 1918; they speak, most poignantly, for themselves. One thousand, five hundred and two officers and twenty-eight thousand sixty-seven other ranks were killed, wounded or reported missing.

Appendix II:
The 1907–1909 British Antarctic Expedition[1]

Shore Party:
Lieutenant James Adams, RNR, meteorologist.
Armitage.
Sir Philip Brocklehurst, assistant geologist and general duties.
Edgeworth David, principal geologist.
Bernard Day, electrician and motor expert.
Ernest Joyce, general stores, dogs, sledges and collections.
Dr. Alistair Mackay, surgeon.
Dr. Eric Marshall, surgeon and cartographer.
George Marston, artist.
Douglas Mawson, physicist.
James Murray, biologist.
Raymond Priestley, geologist.
William Roberts, cook.
Frank Wild, provisions.

***Nimrod* Staff:**
Lieutenant England, R.H.R., master.
John Davis, first officer.
Aeneas MacIntosh, second officer.
Dr. Rupert Mitchell, surgeon.
Harry Dunlop, chief engineer.
Alfred Cheetham, third officer/boatswain.

Appendix III:
The McMurdo Sound Region

Map on following page.

Appendix III

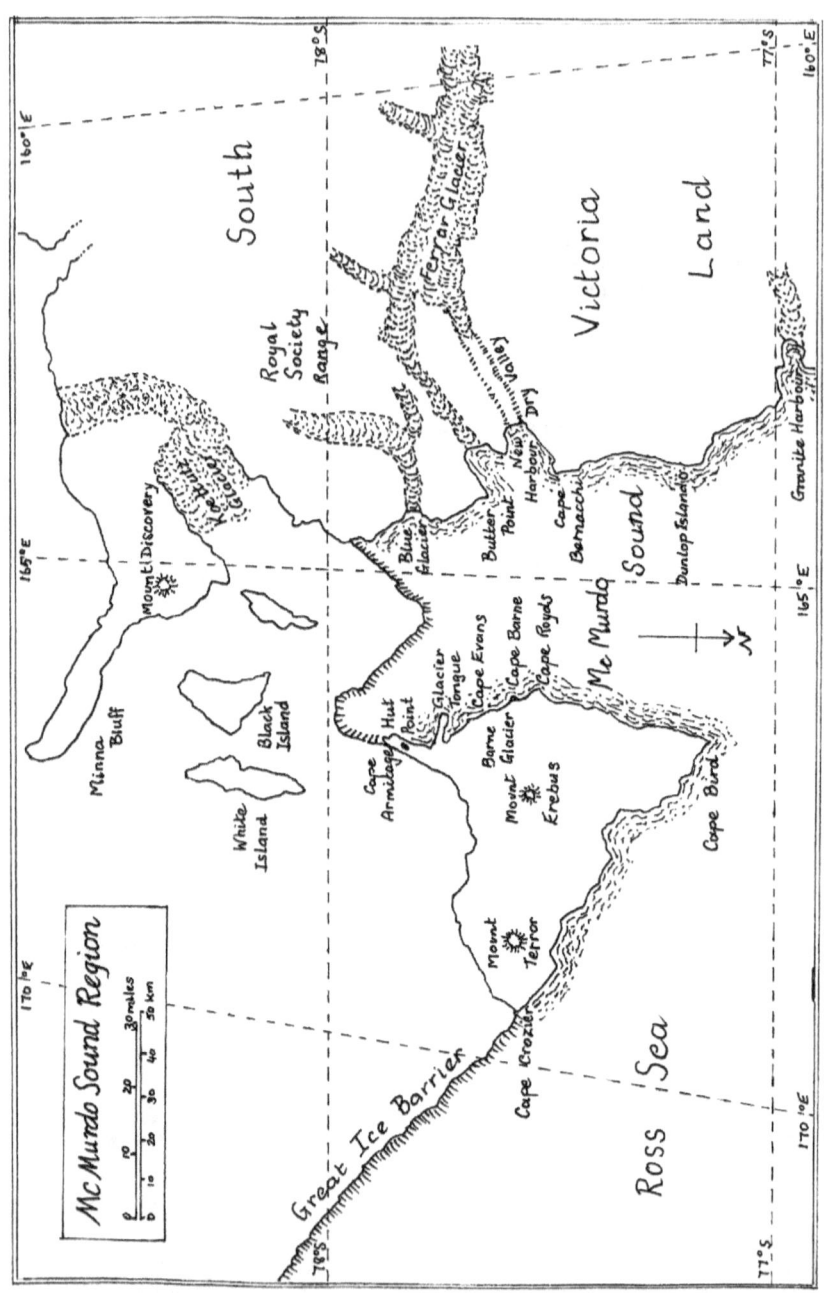

The McMurdo Sound Region (courtesy Frances H. Bullock).

Appendix IV: The 1910–1913 British Antarctic Expedition[1]

Western/Southern Party:
Captain Robert Scott, CVO RN, Leader.
Lieutenant Edward Evans, RN.
Lieutenant Henry Bowers, RIM.
Dr. Edward Atkinson RN, surgeon.
Captain Lawrence Oates, 6th Inniskilling Dragoon Guards, ponies.
Chief Stoker William Lashley, RN.
Petty Officer Robert Forde, RN.
Petty Officer Edgar Evans, RN.
Petty Officer Thomas Crean, RN.
Petty Officer Patrick Keohane, RN.
Thomas Clissold, RN, cook.
Frederick Hooper, RN, steward.
Dr. Edward Wilson, zoologist & chief of scientific staff.
Charles Wright, physicist.
Edward Nelson, biologist.
Aspley Cherry-Garrard, assistant zoologist.
Cecil Meares, dog handler.
Herbert Ponting, photographer.
Tryggve Gran, ski expert and instructor.
Bernard Day, motor engineer.
Demetri Gerof, dog-driver.
Anton Omelchenko, ponies.

Far Western Party:
Griffith Taylor, geologist.
Frank Debenham, geologist.

183

Eastern/Northern:
  Lieutenant Victor Campbell, RN, leader.
  Dr. George Murray Levick, RN, surgeon.
  Raymond Priestley, geologist.
  Petty Officer George Abbott, RN.
  Petty Officer Frank Browning, RN.
  Able Seaman Harry Dickason, RN.

Terra Nova **Staff:**
  Lieutenant Harry Pennell, RN, first officer.
  Henry Rennick, RN, second officer.
  Wilfred Bruce, RNR, third officer.
  Francis Drake, RN, assistant paymaster.
  Dennis Lillie, biologist.
  Alfred Cheetham, boatswain.
  Frank Davies, RN, leading shipwright.
  Walter Archer, RN, chief cook.
  Petty Officer Thomas Williamson, RN.

Chapter Notes

Preface

1. M. Bullock and L. Lyons, *Missed Signals on the Western Front* (Jefferson, NC: McFarland, 2010).
2. Sir R. Priestley, *Work of the R.E. in the European War, 1914–1918* (Chatham: W. & J. Mckay, 1921).

Introduction

1. R.E. Priestley, *Work of the R.E. in the European War, 1914–1918, the Signal Service (France)* (Chatham: W. & J. Mackay, 1921).
2. M. Bullock and L. Lyons, *Missed Signals on the Western Front* (Jefferson, NC: McFarland, 2010).
3. M. Hooper, *The Longest Winter. Scott's Other Heroes* (London: John Murray, 2011) p. xxi/ii.
4. Sue Edlin, the Chairman of the Trustees of the Tewkesbury Town Museum, has taken a lifelong interest in Priestley's history and has been responsible for a dedicated exhibition, within the Museum, devoted to him. Indeed, she was my first point of contact before writing the biography to ensure that she did not wish to claim a justifiable priority to do so. David Villavoys, a local historian, prepared a paper entitled "The Priestley Family in Tewkesbury," which has been invaluable in researching Priestley's family background and early life.
5. R.E. Priestley, *Breaking the Hindenburg Line: The Story of the 46th (North Midland) Division* (London: T. Fisher Unwin, 1919).
6. R.E. Priestley, *Work of the R.E. in the European War, 1914–1918, the Signal Service (France)* (Chatham: W. & J. Mackay, 1921).

Chapter 1

1. Assembled by Sue Edlin, Chairman of the Trustees of Tewkesbury Town Museum.
2. D. Villavoys, "The Priestley Family in Tewkesbury."
3. Priestley wrote some recollections of his youth entitled "Early Days at Tewkesbury" while on the RY *Britannia* in December 1956.
4. A. Cherry-Garrard, *The Worst Journey in the World* (London: Constable, 1922).
5. Sir C. Wright, *Sir Raymond Priestley: An Appreciation* (*Polar Record*, Vol. 17, No. 108, 1974); event held at The Scott Polar Institute, Cambridge.

Chapter 2

1. University College, Bristol, *Calendar for the Session (1904–1905)*.
2. *Ibid.*, p. 117.
3. *Ibid.*, p. 125–6.

Chapter 3

1. R.F. Scott, *The Voyage of the Discovery* (Stroud: Nonsuch, 2005) p. 71.
2. *Ibid.*, p. 99.
3. *Ibid.*, p. 102.
4. Sir E. Shackleton, *The Heart of Antarctica* (Cork: Collins, 2002) p. 1–19.
5. *Ibid.*, p. 24.
6. The remainder of the chapter, unless otherwise indicated, has been compiled from Priestley's personal diaries held at the Scott Polar Research Institute, Cambridge MS 298/2/1–2/2–2/3–2/4–2/5–2/6 B.J.

7. N. Peat, *Shackleton's Whisky* (London: Prefacing, 2012).
8. Capt. R.F. Scott, *The Voyage of the Discovery—Volumes 1 & 2* (Stroud: Nonsuch, 2005).

Chapter 4

1. MS 1097 21/1-8: D *In-Between Expeditions*, Priestley's personal diary covering the period following the Nimrod Expedition and prior to his participation on the Terra Nova Expedition.
2. Sir E. Shackleton, *The Heart of Antarctica* (Cork: Collins, 2002).
3. R.E. Priestley and T. Edgeworth David, *Report on the Scientific Investigations of the British Antarctic Expedition 1907-9* (London: William Heinemann, 1914).

Chapter 5

1. R.E. Priestley and T. Edgeworth David, *Report on the Scientific Investigations of the British Antarctic Expedition 1907-9* (London: William Heinemann, 1914).
2. Hereafter, Priestley's firsthand account of his experiences, compiled from his personal diaries, in a comprehensive paper he wrote entitled "Inexpressible Island," for delivery to or publication by a variety of interested parties and professional journals, forms the framework for this chapter and a copy of which is held at the Scott Polar Research Institute in Cambridge.
3. M. Hooper, *The Longest Winter: Scott's Other Heroes* (London: John Murray, 2010) p. xxii.
4. V. Campbell, *The Wicked Mate: The Antarctic Diary of Victor Campbell*, ed. H.G.R. King (London: Bluntisham Books, 2001); Campbell, as leader of the Northern Party, makes frequent reference to the value of Priestley's role in charge of food supplies.
5. R.E. Priestley, *Antarctic Adventure: Scott's Northern Party* (London: Fisher Unwin, 1915) and M. Hooper, *The Longest Winter* (detailed above) are recommended as complete accounts of the Northern Party's truly incredible survival story.

Chapter 6

1. Priestley compiled a specific war memoir, in addition to his diary record, both of which form the framework of the chapter.
2. R.E. Priestley and T. Edgeworth David, *Report on the Scientific Investigations of the British Antarctic Expedition 1907-9* (London: William Heinemann, 1914).
3. R.E. Priestley, *Work of the R.E. in the European War, 1914-1918, the Signal Service (France)* (Chatham: W. & J. Mackay, 1921).
4. Col. J.H. Patterson, *The Man-Eaters of Tsavo* (London: Macmillan, 1907).
5. M. Bullock and L. Lyons, *Missed Signals on the Western Front* (Jefferson, NC: McFarland, 2010).
6. Ibid.
7. R.E. Priestley, *Breaking the Hindenburg Line, the Story of the 46th (North Midland) Division* (London: T. Fisher Unwin, 1919) forms the framework for the remainder of the chapter along with Priestley's war memoir and, specifically, the summary of the Division's heroic performance during the Hundred Days at Appendix I.
8. Ibid., p. 17-22.
9. M. Bullock and L. Lyons, *Missed Signals on the Western Front* (Jefferson, NC: McFarland, 2010).
10. M. Bullock, unpublished Master of Letters thesis, "The British Army Signal Service 1914-1918," p. 138-139.
11. Dr. John Bourne, the University of Birmingham, kindly provided the details.
12. R.E. Priestley, *Antarctic Adventure: Scott's Northern Party* (New York: E.P. Dutton, 1915).

Chapter 7

1. R. Priestley and T. Edgeworth David, *Report on the Scientific Investigations of the British Antarctic Expedition 1907-9* (London: William Heinemann, 1914).
2. R.E. Priestley and C. Wright, *Glaciology*, 1922.
3. F. Debenham, *Retrospect: The Scott Polar Research Institute, 1920-45* (POL/POL4-29/S ... held at the Scott Polar Research Institute, Cambridge).
4. P. Speak, *Deb: Geographer, Scientist,*

Antarctic Explorer (Guildford: Polar Publishing Limited, 2008).
  5. F. Debenham, *Retrospect*, p. 4.
  6. *Ibid.*, p. 5.
  7. *Ibid.*, p. 7.
  8. *Ibid.*, p. 8.
  9. *Ibid.*, p. 9.
  10. *Ibid.*, p. 9.
  11. *Ibid.*, p. 10.
  12. *Ibid.*, p. 12.
  13. *Ibid.*, p. 13.
  14. *Ibid.*, p. 15.

Chapter 8

  1. R. Ridley, *The Diary of a Vice-Chancellor* (Melbourne: University Press, 2002) p. xxi.
  2. *Ibid.*, p. 2.
  3. The remainder of the chapter is based on the compilation of Priestley's diaries reproduced in Ronald Ridley's excellent book, which has been of inestimable value, in addition to his personal diaries held at the Scott Polar Research Institute, MS 1560/1-/2 BJ.

Chapter 9

  1. The chapter is based on a summation of Priestley's diaries held at the Cadbury Research Library: Special Collections, University of Birmingham.
  U.S. 38/2/1 1938 Diary.
  U.S. 38/2/2 1939–1940 Diary.
  U.S. 38/2/3 1940–1941 Diary.
  U.S. 38/2/4 1941–1942 Diary.
  U.S. 38/2/5 1943 Diary.
  U.S. 38/2/6 1944–1945 Diary.
  U.S. 38/2/7 "Home Record" 1945–1947.
  U.S. 38/2/8 Record 1947–1949.
  U.S. 38/2/9 Record 1949–1951 Volume 1.
  U.S. 38/2/10 Record 1949–1951 Volume 2.
  U.S. 38/2/11 Record 1951–1952.
  U.S. 38/2/12 Malayan Union Voyage and West Indies Voyage diary 1946–1947.
  U.S. 38/2/13 West Indies visit diary 1951–1952.
  U.S. 38/2/14 West Indies journey 1952–1953.
  Dr. Helen Fisher, the Archivist, who was in the early stages of completing a summary for digitization, accelerated the process on being made aware of my intention to write Priestley's biography, which has been an outstanding and invaluable contribution towards its completion.

For those with an interest in the history of the University, Eric Ives' book, with contributions from Diana Drummond and Leonard Schwarz, *The First Civic University: Birmingham 1880–1980* (Birmingham: The University of Birmingham Press, 2000) is highly recommended.

  2. The author was awarded a Master of Letters Degree at one such Congregation in 2008.
  3. Eric Ives, *the First Civic University: Birmingham 1880–1980* (Birmingham: The University of Birmingham Press, 2000), p. 311.
  4. A note provided by Mrs. Anne Howarth, a pupil, teacher and Acting Headmistress, respectively, at Edgbaston High School for Girls, Birmingham.
  5. Eric Ives *The First Civic University: Birmingham 1880–1980* (Birmingham: The University of Birmingham Press, 2000), p. 312.

Chapter 10

This chapter is based on a summation of Priestley's diaries and an accompanying paper, as follows:
  1. U.S. 38/2/12–2/13–2/14, Cadbury Research Library: Special Collections, University of Birmingham; MS 1097/38/1-/2-/3-/4, Scott Polar Research Institute, University of Cambridge; *The Making of a University*, a Paper read to the Cambridge Branch of the Royal Empire Society in May 1951 by the Vice-Chancellor of the University of Birmingham.

Chapter 11

  1. British Antarctic Survey Archive, *BAS History—Administration & Operations* (J. Rae, 1984) includes the background to FIDS prior to Priestley's appointment as Acting Director.
  2. *Ibid.*, AD 6/8/56–57 Wireless Section HQ Stanley.
  3. *Ibid.*, AD 5/1/14/56 Reorganisation of Rear Base.
  4. *Ibid.*, AD 5/1/14/56 Recruitment.
  5. *Ibid.*, AD 8/1/1 Merger of Rear Base & Scientific Bureau.
  6. *Ibid.*, AD 3/1/AS/164/B(4) Director—Priestley steps down.

Chapter 12

1. This chapter is based on a summation of Priestley's diaries held at the Scott Polar Research Institute, Cambridge MS 210/1/1–1/2–1/3–1/4, of which bound copies are held at His Royal Highness, the Duke of Edinburgh's Archive at Buckingham Palace and, personally, by Priestley's grandson John Hubert.
2. Sir D. Mawson, *The Home of the Blizzard* (Edinburgh: Birlinn, 2000).
3. A. Cherry-Garrard, *The Worst Journey in the World* (London: Constable, 1922).
4. Sir E. Shackleton, *South: The Story of Shackleton's Last Expedition 1914–1917* (Oxford: John Beaufoy, 1919).

Chapter 13

1. https://En.Wikipedia.Org/wiki/Operation_Deep_Freeze.
2. The chapter hereafter is based on a summation of Priestley's diaries MS 510/1/1–1/2–1/3–1/4 held at the Scott Polar Research Institute, Cambridge.
3. R.E. Priestley, *Antarctic Adventure: Scott's Northern Party* (New York: E.P. Dutton, 1915).
4. A. Cherry-Garrard, *The Worst Journey in the World* (London: Constable, 1922).
5. Priestley, *Antarctic Adventure*.
6. The author, as a Fellow of the Royal Geographical Society himself, can readily identify with the intense satisfaction which Priestley must have derived from this highly prestigious award.

Chapter 14

1. The chapter hereafter is a summation of Priestley's miscellaneous speeches and notes, MS 1097/40 D held at the Scott Polar Research Institute, Cambridge, personal diaries held by his grandchildren and collected minutes held at the Royal Geographical Society covering Priestley's period of office as President, 1961–63.
2. R. Hallett, ed., *Record of the African Association 1788–1831* (London: Thomas Nelson & Sons, 1964).
3. G. Melvyn Howe, *National Atlas of Disease Mortality* (Geographical Journal, Vol. 130, No. 1, March 1964).

Chapter 15

1. J. Reed, *A Brief History of the Antarctic Club* (Cambridge, 2009), p. 1.
2. *Ibid.*, p. 1.
3. *Ibid.*, p. 2.
4. *Ibid.*, p. 13.
5. *Ibid.*, p. 11.
6. *Conurbation: A Planning Survey of Birmingham & the Black Country, West Midlands Group* (London: The Architectural Press, 1948); *A Planning Survey of Birmingham & the Black Country, West Midlands Group* (London: Faber & Faber, 1946).
7. R.E. Priestley, *Royal Commission on the Civil Service* (London: Her Majesty's Stationary Office, 1955).

Chapter 16

1. H.G.R. King, *Antarctic Past and Present: A Profile of Sir Raymond Priestley* (London: British Science News, 1974).
2. Sir Charles Wright, *Sir Raymond Priestley: An Appreciation* (Cambridge: Polar Record, Vol. 17, No. 108, 1974) p. 215–20.
3. Rev. L.J. Birch, "Address Given at Priestley's Memorial Service" (Tewkesbury Abbey: 3rd July 1974).

Appendix I

1. R.E. Priestley, *Breaking the Hindenburg Line: The Story of the 46th (North Midland) Division* (London: T. Fisher Unwin, 1919) Appendix V.
2. *Ibid.*, p. 22–80.
3. *Ibid.*, p. 81–131.
4. *Ibid.*, p. 132–157.
5. *Ibid.*, p. 158–172.

Appendix II

1. Sir E. Shackleton, *The Heart of Antarctica* (Cork: Collins, 2012) p. 19–23.

Appendix IV

1. M. Hooper, *The Longest Winter: Scott's Other Heroes* (London: John Murray, 2011) p. xxi/ii.

Bibliography

Archival Sources

British Antarctic Survey
  BAS History—Administration & Organisation—Rae, Joanna (British Antarctic Survey Archives Service) 1984.
  AD 6/8/56-57 Wireless Section HQ Stanley.
  AD 5/1/14/56 Reorganisation of Rear Base.
  Ad 5/1/14/56 Recruitment.
  AD 8/1/1 Merger of Rear Base & Scientific Bureau.
  AD 3/1/AS/164/B(4) Director.

Cadbury Research Library: Special Collections, University of Birmingham.
  US 38/2/1-2/2-2/3-2/4-2/5-2/6-2/7-2/8-2/9-2/10-2/11.
  Raymond Priestley: Diaries; Vice-Chancellor of the University of Birmingham, 1939-52
  (US 38/2/12-13-14).
  Raymond Priestley: Diaries; West Indies Journey and Visit 1946-1947.

Royal Geographical Society Library
  LS/329
  Raymond Priestley: The Work of the Northern Party of Captain Scott's Antarctic Expedition (mgZ.137.24).
  Raymond Priestley: The psychology of exploration: Antarctic (Mg635D).
  Raymond Priestley: Twentieth Century Man against Antarctica (Mg639A).
  Raymond Priestley: Antarctic research: A review of British scientific achievement in Antarctica.

Scott Polar Research Institute, Cambridge University
  MS 298/2/1-2/2-2/3-2/4-2/5-2/6 B.J.
  Raymond Priestley: Diaries; British Antarctic Expedition (BAE) 1907-09 (MS 298/4/1: MSM Antarctic *7:91[08]1907-1909).
  Raymond Priestley: Tracing/sketch map; Cape Royds; BAE 1907-09 (MS 1097/20/1-3; D).
  Raymond Priestley: Prelude to Antarctic Adventure (MS 298/6/11; B.J).
  Raymond Priestley: Sledging Diary; Mount Erebus; BAE 1910-13 (MS 1451; D).
  Raymond Priestley: Personnel of polar expeditions (MS 210/1/1-1/2-1/3/-1/4).
  Raymond Priestley: Voyage on RY *Britannia*; 20 Nov 1956-9 Feb 1957 (MS 510/1/1-1/2-1/3-1/4).

Raymond Priestley: US Deep Freeze IV; 10 Nov 1958–2 Aug 1959 (MS 1560/1–/2).
Raymond Priestley: Vice-Chancellor Melbourne; 1 Jan–17 May 1936 (MS 1097/40; D).
Raymond Priestley: misc. speeches & notes; 1950–1962 (MS 1097/38/1–/2–/3–/4).
Raymond Priestley; Higher Education Board for the Colonies.

University Archives, Syndics of Cambridge University Library
O.II 316 Notes on the office of Vice-Chancellor and on the structure and organization of the University.
Explanatory note on the office of Assistant Registrary and Secretary General.

University College, Bristol
Calendar for the Session (1904–1905).

Documents and Papers by Priestley

"Antarctic Diary, Deep Freeze IV" (typescript, 1959).
CONURBATION: *A Planning Survey of Birmingham & the Black Country, West Midland Group*. London: The Architectural Press, 1948.
"The English Civic Universities." (A paper read to Teaching Officers of Overseas Universities at Cambridge, August 1949.)
"Essay on Government" (Melbourne University, 1938).
"Inexpressible Island." (A copy of a report of Scott's Northern Party, 1913).
"The Making of a University." (A paper read to Cambridge Branch of the Royal Empire Society, May 1951.)
"Message to Freshmen." (A paper read at the Freshmen Conference organized by the Guild of Undergraduates, October 1949.)
A Planning Survey of Herefordshire, West Midland Group. London: Faber & Faber, 1946.
"The Psychology of Exploration." *Psyche* Volume II, No.1, July 1921.

General Works

Amundson, R. *My Life as an Explorer*. Stroud: Amberley Publishing, 2008.
Bowmann-Larsen, T. *Roald Amundsen*. Norway: Cappelen, 1995.
Bullock, M., and L. Lyons. *Missed Signals on the Western Front*. Jefferson, NC: McFarland, 2010.
Cherry-Garrard, A. *The Worst Journey in the World*. London: Constable, 1922.
Dagnell, L., and H. Shibata. *The Japanese South Polar Expedition 1910–1912*. Bluntisham: Erskine, 2011.
Day, D. *Antarctica: A Biography*. Oxford: Oxford University Press, 2012.
Fiennes, R. *Mad, Bad & Dangerous to Know*. London: Hodder & Stourton, 2008.
_____. *Cold. Extreme Adventures at the Lowest Temperatures on Earth*. London: Simon & Schuster, 2013.
Giaever, J. *The White Desert: The Official Account of the Norwegian-British-Swedish Antarctic Expedition*. London: Chatto & Windus, 1954.
Herbert, W. *A World of Men, Exploration in Antarctica*. London: Eyre & Spottiswoode, 1968.
Hooper, M. *The Longest Winter: Scott's Other Heroes*. London: John Murray, 2010.
Huntsford, R., D. Rowley, and J. Summers. *The Shackleton Voyages*. London: Weidenfeld & Nicholson, 2002.
Ives, E., D. Drommond, and L. Schwarz. *The First Civic University: Birmingham 1880–1980*. Birmingham: The University of Birmingham Press, 2000.

King, H., ed. *The Wicked Mate: The Antarctic Diary of Victor Campbell*. Alburgh: Bluntisham Books, 1988.
King, H.G.R. *The Antarctic*. London: Blanford, 1969.
Lambert, K. *Hell with a Capital H*. London: Pimlico, 2002.
Lansing, A. *Endurance: Shackleton's Incredible Voyage*. London: Hodder & Stourton, 1961.
Larson, E.J. *An Empire of Ice: Scott, Shackleton and the Heroic Age of Antarctic Science*. New Haven, CT: Yale University Press, 2011.
Mawson, Sir D. *The Home of the Blizzard: A True Story of Antarctic Survival*. Edinburgh: Birlinn, 2000.
Mountevans, Edward Evans. *South with Scott*. London: Wm. Collins, 1957.
_____. *The Desolate Antarctic*. London: Lutterworth Press, 1950.
Mountfield, D. *A History of Polar Exploration*. London: Hamlyn, 1974.
Peat, N. *Shackleton's Whisky*. London: Prefacing, 2012.
Ponting, H. *With Scott in the Antarctic*. Stroud: Amberley Publishing, 1922.
Priestley, R.E. *Antarctic Adventure. Scott's Northern Party 1915*. New York: E.P. Dutton, 1915.
_____. *Breaking the Hindenburg Line: The Story of the 46th (North Midland) Division* London: T. Fisher Unwin, 1919.
_____. *Royal Commission on the Civil Service*. London: Her Majesty's Stationary Office, 1955.
_____. *Work of the R.E. in the European War, 1914-1918. The Signal Service, France*. Chatham: W. & J. Mackay, 1921.
_____, and T. Edgeworth David. *Report on the Scientific Investigations of the British Antarctic Expedition 1907-9*. London: William Heinemann, 1914.
Ridley, R. *The Diary of a Vice-Chancellor*. Melbourne: University Press, 2002.
Riffenburgh, B. *Racing with Death: Douglas Mawson—Antarctic Explorer*. London: Bloomsbury, 2008.
_____. *Nimrod. Ernest Shackleton and the Extraordinary Story of the 1907-1909 British Antarctic Expedition*. London: Bloomsbury, 2004.
Scott, R.F. *Journals. Captain Scott's Last Expedition*. Oxford: Oxford University Press, 2006.
_____. *The Voyage of the Discovery. Volumes I & II*. Stroud: Nonsuch, 2005.
Shackleton, Sir E. *The Heart of Antarctica*. Cork: Collins, 2012.
_____. *South. The Story of Shackleton's Last Expedition 1914-1917*. Oxford: John Beaufoy, 1919.
_____. *Aurora Australis*. Shrewsbury: Airlife, 1988.
Solomon, S. *The Coldest March*. New Haven, CT: Yale University Press, 2001.
Speak, P. *Deb: Geographer, Scientist, Antarctic Explorer*. Guildford: Polar Publishing Limited, 2008.
Strathie, A. *Birdie Bowers: Captain Scott's Marvel*. Stroud: The History Press, 2012.
Swithinbank, C. *Forty Years on Ice: A Lifetime of Exploration and Research in the Polar Regions*. Lewes: The Book Guild, 1998.
Turney, C. *1912: The Year the World Discovered Antarctica*. London: The Bodley Head, 2012.
Tyler-Lewis, K. *The Lost Men: The Harrowing Story of Shackleton's Ross Sea Party*. London: Bloomsbury, 2006.
Wheeler, S. *Terra Incognita: Travels in Antarctica*. London: Vintage, 1996.
Wilson, D. *The Lost Photographs of Captain Scott*. London: Little, Brown, 2011.

Index

Numbers in ***bold italics*** indicate pages with photographs.

Abbott, George Percy 47, ***49***, 52, 149, 184
Acting Chief Wireless Instructor 69
Adams, Lieutenant (Commander) James 13–14, 21, 24–25, 133–134, 137, 140, 164, 180
Adélie penguins 52, 55, 141, 156
Admiralty Bay 140
Admiralty Range 48, 148
Age 84
Alpine Club 163
Amundsen, Roald 41, 47–48, 52, 146, 166, 173–174
Antarctic bases, U.S. 145
Antarctic Circle Certificates 135–136
Antarctic Club Dinner 134, 144, 171
Antarctic Glaciology Memoir 58, 75
Antarctic (Polar) Medal 61, 64, 66, 128, 147, ***172***
Antarctic Survey, British 2, 5, 127, 167, 171–172
Antarctica, West 5, 125, 127–144
aplitic rocks 22
Appointments Board 84
Argus 84
Armitage 25, 29, 32–34, 44, 149
Armstrong-Siddeley car 62
Army Drill Manual 59
Arneb 152, 156
ARP shelters & wardens 95, 103
Arrol Johnson car 153
"Article" (Victorian chamber pot) 147
"attic period" 79
Avamine tablet 145
"Avifauna Britannia Antarctica" 137

Backdoor Bay 24
Bailey, Kenneth 82
Bainbridge, Joseph 84
Balloon Bight 21
Baptist Union of Great Britain and Ireland 95
Barbourne College, Worcester 59

Barlow Commission Report 167
Barrett, Sir James 85, 88–89
basalt 22, 24, 29, 44
Battle of Andigny 73, 179
Battle of Bellenglise 70–72, 177–178
Battle of Neuve-Chapelle 67
Battle of Ramicourt 72, 178
Battle of the Somme 8, 67
Bay of Whales 47
Berber Institute of Fine Art 93
Bewdley 60
Bingham, Surgeon-Commander E.W. 124
Binney, Sir George 78
Bishop of Hereford 11
Bjorn 16
Boobooks Club 85
Bourneville Village Trust 167
Bovril 18, 32–33
Bowers, Henry 57, 183
"Boy" (dog) 28
Boys, General 65
Bredon's Norton 61, 92, 129, 142, 149, 165, 170, 173
Bristol Theatre 27
RY *Britannia* 5, 9, 125–144, 146, 149, 167–168, 170–171, 173, ***174***
British Association for the Advancement of Science 169
Brocklehurst, Sir Philip 25–28, 32, 34, 149, 180
Browning, Frank V. 47, ***49***, 52, 54–56, 149, 184
Buchanan, Dr. Gwyneth 86
Buckingham Palace 2, 131, 170
Burstell, Aubrey 89
Bury St Edmunds 60
Butt, Clara 42
Butter Point 32–35, 151, 158

Cadbury, Paul 94, 100, 167
Cadbury, William 94, 100, 167

193

194 Index

Caldwell, Kenneth 59
California Institute of Technology 86
Campbell, Victor 45, 47, *49*, 50–51, 55, 127–128, 149, 184
Cape Adare 48, *49*, 50, 148–149, 157
Cape Barne 151
Cape Crozier 10, 46, 141, 156
Cape Evans 46–48, 51–52, 55–57, 151–153
Cape Horn 40
Cape Royds 22, 29, *31*, 32, 35–36, 149–154
Captain of Hockey 13
Carnegie Organization 85–86
Carol Concert 135–136
Carrier Pigeon Service 70
Castle Rock 151, 154
Cathedral Rocks 33
SS *Cavina* 111
Ceramic 88
Chamber of Manufacturers 89
Chamberlain, Neville 93, 95, 97
Chancellor's Hall 93, 101
Cherry-Garrard, Aspley 10, 88, 141, 155, 183
Chinnery, Squadron Leader Henry 137
Chittick, Henry 60
Christchurch, New Zealand 38, 44, 113, 130–131, 154
Christchurch College, Cambridge 58, 75
Christian Union 12, 102
Churchill, Sir Winston 97, 100, 102, 105, 108, 110, 129, 171
Cilcennin, Lord 129–131, 136–137, 140
"Cissie" (dog) 28
Clare College 58, 75, 84, 88, 135
Clifford, Max 142
Colonial University Grant's Advisory Committee 120
Commandery House 62
Conscription Bill 95
Copland, Douglas 82, 90
Crabeater seals 20, 50, 138
Crater Hill 154
Crawford, Max 89
cricket 8–10, 13, 35, 42, 59, 62, 83, 88–90, 95, 99, 105, 142, 160
cufflinks 136
Curzon, Lord 134, 161

Darby, Professor 164
Davis, John King 128, 180
Day, Bernard 24–25, 28, 39–41, 153, 180, 183
Debenham, Frank 10, 43, 76–80, 149, 171, 183
Deception Island 124, 130, 140, 147, 171
deck hockey 134, 136
Degree Congregation 76, 105
Deputy Director Signals, First Army 74
Descent Pass 33
Dickason, Harry 47, *49*, 149, 184
Drake, Miss W.M. 80
Dry Valley 32–33, 151, 152
Duke of Devonshire 94
Duke of Edinburgh, HRH (Prince Philip) 2, 5, 9, 125, 127–144, 147, 150, 167–168, 170–171, 173
Dunlop, Harry 22
Duras, Fritz 89

Eadie, Ione 140
Edgbaston High School for Girls 114
Edgeworth David, Professor T.W. 17, 75, 80, 149, 151, 180
Education Act, 1944 108
Elephant Island 143, 166
Elliott, Dr. (dean of Bristol) 11
Endurance 143, 166
England, Captain 21–22, 35, 180
Evans Cove 48

F422 132
F424 132
Falkland Islands Dependencies Survey (FIDS; later the British Antarctic Survey) 5, 123–127, 138–140, 142
feldspar crystals 22, 26
Ferrar Glacier 32, 149, 151
Ferrier Glacier 21
Fiennes, Lady Virginia 167
Fiennes, Sir Ranulph 129
First Assistant Registrary 76
Fitzroy Arts Centre, Tewkesbury 172
46th (North Midlands) Division 4, 67, 70–72, 135, 177–179
Foster, John 84
Fuchs, Sir Vivian 5, 123–126, 157, 171, 173
"Future of Polar Exploration" 78

Gallipoli 60
Geographical Journal 164
geographical Pole 16, 29, 52, 166
"Glennie Nos" (dog) 65
gneiss 22, 50
Gog Magog Hills 59
Gonzales, Lieutenant 145
granite 22, 26, 50
Great Barrier Reef 16
Greig, Alfred 84

Haig, Major Nigel 72
Handley, Major 61–62
Hartley, Sir Harold 127
Haynes Park 65–66
Herbert, Wally 171, 173
Heroic Age 1, 21, 123, 166, *172*, 173
Hillary, Sir Edmund 5, 123, 132
Hindenburg Line 66, 69–70, 73, 178
"Hints to Future Assistants" 80
Hope Bay 124
Horseshoe Bay 30
Howarth, Anne 114
Hundred Days 66, *68*, 69–70, 73, 135, 177–179

"igloo back" 55
Illustrious 132

Index

Imperial College, London University 120
Imperial College of Tropical Agriculture 111–112, 120
Inaccessible Island 151
International Date Line 133
Irvine, Sir James 116–117, 119, 121–122
Irving, Captain 145–150, 152, 154, 156

Johansen 41
John Biscoe 124, 132–133, 137–140, 142
Joint Recruitment Board 95, 100–101
Jowett, Dr. 11
Joyce, Ernest 18–19, 21, 24–25, 27–30, 35, 39–41, 180

killer whales 20, 35, 40
King, H.G.R. 174
King Edward VII 16, 20, 153
King Edward VII Land 16, 21, 47
King George's Island 140
King's School, Worcester 61
Kinsey, Baines and Co. (shipping agents) 20
knighthood 1, 5, 111
Koonya 17, 20

Laurie Island 124
Lawn House, Birmingham 98
Lemaire Channel (later Kodak Alley) 139
LeMay, Commander 145, 147, 149, 151
Lensfield Road 80
leopard seals 20
Levick, Dr. George Murray 47, *49*, 53, 55, 149, 184
limestone breccia 41
Loewe, Fritz 89
Lowther Lodge 165
Lyttleton Harbor 17, 39

MacDonald, Captain 150–151
MacFarland, Sir John 85
MacIntosh 17, 23, 180
Mackay, Dr. Alistair 18, 20, 25, 28, 32
MacKinlay's Rare Old Highland Malt Whisky 20
Magnetic Pole, North and South 28–29, 32, 36, 40, 80, 128, 162
The Man-eaters of Tsavo 63
Marconi 65
Marr, Commander J.W.S. 123–124
Marston, George 19, 24, 29–30, 40, 42, 180
Masefield, John 135–136
Mawson, Sir Douglas 17–18, 22, 25, 28, 32, 34, 36, 48, 76, 128, 180
Mayor of Bristol 11
McMurdo Base & Sound 16, 21, 36, 46, 138, 146, 148–152, 156–158, 181–182
Medical Research Council 94, 164
Medley, John 90–91
Melbourne Club 85
mess deck 51, 131, 136, 147
metamorphic rock 33

meteorology 16, 18, 32, 37–38, 48, 89, 160, 180
Methodist Guild 8–9
Midwinter's Day 28, 54
Military Cross 1, 3, 72–73, *172*, 178
Millikan, Dr. 86
"Misery Nunatek" 31
Mitchell, Commander 130
Moeraki 44
Montagu-Stuart-Wortley, Major-General the Hon. E.J. 67
Moore, Professor Harrison 86
Mount Bird 27, 155
Mount Discovery 152–153
Mount Erebus 22, 25–27, 36, 38, 40, 76, 151–152, 155–156, 162
Mount Everest Foundation 163
Mount Lister 151
Mount Morgan 44
Murray, James 23–26, 29, *31*, 34

USS *Nespolen* 145, 150
Nestor 82
Norton Barracks 62
Nuffield, Lord 93, 106, 173

O'Brien 136
Observation Hill 151, 154
Observer Corps 103
Operation Taberin 123

Paperoa 40
Parker, Lieutenant-Commander Mike 128–129, 134–138, 140–141, 143, 170
Pegasus 17
Pembroke College 59
pemmican 30, 32–33, 48, 56, 149
Percy 13
petrels 21, 138
Philharmonic Hall 14
Pilgrim Trust 164
Pluto 132
plutonic rock 33
Polar Record 81
Port Lockroy 124, 139
Portuguese allies 70
Potts, Frank 59
Powerful 17
Pram Point 29, 152
Priestley, Donald (younger brother) 8, 10, 65
Priestley, Doris (sister) 10
Priestley, Edith (sister) 10, 88, 110
Priestley, Jocelyn (elder daughter) 61, 82
Priestley, Joseph (grandfather) 7
Priestley, Joseph Edward (father) 7,.
Priestley, Joseph Hubert (eldest brother) 7, 10–11, 13, 36, 106
Priestley, Joyce (sister) 10, 41, 88
Priestley, Margaret (younger daughter) 61, 88, 92, 96–97, 99, 102, 105, 110–111, 136, 170
Priestley, Marie (sister) 10

Priestley, Phillis (née Boyd; wife) 40, 58, 60, 82, 90, 92, 96–99, 109–110, 132, 136, 170
Priestley, Raymond 174
Priestley, Stanley (youngest brother) 8, 10, 65
Princess Alice of Athlone 111, 121–122
Protector 133, 137, 141–142
ptomaine poisoning 55

quarter deck 51
Queen Alexandra 16, 153
Queen Anne's Chambers 124
Queen Elizabeth Hospital 95
Queen's Speech 136

Rathbone, Captain 61
Razorback 151, 153
relief party 53
Reynolds, Professor S.H. 12
Riding School 61, 64, 66–67
Roberts, William 19, 23, 28, 180
Robertson, Charles Grant 92, 112
Robinson's of Tewkesbury 23
Rockefeller Foundation 94–95
Ross Island 39, 156
Ross Sea 21, 149
Ross seals 20
Royal Charter for University College 117
Royal Geographical Society 2, 5, 16, 78, 80, 101, 105, 108, 128, 134, 161–165, 170–171; Founder's Medal 158, *159*
Royal Grammar School, Worcester 61
Royal Society 11, 127–128, 153, 169, 172
Royal Standard 131
SS *Runic* 14, 16, 40, 131

St. Martin's Gate, Worcester 61–62
Sandra 137
School of Architecture 80
Scott, Lady Kathleen 77, 80
Scott, Captain Robert Falcon 1, 12, 15–16, 35, 39, 44–58, 64–65, 75–81, 88, 93, 112, 123, 127, 129, 138, 141, 144–146, 153–154, 160, 162, 166, *172*, 173–174, 183
Scott Base 146, 155, 158
Scott, "Message to the Public" 77
Scott Polar Research Institute (originated as Scott Memorial Mansion House Fund) 2–4, 10, 43, 58, 75–81, 88, 93, 103, 127, 149, 171, 174
Scott's Discovery Base 16, 21
Scott's Discovery Expedition 15, 16, 21
Scott's Discovery Hut 21
Scott's Northern Party 3, 9, 32, 44, 46–57, 128, 134, 137, 146, 147, 149, 154, 173
Scott's Terra Nova Expedition 4, 10, 46–57, 106, 128
screw-ice 26
sea sickness 18–19, 21, 45–46
Seago, Edward 129–133, 135–137, 143, 170, 173
seal hoosh 51–52, 54–55
Secretary General to the Faculties 76, 82

Secretary to the General Board 76
Sedgwick Museum 78–80
sedimentary rock 33
Seward, Professor 79
Shackleton, Sir Ernest Henry 1, 3, 12–46, 48, 62, 64, 75–76, 78, 80, 93, 123–124, 127, 129, 135, 142–146, 152–154, 160, 166–167, *172*, 173–174
Sherlock, Philip 116, 120
Sherwood Foresters   69, 177
Shipley, Sir Arthur 77
Signal Service Training Centre (S.S.T.C.) 65
Sixth Division 59
Smith, Vice-Admiral Sir Connolly Abel 128
snow cave 50, 51, 149, 154, 173
South Georgia 127, 143, *144*, 166
South Wales Borderers 60
Southern Army Troops Wireless Telegraphy Section 61
Southern Harvester 133, 137
spring sledging 56
Springer, Hugh 116
Stanley, Rupert 69
USS *Staten Island* 148, 150–152, 154–160
Stevenson, Anne (now Dame Anne Griffiths) 140
Stewart Island 38
"Sticky Glew" 66
Stonington Island 124
Stratton, Colonel F.J.M. 58, 69
Students Union 83, 88, 90–91
Survey and Instruments Committee 163
Sydney Town Hall 43

Taylor, Captain A. 124
Taylor, Griffith (brother-in-law) 10, 41, 75, 149, 183
Taylor, Dr. W.J. 119
Tent Island 22, 151
Tewkesbury Abbey House School 7
Tewkesbury Grammar School 7–8, 59
Tewkesbury Town Museum 2–3, 7, 185
Thomson, Allan 46
Thwaites, Major-General W. 68
Tyree, Rear Admiral 145–146, 150, 152

Universities Act 1933 82
University Disciplinary Committee 103, 106
University House, Birmingham 93, 95
University of Adelaide 17, 83, 89
University of Birmingham 2, 4, 76, 89–115, 140, 157, 167–168, 170
University of Cambridge Officers' Training Corps 58
University of Sydney 17, 41, 44, 84, 90, 112

Vernon, Sydney 110, 113
Victorian Legislative Assembly 82
Victorian Order 16
Victorian State Government, Australia 89–90
volcanic dust, gravel, rock 12, 26, 29, 33, 132

War Damage Act 99
Wave Chief 134–135
Weddell seals 20, 55, 138
Wellcome Research Institution 106
White Star Line 16
Wild, Frank 18, 21, 24–25, 27–28, 33, 38–42, 44, 143, 149, 180
HMS *William Scoresby* 124
Wilson, Dr. Edward 15, 57, 173, 183
Wireless Section T.F. 58, 60–61, 63, 125

"Woodbine Willie" 62
Wordie, J.M. 78, 80, 123
Wright, Sir Charles (brother-in-law) 10, 57–58, 60, 75, 88, 106, 149, 173–174, 183
USS *Wyandot* 145–152, 154, 156, 160

Yalta Conference 108
Young Officers School 64
Younghusband, Sir Francis 77

www.ingramcontent.com/pod-product-compliance
Lightning Source LLC
Chambersburg PA
CBHW032100300426
44116CB00007B/827